Thinking on Screen

'This book is a powerful defense of the view that films can philosophize. Characterized by its clear and lively presentation, and by its intertwining of philosophical argument with detailed discussion of several important films, it will be of interest not just to those studying philosophy and film but to everyone who believes in the importance of film to our cognitive life.'

Berys Gaut, University of St Andrews, UK

Thinking on Screen: Film as Philosophy is an accessible and thought-provoking examination of the way films raise and explore complex philosophical ideas. Written in a clear and engaging style, Thomas E. Wartenberg examines films' ability to discuss, and even criticize, ideas that have intrigued and puzzled philosophers over the centuries, such as the nature of personhood, the basis of morality, and epistemological skepticism.

Beginning with a demonstration of how specific forms of philosophical discourse are presented cinematically, Wartenberg moves on to offer a systematic account of the ways in which specific films undertake the task of philosophy. Focusing on the films *The Man Who Shot Liberty Valance*, *Modern Times*, *The Matrix*, *Eternal Sunshine of the Spotless Mind*, *The Third Man*, *The Flicker*, and *Empire*, Wartenberg shows how these films express meaningful and pertinent philosophical ideas.

Thinking on Screen: Film as Philosophy is essential reading for students of philosophy with an interest in film, aesthetics, and film theory. It will also be of interest to film enthusiasts intrigued by the philosophical implications of film.

Thomas E. Wartenberg is Professor at Mount Holyoke College and author of *Unlikely Couples: Movie Romance as Social Criticism* and *The Forms of Power*. He has edited four anthologies on the philosophy of film and aesthetics, and is film editor for *Philosophy Now*.

Thinking on Screen

Film as philosophy

Thomas E. Wartenberg

Routledge
Taylor & Francis Group

LONDON AND NEW YORK

First published 2007
by Routledge
2 Park Square, Milton Park, Abingdon, Oxon, OX14 4RN

Simultaneously published in the USA and Canada
by Routledge
270 Madison Ave, New York NY 10016

Routledge is an imprint of the Taylor & Francis Group, an informa business

Transferred to Digital Printing 2010

© 2007 Thomas E. Wartenberg

Typeset in Sabon by Taylor & Francis Books

British Library Cataloguing in Publication Data
A catalogue record for this book is available from the British Library

Library of Congress Cataloging in Publication Data
A catalog record for this book has been requested

ISBN 10: 0-415-77430-6 (hbk)
ISBN 10: 0-415-77431-4 (pbk)
ISBN 10: 0-203-03062-1 (ebk)

ISBN 13: 978-0-415-77430-7 (hbk)
ISBN 13: 978-0-415-77431-4 (pbk)
ISBN 13: 978-0-203-03062-2 (ebk)

Contents

Figures

Preface

As I cast a backwards glance over the process that eventuated in the writing of this book, I am struck by a sense of arrival, both for me professionally and for the field of film and philosophy. When I began to argue that films could be relevant to philosophical concerns, that claim was met with a rather stony silence in the world of Anglo-American professional philosophy. Now, more than a decade and a half later, I feel privileged to be a member of a thriving sub-discipline of philosophy that takes films seriously not just by thinking about philosophical issues concerning the nature of the medium as such, but also by using films as a way of addressing philosophical issues. I am gratified to note that there are now sessions at the meetings of both the American Philosophical Association and the American Society for Aesthetics on film, something that was a rarity when I first began writing on and speaking about films.

Personally, I also feel a sense of fulfillment, but not completion. When I wrote my first book on film, *Unlikely Couples*, I felt a sense of embattlement with the philosophical community, for I didn't feel that my efforts to wrest philosophical significance from romance films had a sympathetic audience of response. Indeed, I had a growing sense of myself as becoming increasingly marginal from a philosophical community to which, as a young Kant scholar, I had clearly belonged. But now, as I glance over the completed text of this book, I can visualize a virtual but nonetheless real community of readers and friends who have helped create the philosophical community of which I now am a committed member. To all of them – many of whom I cannot thank explicitly here – I express my thanks for their support and interest. You do not know all that it has meant to me.

The actual writing of this book began with a series of lectures I presented at the University of Kent-Canterbury during the winter and spring of 2003 as the Leverhulme Visiting Professor to the Film Studies Department. I owe an immeasurable debt of gratitude, not only to the Leverhulme Trust for giving me the opportunity afforded by the lectureship, but also and especially to Murray Smith for facilitating my visit there and for all the support he has given me while working on this project even as he continues to disagree with my basic contention. Without our spirited disagreement, this book would have been significantly poorer. I also want to thank Sarah Cardwell for first suggesting that I come to Kent. Without that prescient suggestion, this book might never have been written. All the members of the Film Studies Department and many in the Philosophy Department at Kent were so enthusiastic in their response to my lectures that I became hopeful that there really was something worthwhile saying in them. During my time in England, I also read early versions of some of these chapters at the Universities of Southampton, Nottingham, and Lancaster, and I received useful feedback at each of them. I thank everyone who attended the lectures, but particularly Gregory Currie, Annette Kuhn, Alex Neill, and Jackie Stacey for their hospitality and support.

Mount Holyoke College provided me with the financial support in the form of Faculty Fellowships and Sabbaticals that gave me the time to write this book. As I began to write the final text, the opportunity to give a series of lectures at the Beijing Language and Cultural University focused my energy and allowed me to make good use of the time the College had given me. My thanks to all involved!

Throughout my work on this manuscript, a few individuals gave me the support and encouragement – not without critical reminders – that kept me on track. Christopher Grau read the entire manuscript with a keen philosophical eye, helping me articulate my ideas more clearly and forcefully. Joseph Kupfer also read the manuscript and helped me avoid both infelicities of style and mistakes in content. Angela Curran and I have been friends and colleagues for over a decade now and she continues to inspire me with her acute understanding of the philosophical issues pertaining to film. The person who has been for nearly two decades my primary critical reader and philosophical interlocutor, Alan Schiffmann, is unfortunately now too ill to have read the entire manuscript with his highly skilled and perceptive eyes. Nonetheless, specific chapters, as well as whatever stylistic fluidity I now possess, owe more to him than I can say.

Members of the Five College Philosophy Discussion Group (still anachronistically known as the Propositional Attitudes Task Force) – Ernie Alleva, Bert Bandman, John Connolly, Owen Freeman-Daniels, Jay Garfield, Murray Kiteley, Sam Mitchell, Allyson Mount, and Barry Smith among others – spent three weeks discussing the penultimate version of this manuscript. I am so grateful to them for giving me the opportunity to discuss the entire manuscript in a critical yet supportive environment. A special nod of thanks to Ernie Alleva for organizing those meetings, bringing the wonderful refreshments that fueled the discussions, and keeping me on my philosophical toes with his astute criticisms and corrections.

At various stages in my work on the manuscript, I gave portions of it at various different venues. Among those venues were the Institute for the Advancement of Philosophy for Children at Montclair State University, the Thinking on the Boundaries Conference at the University of South Carolina, the Philosophy Department at Carleton College, the 2004 meeting of the Center for the Cognitive Study of the Moving Image at Calvin College, the 2006 Eastern as well as the 2006 Pacific Meeting of the Society for the Philosophical Study of the Contemporary Visual Arts, and the 2007 Meeting of the Pacific Division of the American Philosophical Association. All of the people who responded to these lectures have both encouraged me to keep working while offering numerous useful suggestions and corrections. I would particularly like to thank Martin Donougho, Kathleen Rowe Karlyn, and Megan Laverty for their insightful criticism and comments.

My colleague in Film Studies at Mount Holyoke, Robin Blaetz, gave me useful feedback on **Chapter 7** that helped me better understand the significance of my own argument. Other members of that program – especially Paul Staiti and Elizabeth Young – have supported my ventures over the years and for that I am very grateful to them. My colleague in the Philosophy Department, James Harold, read the penultimate draft of this book and gave me both helpful suggestions and useful criticisms. Ed Royce read a number of chapters and also gave me excellent advice and feedback. Doug Amy was a supportive friend and colleague who helped me see this project through to fruition. Daniel Barrett and Jonathan Frome's comments on an earlier version of **Chapter 6** were extremely helpful and spurred me to think more deeply about the issue it addresses.

I want to thank my son, Jake, and my wife, Wendy Berg, for their support during the writing of this book. Jake deserves special thanks for his help with some of the illustrations in this book. His computer skills and enthusiasm were always there for me when I needed them. I am glad that he shares my enthusiasm for film, even if we occasionally have disagreements about how many he should watch. Wendy's willingness to allow me the travel and the free time to pursue this project was a necessary ingredient in its success. Both of their enthusiasm for this project and their patience with my execution of it helped me keep my nose to the grindstone. Not that watching films and writing about them deserves that grim metaphor. For even if there were times when it did seem like work, writing about film philosophically has come to be an activity that gives me the highest degree of intellectual satisfaction I can imagine. For their help in getting me there, I owe them both a huge debt.

At Routledge, Tony Bruce and Amanda Lucas were joys to work with. I am grateful for their help with this project. My departmental assistant, Anna May Dion, deserves more than the nod of thanks I can give her for her reliable assistance and cheerful attitude in all she has done to help with this project.

Some of the material contained in this book was published previously in different form. Portions of **Chapter 3** were previously published in *The Journal of Aesthetics and Art Criticism* 64 (2007); of **Chapter 4** in *Midwest Studies in Philosophy* 27 (2003); and of **Chapter 5** in *Film Studies: An International Journal* 8 (2006). **Chapter 7** is a much revised version of a chapter to be published in *Ethics in Film*, Ward Jones and Samantha Vice, eds (Oxford: Oxford University Press, forthcoming).

1   Can philosophy be screened?

As the film opens, the camera reveals a young couple taking a journey through the country. The film continues in an artistic mode, showing us what appear to be random glimpses of their travels. Suddenly, a rogue highwayman appears and soon the man is dead and the woman raped. Cut. We are now in a courtroom and each of the four witnesses' testimony opens up into a virtual reconstruction of the crime. The tale we are presented with in each version shows its narrator in a favorable light and the others acting badly. Whom are we to believe? Is truth relative? How should this affect our attitude towards life?

The year is 2019 and the world, as well as being populated by human beings, sports manufactured creatures – *replicants* – who look and act just like human beings. Indeed, only an expert can tell them apart. Some of the replicants have rebelled and are being hunted down and "decommissioned" by special agents called blade runners. Is there anything morally wrong with decommissioning a replicant? Is it any different from killing a human being? What makes something a person? Why do we have to die?

The mistress of a successful ophthalmologist threatens to reveal their affair to his wife. The revelation would result in the destruction of his reputation as a pillar of society. At the suggestion of his brother, the ophthalmologist agrees to have his mistress killed. The murder is successful and, after a brief period of guilt and remorse, the ophthalmologist lives a happy life, his public image unblemished. If one can commit a crime with impunity, is there any reason not to? If people who do evil do not suffer some form of punishment, what reason is there to live morally? If the guilty go unpunished, does belief in God make sense?

Many film lovers will recognize these three scenarios as very sketchy summaries of the plots of three very different films: Akira Kurasowa's 1950 art film masterpiece, *Rashomon*; Ridley Scott's 1982 science fiction classic, *Blade Runner*; and Woody Allen's 1989 tour de force, *Crimes and Misdemeanors*. Despite the myriad differences among the films – one is an art film made for a sophisticated audience, one is a dark, ruminating, Hollywood-produced science fiction film, and one a funny but dramatic independent film – all three pose philosophical questions and even take stabs at answering them.

This suggests that one cannot really understand these films without thinking about the philosophical issues they raise. Invoking philosophical questions seems to be part of what these three films are about, part of what makes them the remarkable films they are. They present and take a stand upon such deep philosophical issues as epistemological relativism, the nature of personhood, and the basis for morality. Despite the difference in the films' genres and intended audiences, they all have philosophical concerns at their centers.

But this, in turn, suggests a more general question about the relationship between film and philosophy: To what extent are films capable of actually doing philosophy? In asking this question, I am not suggesting that *all* films have philosophical significance, but, as the three films I have chosen suggest, some films do seem to stake out a claim to be doing philosophy. The question facing us is exactly in what sense can they be said to do so.

One option is to make the strong claim that films are capable of actually doing philosophy in something like the sense we think of the classical texts of the Western tradition – such as Plato's *Republic* and Descartes' *Meditations on First Philosophy* – doing philosophy. Of course, there are differences between films and traditional philosophical texts. At a minimum, the former are visual and seek to entertain their audiences while the latter are written and aim at establishing the truth of their contentions. Nonetheless, one might hold, taking account of the films we have just considered, that films can do philosophy in pretty much the way that the traditional texts of the Western tradition do.

At the opposite pole, one could admit that some films do have a relationship to philosophy but deny that it is anything like that exhibited by the founding texts of the Western tradition. Here, the contention might be that film is a medium that is very adept at *popularizing* philosophical issues but lacks the capacity to actually produce original philosophy itself. So one could grant that a film like *Blade Runner* has gotten many more people to think about the question "What is it to be human?" than the works of such philosophers as Bernard Williams and Derek Parfit without additionally attributing to the film the ability to make an independent contribution to philosophy.[1]

The two views I have just outlined mark out the two extreme positions in the debate about the relationship between film and philosophy. In this book, I shall defend a moderate form of one of them: that films can do philosophy. As a way of initiating my brief for this view, let me just say that it seems quite natural to think of films as sometimes addressing philosophical issues. After all, in one sense of the word, "philosophy" is the name given to the most basic issues that concern us as human beings. In the *Critique of Pure Reason*, Immanuel Kant characterized philosophy as the attempt to answer three basic questions: What can I know? What should I do? What can I hope for? Although these questions do not adequately capture all the problems, issues, and questions that philosophy has addressed through the ages, they are a good initial attempt at characterizing the concerns that are essential to philosophy.

From our standpoint at the beginning of the twenty-first century, it is clear that film was the predominant artform of the twentieth century. From its somewhat dubious beginnings in vaudeville peepshows and nickelodeons, film became not only a major industry, but also a cultural form that can no longer be ignored by anyone. For many people, the latest Hollywood blockbuster or independent feature is a "must," something they have got to see in order to remain au courant.

As a result, we can understand why some films might want to confront philosophical questions. After all, as a popular artform, film needs to attract a mass audience. And if, as we have seen, philosophical issues include the most basic concerns we all share as human beings, then it makes sense for films to raise them, for these are questions in which we naturally take an abiding interest.

But no sooner is this claim articulated than reservations surface. Sure, it might make sense to hold that an art film like *Rashomon* and an independent feature like *Crimes and Misdemeanors* actually focus on philosophical concerns, for these films are regarded as the work of *auteurs*, directors who think of themselves as artists and who have a great deal of control of the production process of making their films. But what about a Hollywood film like *Blade Runner*? Such films are the products of a studio system in which directors' ideas are subordinated, often forcibly, to the demands of producers and their concern for the bottom line. As a result, these directors need to be more worried about the marketability of their films than their *auteur* colleagues. Aren't films made under these conditions more likely to be tailored to their ability to attract audiences – and hence make enough at the box office to justify their production costs – by keeping them entertained rather than by trying to incorporate heady questions about the nature of human existence? Philosophy is hardly a popular endeavor in contemporary America. Why think that popular films attempt to address its concerns?

This is a telling response that shows that arguing that films – including popular fiction films – not only address philosophical issues but also make contributions to philosophy itself is a hard row to till. Film and philosophy appear to have such different basic concerns that any initial enthusiasm for the idea that films could do philosophy might now appear to have been misguided.

Nonetheless, more and more Anglo-American philosophers are trying to show that films can be a form in which philosophy is done. Beginning with Stanley Cavell's groundbreaking interpretations of 1930s American films, philosophers have been arguing with increasing frequency that popular narrative films have philosophical depths that previous scholars denied them.[2] In addition to books by philosophers such as Christopher Falzon and Stephen Mulhall, two anthologies have recently appeared that contain essays discussing the philosophical contributions made by film.[3] And this is in addition to the many books that discuss the philosophical implications of film and popular culture more generally.[4]

In defending the idea of film as capable of philosophy, I am not defending all of the recent contributions to this field, for there are some that I find quite problematic, as will become evident in the chapters that follow. Still, from my point of view, the philosophical discussion of film is one of the most interesting and dynamic fields of contemporary philosophy. One reason for this is that films are capable of giving philosophical ideas a liveliness and vivacity that some may find lacking in the written texts of the tradition.

In order to show this, I turn now to John Ford's 1962 western, *The Man Who Shot Liberty Valance*, a film that I see as making an interesting intervention into the philosophical discussion of whether history is progressive. In order to see the film as doing so, it will be helpful to get a sense of what was at stake in the philosophical debate about this issue. Since at least the late 1800s, philosophers have asked whether changes in human social organization can be seen as progress towards some goal or whether, as the old saw has it, the more things change, the more they stay the same. In the early nineteenth century, G. W. F. Hegel gave the idea of progress its most rigorous philosophical defense by attempting to show that the entire course of human history – as well as the differentiation of aspects of non-historical reality itself – had to be viewed as a progressive development that eventuated in the completely self-conscious existence of humanity. As overly ambitious as this undertaking might seem, Hegel did an amazing job of presenting the vast array of existing things and processes as part of an overarching story of progressive self-development.[5]

Many have disputed Hegel's optimistic vision of the often-bloody course of human history. Here, I will only discuss Friedrich Nietzsche's claim that there are reversals in history, declines as well as advances. For him, most of the history of Western civilization represented a decline from the zenith that had been attained in ancient Greece. And while he saw the possibility of the West attaining new heights, that future was not one that he could be certain would come to pass. So his critique asserted that Hegel's notion of "the cunning of reason" concealed a facile optimism that obscured the actual costs of historical "advances."

There are similarities between this aspect of Nietzsche's claim and that made by Ivan in Fyodor Dostoyevsky's masterpiece, *The Brothers Karamazov*. Like Nietzsche, Ivan argues against the possibility of attaining a perspective from which suffering can be rationalized as a necessary cost of progress. Indeed, Ivan is even willing to sacrifice his own rationality if that is the cost of affirming the absolute significance of the suffering of innocent people.[6]

That a great work of literature is able to raise and discuss philosophical issues is probably not surprising.[7] If nothing else, the realist Russian novel allowed its author sufficient space to include what are very nearly philosophical tracts. But what about a Hollywood fiction film? They generally have only two hours or so to resolve everything. Can I seriously maintain that a fiction film can address a philosophical issue in as interesting a manner as a great novel?

Despite its paradoxical air, this is exactly what I believe. Indeed, I think that *The Man Who Shot Liberty Valance* presents its own version of Nietzsche's criticism of Hegel's conception of history by examining one small slice of history through a fictional story about the so-called Wild West. The film depicts the transition from the gun-toting age of Western cowboys and bandits to the civilized order associated with the East and the coming of the law. Generally, when Americans think about the process of "taming" or "settling" the West – note the view implied by this terminology – they rely on an implicit idea of progress as inherent in the development of American society as progressive. Ignoring the presence of another civilization on the very land onto which a civilized order was inserted, they see the spread of European-inspired institutions as simply an advance over the lawlessness that was previously dominant.

As I have said, *The Man Who Shot Liberty Valance* presents the development of the American West from a society ruled by the gun into one ruled by law. Its two male heroes – played by John Wayne and Jimmy Stewart (see Figure 1) – personify the conflict between these two principles. In the course of the film, we are led from the dominant view that the spread of law to the West marked an important advance in human attainments to the contrary perspective: that the replacement of the gun by law resulted in the triumph of less than admirable human capacities, including deception, over some more honorable traits, such as honor and valor. Because the film personifies these two principles in Wayne and Stewart, the story of the defeat of Wayne by Stewart vividly demonstrates the human costs of the so-called civilizing process. It is easier to see these costs when they are presented through the fate of two human beings than when they remain only abstract ideas. Thus, we can say that film is able to give philosophical concepts and ideas a human garb that allows their consequences to be perceived more clearly.

In the film, the Stewart character's ascension – he is an Eastern tenderfoot who "gets the girl" and attains fame as a politician in the newly settled territories – is purchased through the misattribution to him of the role of Liberty Valance's killer, when it was actually the Wayne character – the real cowboy – who shot the outlaw. But this admirable man ends up – the misattribution of Valance's killing results in the loss of his sweetheart and the homestead he built for her – the anonymous town drunk, at whose nearly unmourned coffin we see Stewart and a few others at the start of the film.

Figure 1 The cowboy and the tenderfoot. From *The Man Who Shot Liberty Valance.*
Source: Paramount/The Kobal Collection.

Some may still dismiss this film as just a cowboy story, but the film's perceptive association of the rise of the legal order with the concomitant rise of a press more concerned with images than truth asks its viewers to see two fundamental social institutions of our society – the legal order and the press – as linked in their adherence to deception over truth. Particularly in our own time, when the spread of images has all but totally obscured the search for truth, we cannot but be admiring of the prescience of this film.

Maybe a discussion of one scene will nail down this point. The bulk of the film is a visualization of the narration that the Jimmy Stewart character gives about events that happened some thirty or so years before the present of the frame story. When he's done and has revealed to the current editor of the *Shinbone Star* that his entire political career had been founded on the lie that he

Figure 2 Liberty Valance is shot, but by whom? From *The Man Who Shot Liberty Valance*.

Source: Paramount/The Kobal Collection.

had been the one who had shot Liberty Valance (Figure 2), the editor remains nonplussed. In response to the Jimmy Stewart character's somewhat perplexed question, "Well, you're not going to use the story, Mister Scott?" the editor proudly replies, "This is the West, sir. When the legend becomes fact, print the legend." In so doing, he reveals that, in the modern West, newspapers are less concerned with unearthing the truth than they are with maintaining the image.

So *The Man Who Shot Liberty Valance* – which, on one level, is simply a western, one of Hollywood's most popular film genres – reveals itself as having a deeper agenda that cannot remain hidden from an audience that is primed to think of films as more than mere entertainments. The excitement I find in paying attention to the philosophical aspects of films is that it allows the films' own interest in serious social and intellectual issues to emerge. Engaging with films as philosophy allows us to see that, despite their form, films can have serious aspirations.

It is my view that many fiction films embody philosophical ideas much in the way that *The Man Who Shot Liberty Valance* does Nietzsche's criticism of Hegel's view of history, that is, by providing vivid examples that make it clear what the stakes are in an otherwise quite abstract philosophical debate. These films provide philosophy with an empirical content that shows why philosophy is more than the mock combats Kant claimed many saw in traditional philosophical debates. Taking films seriously is one way to help people see the importance of philosophy.

A reader skeptical about the philosophical potential of film might respond to my invocation of *The Man Who Shot Liberty Valance* with a number of arguments designed to show that the film is not capable of making the philosophical point I attribute to it. He might begin by admitting that the film was, in some sense, about the underside of the settling of the American West, but object that this does not justify seeing the film as making a specifically Nietzschean objection to a specifically Hegelian conception of progress. The film simply lacks the means for articulating the conceptual structures necessary to embody the view of either of these great philosophers.

My critic might also claim that a film cannot make the sort of general claim that I have attributed to *The Man Who Shot Liberty Valance*. Although the film is certainly about the rise to power of a man who has concealed an important truth about an event that was pivotal in his ascent to power, this specific story about specific individuals and events is not even of the right level of generality to make the sort of general claim that I attributed to it.

Finally, this skeptical reader might even admit that he found my interpretation of the film interesting, maybe even compelling. But that, he would add, does credit to me – the philosophical interpreter – rather than to the film. If my interpretation points out that the story the film presents has philosophical implications, then that is an interesting way to *use* the film. The film itself, according to the skeptic, makes no such philosophical statement. That is something imposed upon it by me, the philosophical interpreter.

These three objections – the *explicitness, generality,* and *imposition objections* – although presented here in the context of a specific film, can be generalized into in principle arguments against the possibility of films doing philosophy. Staving them off may be a difficult task, but it is one that is necessary in order to justify my claim that films can do philosophy. Although I will undertake a theoretical refutation of each one, the real proof of films' philosophical abilities occurs through careful investigations of individual films. In the course of the next seven chapters, I will show that some films do philosophize and thereby refute each of these objections.

In developing my answer, I begin in the next chapter at the very general level at which these objections are made, but then turn in the following ones to an investigation of specific philosophical techniques that actually have been employed by films to do philosophy. I will show that films not only have the ability to illustrate philosophical claims or theories in a way that provides genuine illumination, but I will show that films can *make arguments, provide counterexamples* to philosophical claims, and *put forward novel philosophical theories.* Their ability to do these things justifies claiming that, in those specific instances where they do these things, they are doing philosophy. Sometimes, to put my thesis provocatively, *philosophy can be* – and has been – *screened,* that is, shown to us in what we see while watching and listening to a moving picture.

For now, let me just say that, skeptical doubts to the contrary notwithstanding, I do think that *The Man Who Shot Liberty Valance* puts forward the Nietzschean objection with which I credited it. Although I will not now justify this claim fully, let me simply say that this does not entail that John Ford actually had to have Hegel or Nietzsche in mind. All that is necessary is that he was thinking about the philosophical views that *we* can trace back to these great philosophers and that it makes sense to think of him as attempting to respond to one and defend another in the specific context of the Hollywood western. Certainly, more has to be said to justify this, but that is one of the tasks I undertake in the balance of this book.

It may seem odd that I have chosen to begin my defense of the idea that films can be philosophy with a discussion of a film from a popular genre like the western instead of an artfilm like *Rashomon.* After all, it is pretty clear that *Rashomon* presents the philosophical themes of relativism – the idea that there can be multiple, equally (in)valid interpretations of a given event – in a vivid and compelling manner.[8] And among art films such engagement with philosophical ideas is not uncommon. Thus, Ingmar Bergman's 1957 film, *The Seventh Seal,* presents an allegorical tale of a medieval knight on a journey through a plague-ridden landscape. During his journey, the knight shows his doubts about God's existence and questions life's meaning in the face of death. Clearly, these are philosophical issues and the film portrays one man's attempt to find answers to them.

There are a variety of reasons why I do not focus upon such films in this book, despite their obvious philosophical concerns. For one thing, the art film is no longer the central form of filmmaking that it was in the 1950s and 1960s. It therefore seems ill advised to base an argument about the philosophical potential of film as an artform on a mode of filmmaking that is no longer in its ascendancy, no matter how much I personally feel drawn to it. In addition, it struck me that some of the central films in the genre were philosophical more in a layperson's sense than in a way that a professional philosopher uses the term. Since I did not want to limit my attempt to legitimate film's philosophical capacities only to general readers interested in the relationship between film and philosophy, I realized that it would be a mistake to endorse as philosophy forms of reflection that many professional philosophers would take to be philosophy only in a loose sense. While I do not wish to denigrate such films – I am a real fan of art films as well as popular cinema – I made the decision to avoid using them as central examples in making my argument.

Despite what I have just said or, perhaps, because of it, it might be tempting – at least to some readers – to dismiss the growing popularity of using films as vehicles for philosophical discussions as an attempt by an esoteric academic field to gain popularity among an undergraduate population and a general public that is increasingly unable and/or unwilling to read difficult texts, preferring to watch films, television, and related visual media instead. And although there is certainly some truth to this contention, it would be a mistake to think that it accounts for *all* the recent philosophic interest in film and popular culture. There is more at issue in this trend than such a dismissal acknowledges.

Consider, for example, the changed conditions of film viewing in the last twenty or so years. When I began teaching philosophy and film in the late 1970s, the technological requirements for doing so were a daunting problem. I had to get a special grant to buy a projector, a screen, and celluloid copies of the films I wanted to show my class. In order to screen the films, I had to lug to class a heavy projector, a bulky screen, and two or three cumbersome metal cans that held the film reels. Once the film had been shown – usually in only a semi-dark classroom – it was nearly impossible to look at specific scenes again. At most, we could watch one scene in the following class. To screen it, I had to get to the classroom early, run the film through to the scene I wanted to show, and only then could we watch it. Obviously, the possibility of doing so depended upon, among other things, classroom schedules. I think you get the picture.

It's hard for people brought up in the digital age to imagine how much things have changed. Now watching a film seems "second nature." All you have to do is to pop a DVD into the drive of your computer and you're off and running. Films are so completely available for our viewing pleasure that it's hard to imagine how special an occasion film viewing was for those of us raised in earlier times. While I remember fondly the specialness of the Saturday matinee film viewings during which I first encountered some of the classic films I still love, my thirteen-year-old son had experienced films for years before he even entered a theater. And it was quite a while before he understood that films were actually recorded on celluloid rather than on videotape.

The fundamental changes in the accessibility of films has affected not only the teaching of film – paving the way for Film Studies to become a serious academic discipline – but also our viewing habits. Here, I only want to call attention to the fact that it is now standard practice to watch a film repeatedly. In earlier times, viewers saw films only on special occasions and it was rare to see a film more than once. There were, even then, cult films that people flocked to again and again, but standardly one had access to films only during their theatrical release, so that it was expensive and thus unusual for most people to watch a film repeatedly.

Now, however, we have such easy access to reproductions of films in the forms of videos and DVDs that it is standard practice to watch them a number of times. Among my students, it seems common practice to purchase a DVD and then watch a film over and over – often in tandem with visiting its website and playing a range of "special features" available only on the DVD. The technological barriers to repeated viewings of a film have simply vanished, so that films are now viewable as often as one wishes whenever one wishes.

This change in viewing habits has impacted film production. After all, if films are routinely going to be watched more than once, there must be something about the film to justify repeated viewings. Cult films are only one example of a strategy for encouraging multiple viewings of a film. Another involves the bonus material only available on the DVD. A third that is more relevant to our concerns is the increased use of "twist" narratives. Such narratives mislead viewers about important facts until some point late in the film. Once the twist has been revealed, viewers will often experience a desire to see the film again in order to watch it with knowledge of the revealed fact(s). *The Usual Suspects* (Bryan Singer, 1995) – in which a crucial character's real identity is concealed until the end – is an early example of this new trend in films.

This new demand on filmmakers provides a partial explanation of the increased frequency of philosophical films, for the philosophical content of a film won't reveal itself completely on a first viewing. Couldn't making a philosophical film simply be a response to the new demands made by changes in the conditions of film viewing?

Of course, this can't be a complete answer to the question of why films address philosophical issues. After all, as a number of philosophers have claimed, films were doing so well before the digital revolution and we have looked at a number of possible explanations for their doing so. Still, films' newfound interest in philosophy can be at least partially explained by the changes brought about by digital and other means of mechanical reproduction.

It is now time to address what might seem to be simply a terminological issue, but actually has some deep implications. So far, I have generally used the phrase "doing philosophy" to characterize my understanding of film's relationship to philosophy. This way of talking might seem problematic for a variety of reasons. The first is that it attributes agency to films, something that some may object to.[9] From their point of view, only animate creatures are able to do anything, so it is a mistake to attribute to films the capacity to *do* philosophy. I have two responses to this concern. The first is to concede its validity, but to add that my attributing to films the ability to do philosophy is only a *façon de parler*. When I say that a film philosophizes, it is really a shorthand expression for stating that the film's makers are the ones who are actually doing philosophy in/on/through film. The second is to note that philosophers do often attribute actions to written texts, as when they say, for example, that *The Phenomenology of Spirit* develops an idealist metaphysics. While this might also be simply a figure of speech, I intend my attribution of philosophical abilities to films to be on a par with the standard treatment of written works. There is nothing special about my use of this way of talking.

But if I am comfortable claiming that films can do philosophy or, even, philosophize, this is a different claim than saying that films are (works of) philosophy. It would take us far afield to discuss the nature of the various classificatory schemes in which the term "philosophy" occurs. Here, I only want to point out that asserting that a film is (a work of) philosophy makes a stronger claim than saying that it philosophizes. This is because there are various other types of works that might contain some philosophizing without themselves then counting as works of philosophy. *The Brothers Karamazov*, to which I referred earlier, is a good example of such a work. I think it is plain that this novel contains a great deal of philosophy in it without thereby being itself a work of philosophy. For this reason, I generally avoid claiming that a film is (a work of) philosophy. Although I will discuss this issue more fully in **Chapter 7**, at this point I do want to admit that there are certain special cases in which this stronger claim is justified. One example is John Berger's BBC series, *Ways of Seeing*, a work that I will discuss in more detail in **Chapter 5**. So only in special cases will I claim that a film's philosophizing justifies its counting as a work of philosophy.

There is one final locution that I employ that calls for some comment. When a film is able, for example, to develop a counterexample to a philosophical claim or present a philosophical argument, I will generally claim that the counterexample or argument has been *screened*. This way of articulating my assertion makes it evident that the claim or argument has been made in what I would like to call a "specifically cinematic manner." Of course, the assertion that films have to be projected onto a screen is itself a highly contested philosophical issue. We need not go into this question here, but can just stipulate that *screening* refers to a specifically cinematic technique for presenting a philosophical view, claim, or argument. So I will use the phrase "screening philosophy" to refer to the specifically cinematic way in which a film presents a philosophical issue, one that depends upon features of the film medium itself.

The idea of the "specifically cinematic" is also a difficult one to characterize precisely. For example, a film could present a philosophical argument by having the content of a written argument included on its soundtrack while anything whatsoever appeared on the screen. This would not, in my terminology, count as a *screening* of the philosophical argument, for there is nothing inherently cinematic to the argument's presentation. From this point of view, seeing the written text of Kant's Transcendental Deduction of the Categories presented on film – in the manner, say, of silent intertitles – is not a screening of that famous and immensely complex philosophical argument, for one could just as easily have read it in a book, as we normally do. On the other hand, when a fiction film supplies a counterexample to a philosophical theory by means of a specific narrative, I will claim, as I do in **Chapter 5**, that the film has screened the philosophical counterexample, in that case to the principle of utility as the foundation of morality.

I acknowledge that this distinction is a difficult one to draw carefully. If, to choose a different example, Descartes' first *Meditation* were presented in a film version in which it appeared as a receding, scrolling fade like that at the beginning of *Star Wars* (George Lucas, 1977), its presentation would rely on film's ability to so present it, for the scrolling of a visual text is something that only a film can achieve. But this would not count as a *screening* of the first *Meditation*'s argument, because there would be nothing *necessary* about the argument being presented in precisely this way rather than, say, in its standard form in a book.

So it is tempting to say that a philosophical argument or claim is *screened* only when it is *necessary* that the argument or claim be presented in the way that it is in the film. But then we bump up against another philosophical question: Is there anything about the screened philosophy that *requires* that it be presented on film rather than verbally? If we say there is, then we seem to make writing philosophical discussions of the film impossible, while if we say there is not, then we have contradicted the claim of necessity.[10]

Despite the difficulties in formulating this position precisely, I am content to employ this manner of speaking in this study because we have a general idea of paradigm cases of what would constitute screened philosophy. Its general claim can then be phrased as asserting that philosophy can be screened, and I will establish this claim by looking at specific means whereby films can screen particular philosophical techniques.

Earlier, I mentioned that our position at the beginning of the twenty-first century has a bearing on how we think about the relationship between film and philosophy. It also makes a difference in how we think about film itself. When theorists began writing about film in the first decades of the twentieth century, it seemed to be a unique artform, one in which the visual and aural were joined in a unique way. Rudolph Arnheim is one of the classical film theorists who spent a great deal of time and energy reflecting on what made film unique and what the resulting implications were for film style.[11] His idea was that film, in order to qualify as an artform, had to depart from the realistic potential it inherited from its basis in photography.

Now, however, with the advent of alternative means for photographic reproduction such as video and the development of digital technology such as DVDs and digital imaging, film – if we restrict that term to the use of celluloid film strip to project visual images – seems but one of a number of what I call *cognate* media. That is to say, we generally think of films as naturally being reproduced on DVDs and don't always take care to say that what we saw last night, for example, was a DVD reproduction of a film. We just say that we watched the film.[12]

What this imprecision in our speech practices reveals is that film is no longer a unique artform. Rather, film has to be seen as the historically privileged member of a group of cognate artforms all of which involve screened visual images accompanied by (potentially) synchronous sound. There have been various suggestions about how this fact should affect our use of the term "film."[13] Suggestive as many of these proposals are, I will generally retain the use of the term "film" in this study. I usually intend it to stand for the more correct term "film and its cognate media," for I do not want to restrict my argument to celluloid but wish it to include DVDs, VHS, and other related media as well. So when I ask whether philosophy can be *screened*, I explicitly intend that term to include the variety of different modes for presenting moving audio-visual material that now exists – as well as those that may come to be in the future.

But it's high time to move beyond these preliminaries and actually confront the question of how films screen philosophy.

2 Are there limits to film's philosophical capabilities?

It has become something of a commonplace for philosophers of film to remark on the similarity between the situation of the prisoners in Plato's Allegory of the Cave and that of film viewers. In an attempt to explain his metaphysics of Forms in *The Republic*, Plato analogizes our everyday belief in the reality of the physical objects that surround us to that of prisoners in a cave who, able to see only shadows projected on the cave's wall, take these shadows to be completely substantial entities.[1] One of Plato's goals in developing the allegory was to provide his readers with a way of understanding the puzzling claim that what they take to be fully real things – the ordinary objects of their experience, tables and chairs, etc. – might be, from a more adequate metaphysical point of view, as insubstantial as the shadows the imaginary prisoners perceive on the wall of their prison-like cave.[2]

The fascination that Plato's image has for contemporary scholars of film does not stem, however, from their interest in his metaphysics. What mesmerizes them is the fact that – nearly two and a half millennia before its technological realization – Plato appears to have invented the cinema.[3] Without the benefit of either electricity or advanced technology, he was able to envision the "magic lantern show" that has so captivated mass audiences since its inception in the final years of the nineteenth century.[4]

Many contemporary film theorists are also sympathetic to Plato's denigration of visual images. For him, truth – the object of philosophic investigation – must have as its object those eternal and unchanging entities he designates the Forms. Even ordinary physical things are insufficient as the objects of philosophic truth, for they are subject to change and degeneration, while the truth must be eternal and incorruptible. Images are, from Plato's point of view, twice removed from the fully real, mere copies of copies, and so are doubly disenfranchised as suitable objects for philosophical truth.

In contemporary hands, Plato's view has become the notion that artforms that traffic in images cannot produce knowledge. Film and its cognate artforms – television, video, DVD, CGI, etc. – are banished from the realm of truth, that land which philosophy deems its own. Although there are several basic reasons why film is seen as inimical to philosophy, at base they rely on a view similar to Plato's: Images are not adequate as a source of conviction that can be valorized philosophically. While film has the power to ensnare its viewers – indeed, a power that is unparalleled in our culture – the beliefs so inculcated lack the pedigree awarded by philosophical procedures of justification. From this point of view, the idea that films could screen philosophical truth seems absurd.

In order to ascertain whether there are good reasons to accept the philosophical disenfranchisement of film, I will examine closely the three a priori objections to the idea that film can screen philosophy that I introduced in the last chapter. These objections are a priori in that they do not refer to actual films, but make general claims about what films cannot do. As a result, they posit a fundamental theoretical problem at the root of the attempt to view films as philosophy. What we shall ask is whether the problem does not lie with assumptions made by the objectors themselves rather than with the thesis that films can philosophize.

The explicitness objection

We have already encountered the first type of a priori objection to cinematic philosophy, one that takes off from the relegation of art to a realm of reality inferior to that reserved for philosophy that we detected in Plato's Allegory of the Cave. In its twenty-first-century form, this objection contrasts film's visual nature to the conceptually determinate form in which philosophy is written. It asserts that film lacks the explicitness to formulate and defend the precise claims that are characteristic of philosophical writing.

Although Murray Smith makes this claim in his article, "Film Art, Argument, and Ambiguity," he begins with a different criticism. Smith points out that there is an uncanny similarity between a thought experiment envisioned by Bernard Williams in which the minds and bodies of an emperor and a peasant are switched and the plot of Carl Reiner's 1984 romance, *All of Me*. In the film, the Steve Martin character's body becomes possessed by *two* minds: one, his own; the other, that of a rich female client. But, Smith claims, these similar narratives are used to different effect in the philosophy text and the film. Whereas the narrative in the philosophical thought experiment is structured with epistemic issues at the forefront, in the film it is artistic matters – in this case, comic ones – that trump other concerns. So despite the presence of similar narratives, the philosophical text and the comic film actually have very different structuring interests. Parodying Sam Goldwyn's famous remark denying that films have *messages*, Smith avers, "Pictures are for entertainment – if I wanted to make a philosophical point, I'd publish an essay in *Proceedings of the Aristotelian Society*."[5]

What troubles me most about Smith's argument is its methodology. Rather than criticizing a proposed philosophical interpretation of a film, he begins his argument by focusing on a similarity that *he* has noted between a film and a philosophical text only to insist that those similarities are subordinate to important differences between them. One could easily agree with Smith about the case he puts forward without accepting the general claim he thinks his example supports, viz. that no film can actually do philosophy. Maybe *All of Me*'s similarity to Williams' thought experiment is just coincidental. And even if the film were a failed attempt to provide a direct cinematic equivalent for the thought experiment, that would not show that *no* such attempts would result in the production of a philosophically significant film.

Maybe because he realizes that his example cannot bear the philosophical weight he needs it to, Smith supplements his argument by emphasizing a generic difference between film and philosophy. Relying on an idea developed by the so-called New Critics of the 1950s, Smith claims that works of art are inherently ambiguous, but not so philosophical texts: "Few criticisms are more apt to strike terror into the heart of the philosopher than the assertion that such-and-such a proposition is 'ambiguous,' while in the world of art, that term is more apt to be used as a term of praise."[6] Smith's point is that, if films – and works of art, more generally – are ambiguous, then they cannot present the sort of precision that is necessary for articulating and defending philosophical positions.

You will recall that Plato's denial of art's capacity to reveal the truth was based on a metaphysics that placed art into a category so far removed from reality that its ability to state truths could not be defended. Smith reinscribes this Platonic metaphysics into a difference between epistemic and artistic interests that once again erects a barrier between art and truth. For this, if for no other reason, the argument should raise our suspicions that Smith is not alone in echoing Plato's denigration of the epistemic function of art. Bruce Russell makes a very similar claim but, unlike Smith, focuses upon an actual attempt to demonstrate the presence of "cinematic philosophy": Herbert Granger's reconstruction of Louis Malle's 1963 film *Le Feu follet* as showing its protagonist, Alain Leroy (Maurice Ronet), actually philosophizing about the meaning of life. "*Le Feu follet* is special," Granger tells us, "in that it gives us a cinematic narrative of someone engaged in *philosophical inquiry* at the deepest and most personal level."[7] So what we witness in the film, according to Granger, is someone actually philosophizing and it is in virtue of this that he claims the film deserves to be called "cinematic philosophy."

But why is this so? A film can show someone painting without itself being an example of a supposed "cinematic painting."[8] Why should a film about a person actively philosophizing be an example of a film that itself philosophizes?

Le Feu follet is an example of what we might call an *overtly* philosophical film. No one watching the film can miss its philosophical content for it is explicitly presented in the film's soundtrack in which Leroy explains both his quest to find a life worth living and his decision that he cannot. We witness a person engaged in the process of doing philosophy. Doesn't this mean that the film should count as philosophizing?

A similar claim could be made for Richard Linklater's 2001 film, *Waking Life*. The film is visually unusual because it is rotoscoped and animated, a technique that has since become so common that it is featured in numerous advertisements. The film presents a young man in a persistent dreamlike state conversing with many people – including the late philosopher Robert Solomon and the film scholar Steven Prince – on a wide range of topics that repeatedly bring up the question of the relationship between dreams and reality. Although the film does not endorse any particular view, it prompts viewers to ask whether life might be nothing but a dream. Shouldn't its stimulation of philosophical reflection qualify this film as also an instance of cinematic philosophy?

Granger answers the question of why *Le Feu follet* should be seen as doing philosophy by pointing to the film's actual presentation of philosophical argumentation: "Philosophical argumentation must be an *essential feature* of a story for it to be fully philosophical."[9] Because *Le Feu follet* presents a series of Leroy's encounters with people leading different types of lives who cannot provide a justification for their mode of conduct that Leroy finds adequate, Granger sees the film as presenting an argument against the idea that life has meaning.

> Alain [Leroy] concludes: the thing well done [which he believes would give life meaning] is beyond us; indeed, it is beyond life; it is *le feu follet*, 'the will-o'-the-wisp'; excellence does not exist, and we are always left with something less. At its best, life only offers us the infinite forms of mediocrity that result from the compromises of adulthood. ... The mediocrity of life and the absence of excellence are where life's horror lies.[10]

Granger sees *Le Feu follet* as a paradigmatic example of philosophizing on film because in it we witness Leroy developing his own philosophical answer to the question of whether life is worth living. This is, after all, a question that most people see as *the* basic philosophical one. If the film really does present a case that life is *not* worth living, shouldn't that qualify it as really doing philosophy? And a similar case could be made, *mutatis mutandi*, for *Waking Life* philosophizing.

Russell answers this question with a resounding, "No." In response to Granger, Russell avers, "Narrative films so lack explicitness that it is not true that there is some particular argument to be found in them."[11] Russell begins his criticism by pointing out that the argument that Granger finds in the film is *implicit*. That is, the film does not explicity present this argument; it has to be flushed out by perceptive philosophical critics like Granger who make explicit to us what they take the film to be saying implicitly.

But, Russell continues, why accept Granger's interpretation of the film's argument? There are alternative arguments that are equally plausible candidates for the film's argument. In response to Granger's interpretation of the film as showing that life is not worth living, Russell asks the following questions:

> Is it that life is not worth living *for him*, a depressed man who does not have the ability, or the desire, to live types of lives other than those he considers? Or is it the general claim that life is not worth living for anyone? And is the argument that the various types of lives Alain considers to be not worth living are not worth living because they are lived in a poor way by the people Alain considers, or that they couldn't be lived by anyone in a way that would make them worth living?[12]

We may presume that Russell takes these to be rhetorical questions rather than alternatives from which one should make a choice. But why accept this? What if Granger simply responded by saying that Alain was making the second argument described by Russell – that life is not worth living for anybody – and that he had simply not thought about the distinction Russell makes in the third between specific and general ways of assessing the types of lives that Leroy considers? After all, Granger concedes that Alain's philosophical arguments are not good ones. Why should we accept Russell's contention that the film is ambiguous rather than saying that its philosophical argument is not sufficiently well developed to be a valid argument that we could accept?

The answer is, I think, that Russell does not think that films are capable of making philosophical arguments in any sense. Rather, he sees film as raising philosophical questions that viewers or interpreters – the actual philosophers – must develop into philosophical arguments proper. As Russell says, "non-documentary films provide occasions for us to do philosophy, but they do not themselves do it."[13]

Once again, we find art and philosophy compared to one another with the former found wanting – of course, by a philosopher not an artist. And, also once again, we find the explicitness of philosophical texts valorized over the supposed ambiguity of artistic objects, specifically film narratives. Russell's charge is that films lack the explicitness necessary for philosophy.

There is, I think, an invidious comparison at work in Russell's thinking between philosophical texts and films (or artworks). While philosophical texts are taken to unproblematically present arguments, it is maintained that it is not films but their interpreters who make the arguments. But this, I believe, represents a misunderstanding of both philosophical texts and works of art. It certainly is true that the claims that artworks make are often implicit and therefore require the viewer to make them explicit. But this does not mean that the viewer is the one who constitutes a work's meaning as some have argued.[14] Indeed, it would be paradoxical, for example, to say that I, rather than *Guernica*, express outrage against the atrocity perpetrated by Franco because I have to see that this is what the painting expresses. And, similarly, just because an argument is implicit, it does not therefore have to be imprecise. Finally, it is worth noting that interpretive disagreements about what and how philosophical texts argue remain unresolved after centuries of ongoing debate. One notorious example is the ongoing dispute about how to characterize the precise conclusion of Kant's Transcendental Deduction of the Categories.[15] Just because an argument is philosophical, it need not be unambiguous.

Still, I imagine that Russell would not be satisfied with this response. While he probably would allow that films (and artworks) can express attitudes such as that of outrage or love, I expect that he would still deny that works of art can actually *make* arguments. And if we have to attribute *implicit* arguments to them, then he would once again claim that they lack the determinate structure necessary for making those in a precise manner.

But what exactly is it about non-documentary film that makes it incapable of presenting an argument according to Russell? Is it its visual nature? Since he excludes documentary films from the scope of his argument because he believes them to be capable of presenting arguments, this cannot be the case. Is it, then, the films' narrative structure? Since Russell objects to Noël Carroll's claim that non-narrative avant-garde films such as Ernie Gehr's *Serene Velocity* (1970) present arguments for philosophical conclusions, this also cannot be the ground for his claim.[16] Is there ambiguity in Russell's grounds for this assertion? Does this mean *he* is not making a philosophical argument?

Most likely, Russell is bothered by the implicit nature of the arguments that have been attributed to films. He seems to think that, because the arguments are implicit, they cannot be formulated precisely. But this seems to me simply a mistake. It may be that the philosophical claims and arguments that have been attributed to films have not always been formulated as precisely as they should be by their philosophical interpreters. But this does not establish the claim that the films themselves are inherently ambiguous and their arguments incapable of precise formulation. Russell has not presented an argument that is adequate to establish *this* claim.

What he has established is the need to present philosophically precise interpretations that demonstrate in clear and explicit terms exactly what philosophical claims films have established and what the exact argument is that the film makes. But these are simply important regulative ideals that should govern philosophical interpretations of films, not in principle arguments against their possibility. In order to reject the possibility of films making arguments, Russell would need to either show that there are the problems dogging *any* attempt to formulate a philosophical argument made on film or provide a more convincing argument that explained exactly why it was not possible for films to present philosophical arguments.[17]

The generality objection

There is another reason why some philosophers and film theorists have denied that film is capable of screening philosophy. Philosophy is – by its own accounts – one of the oldest intellectual pursuits, with roots extending back into most ancient cultures. The questions that characterize philosophy as a specific mode of inquiry – such as "What is the nature of existence?", "What can we really be said to know?", "Is there a correct way to live one's life?" – are nearly as old as humanity itself and probably incapable of that final answer that most great philosophers seemed determined to provide.

In measuring the distance between these questions and film, what stands out is the abstractness and generality of the issues that characterize philosophy. In order for something to qualify as even a possible answer to a philosophic question, it therefore has to be formulated as a universal claim that purports to provide general knowledge.[18] Indeed, on many accounts philosophy's birth in fifth century B.C. Athens comes about precisely at the moment when abstract principle begins to rival narrative as a way of understanding the place of human beings in the universe as a whole. So, for example, instead of relying on stories about the gods to answer questions about the natural world, philosophy puts forward abstract accounts to serve as explanations of natural phenomena. We therefore find Xenophanes denying that the rainbow is a god and positing instead a naturalistic explanation for its colorful appearance: "She whom men call Iris (rainbow), this also is by nature cloud, violet and red and pale green to behold."[19] So if philosophy can be characterized as involving a rejection of narrative in favor of an alternative style of explanation, fiction films appear to be the wrong type of entity to embody philosophic reflection. Like the Greek myth, a film like *The Man Who Shot Liberty Valance* tells us a story that *the generality objection* contends stands at odds with the generality of philosophical argumentation.

In order to respond to this objection, I first need to distinguish two genera that films fall into: fiction and non-fiction films, with the latter being subdivided into documentary and experimental films.[20] This set of distinctions is important because we need to be clear whether the generality objection is meant to apply to all three types of films – fiction, documentary, experimental – or only to one of these. It certainly is intended as an objection to fiction films doing philosophy and, indeed, to any narrative artform doing so.[21] But whether, and if so how, it applies to the other two categories of films remains to be seen.

So, let's ask why anyone might expect there to be a connection between fiction films and philosophy. After all, consider the relationship between fiction films and mathematics. Mathematics is an example of a field of knowledge whose nature is so remote from film that the idea that a fiction film could actually develop mathematical knowledge strikes us as absurd. Mathematical knowledge involves proof and demonstration, which means that the linkage between different mathematical statements is a matter of logic. With narrative films, however, linkages are generally temporal, with one scene preceding or following another. This difference in fundamental structure or the "grammar" of the two areas makes it difficult to imagine mathematics actually happening on screen.

Of course, it is possible to film a mathematician proving, say, the Pythagorean theorem. And, indeed, something analogous can be done with philosophy. However, this is not what is at issue, for we are now considering the question of whether a fiction film can qualify as a work of mathematics or philosophy, whether either of these disciplines can, as I like to put it, be screened. Certainly, a film can *record* mathematics being done, just as it can a philosophic argument being articulated.[22] But this is not to say that a film can make a contribution to either of these two disciplines, the possibility that we are envisioning in claiming that philosophy might actually be done on screen.

Some recent films have made the attempt to represent mathematical thinking to their audiences. The eponymous hero of Gus Van Sant's *Good Will Hunting* (1997), for example, is a mathematical genius and the film shows us blackboards filled with equations he has written. Similarly, Ron Howard's *A Beautiful Mind* (2001) tells the story of a troubled mathematical genius, John Nash, and makes a few stabs at presenting his mathematical insights to us. And the hero of Darren Aronofsky's 1998 film, π, is certainly tormented if not a genius, as he looks for the numerical pattern that will decode the mysteries of existence. Yet despite their having some mathematical *content*, I think it beyond dispute that none of these films actually *does* any mathematics at all. While the films may allow us to become privy to some of the joys and torments of this highly abstract field of knowledge, the films cannot convey the nature of actual mathematical activity. The sort of intellectual operations that are characteristic of mathematics are so different from the ways in which film operates that it is hard to even begin to speculate on how a fiction film might be able to count as a screening of mathematical knowledge.

History, on the other hand, is an example of a field of knowledge to which a film can – and does – make contributions. Now the term "history" is itself ambiguous, referring both to the actual temporal development of human affairs and its reflection in an intellectual discipline whose object it is to understand history in the first sense. The issue we are concerned with is whether film can screen history in the second sense, that is, itself qualify as a scientific or scholarly investigation of actual historical events themselves.

Like philosophy, history is explored through a variety of different methods. One of the best-known efforts to distinguish them was made by Nietzsche in *The Use and Abuse of History*. He distinguished between three different historical methods "a *monumental* method, an *antiquarian* method, and a *critical* method."[23] For our purposes, we need only consider one method that historians use to present the results of their research: narrative.

What is a narrative? *The Concise Oxford Dictionary of Literary Terms* defines a narrative as "a telling of some true or fictitious event or connected sequence of events, recounted by a *narrator* to a *narratee* (although there may be more than one of each)." While this definition is itself subject to philosophic debate – some philosophers have maintained there must be at least two events and a narrator need not recount them – it does give us a working idea of what a narrative is. It is a story that is told by one person, usually to another, that provides an account of something that happened.[24]

From this definition, it is obvious why history employs narratives. Historians use them to make intelligible to us occurrences or tendencies that we otherwise might find problematic or unintelligible. The function of a narrative is to provide the scaffolding that joins events into a pattern that allows us to comprehend their significance.

Take, for example, Lorraine Gray's 1977 documentary, *With Babies and Banners*. This film presents a feminist reinterpretation of the events of the famous sit-down strike that the United Auto Workers waged against General Motors in Flint, Michigan, during the winter of 1936–37. While standard histories of the strike credit this as a turning point in the labor wars of the 1930s, they minimize or omit the role that women played in the strike. Through a combination of interviews, photographs, and newsreels, the film puts forward an interesting thesis: That without the efforts of the Women's Emergency Brigade, the UAW would have lost the strike when the police charged at the so-called Battle of Bull Run. This was an attempt the police made to force the workers out of the main GM plant. But because the women placed themselves between the police and the striking workers, the men were able to secure the plant and thus win a victory of the union. The importance of this strike is recognized by Sydney Lens: "It was at General Motors in Flint, Michigan, where the CIO [the parent union of the UAW] was 'made,' and where American labor came of age."[25] What he fails to acknowledge, from the point of view of the filmmakers, is the role that women played in that victory.

Now my concern here is not with whether Lens' written account of the strike is superior to the film's audio-visual one, but only in pointing out that both are attempts to present an accurate history of the events of the Flint Sit-Down Strike.[26] And it needs to be noted that this film is not simply a recording of historical events, a possibility that we noted could be achieved in a film of either mathematics or philosophy being done but that would not amount to a genuine screening of either discipline. Although *With Babies and Banners* includes a great deal of documentary footage, what constitutes it as a work of history is that manner in which this footage is edited into a coherent narrative that is an essential component of an historical work of this type. To see a documentary film as simply a recording of the actual historical events is to ignore the complexity of the process by which records of events are put together into a coherent narrative, whether through film or words on a page.[27]

Both *The Labor Wars* and *With Babies and Banners*, then, are works of history because each presents us with a narrative that gives us a new understanding of the events it describes/depicts. Although the book develops its narrative completely linguistically, while the film uses images, language, and sounds, it is because the two objects share the property of being narrative works that they can both be instances of genuine historical research and understanding that offer competing narratives of the same events. There can be different forms in which historians present the results of their research. And each of those forms can constitute a different mode of history as a discipline that aims at understanding the past.[28]

What this discussion of history might suggest is the possibility of giving an affirmative answer to the question of whether philosophy can be screened by specifying an element that can function as narrative did in the case of history. That is, if we could specify an element that film and philosophy have in common, then we might be able to explain how film was capable of screening philosophy.

Still, understanding the possibility of screening philosophy does not seem as easy to map out as was the case of screening history. We have already acknowledged that philosophy, however else it might be characterized, presents universal truths such as: knowledge is justified true belief; an action is moral if and only if it, more than any alternative, contributes to the general welfare; art is the figurative expression of an idea. These philosophical claims – chosen more or less arbitrarily from the theory of knowledge, ethics, and the philosophy of art – present definitions of philosophical concepts that are central to their fields. In each case, the definition is an answer to a very general question: What is knowledge? What makes an action moral? What is art? Narratives – visual or otherwise – are, however, about specific events and individuals, such as the success of a strike. On the face of it, they don't involve general truths at all. But in so far as philosophy is inherently general – and here we encounter the generality objection once more – there seems an unbridgeable gulf between it and narrative film. How could an inherently narrative medium establish general truths? Film by its very nature seems as unable to perform the sort of intellectual operations that are central to philosophy as an intellectual discipline as it was in the case of mathematics.[29]

The generality objection, then, presents another significant obstacle to seeing how films could screen philosophy. It contends that the two media are just too different in their natures for film to be able to present philosophy on screen.

But we are actually in less desperate straits that this suggests, for the example of history can give us a clue to a response to the generality objection. The reason that history could be screened was that narrativity provided a link between film and history. Perhaps we were too quick to claim that philosophy did not involve narratives. For if there were a distinctive philosophical use of narrative, then this might provide the required link between philosophy and film.

And, indeed, there is a well-developed philosophical technique that involves narratives, indeed, fictional ones at that: the thought experiment. Although I postpone a full discussion of thought experiments until **Chapter 4**, let me just note that thought experiments do involve hypothetical narratives and thus provide a way out of the dilemma proposed by the generality objection: that films are inherently specific while philosophy is inherently general. Even though I have yet to present a full explanation of how films function as philosophical thought experiments, we can already see how the presence of such narrative episodes in the heart of philosophy provides one avenue of escape from the generality objection.

The imposition objection

Let's now turn to a third in principle objection to film screening philosophy. *The imposition objection* recognizes that films can be used for philosophically interesting purposes. For example, a professor might get his introductory class in philosophy to think about the question of civil rights for robots by having them watch Alex Proyas' 2004 film, *I, Robot*. In so doing, the professor might not believe that the film actually raises this question itself, but that she can use the film in order to get her students to think about this question in a more engaged manner than they would without having seen the film's depiction of robots as capable of thought and emotion.[30]

In teaching elementary school children philosophy, I do very much the same thing except that I use children's books. If I discuss the nature of knowledge by using James Thurber's *Many Moons*, I don't claim that the book has made a contribution to philosophy but only that it can be a useful *prompt* for getting the children to engage in a philosophical discussion of knowledge.[31]

Someone might maintain that my position vis-à-vis *Many Moons* is valid as a general characterization of the relationship between films and philosophy. Although films can be useful ways to introduce the discussion of philosophical issues and may even help us think about those issues in deeper and more adequate ways, the films themselves do not contribute to our store of philosophical knowledge, assuming that there is such a thing. The philosophizing is being done by a philosopher using a film, but not by the film itself.

Recall Russell's objection to Granger's interpretation of *Le Feu follet*. In the present context, we can reinterpret Russell as arguing that, were Granger to provide a sufficiently explicit version of the argument about the meaninglessness of life, it would be *Granger* and not the film that should be credited with doing so. While the film raises important questions about the meaning of life, it is only the philosophical interpreter who can organize these into a coherent philosophical claim or argument.

As with the explicitness objection, I am troubled by the a priori character of the imposition objection when it is taken as a general argument against the possibility of cinematic philosophy. In fact, I actually employ this criticism myself, but not as a general criticism of the possibility of screening philosophy. Rather, I criticize particular interpretations of films as imposing the author's ideas on a film. So, for example, I raise precisely this objection in **Chapter 6** when I criticize Noël Carroll's interpretation of *The Third Man*.

Rather than an argument against film being philosophy, I take the imposition objection to be a warning that can be made into a regulative principle:

(PI) When making an interpretation of a film, take care not to *impose* an interpretation on a film that is inappropriate.

Of course, this leaves the question of when an interpretation makes an *inappropriate imposition* of philosophical concerns onto a film.

There is an important distinction between creator-oriented and audience-oriented interpretations that can help us resolve this issue.[32] One important type of interpretation of works of art attempts to reconstruct the meaning that the creator of the work of art could have intended the work to have. Such creator-oriented interpretations have many constraints that audience-oriented interpretations need not heed. For example, the following principle makes sense for creator-oriented interpretations:

(PCI1) Do not attribute to the work of art a meaning that could not have been intended by the creator of the work.

This principle entails, for example, that seeing an artwork from the seventeenth century addressing Einstein's theory of relativity makes no sense as a *creator-oriented* interpretation, even if it can be a profound *audience-oriented* one, for the obvious reason that no one living in the seventeenth century could have had any knowledge of Einstein's theory.[33]

This allows us to understand at least one-way in which an interpretation can be inappropriate: If it is a creator-oriented interpretation and it violates PCI1. The significance of this is that it allows us to have a more determinate sense of when an interpretation might illicitly attribute a philosophical interest to a film and when such an attribution would be legitimate. For a philosophical film interpretation to be at least *prima facie* plausible, it needs to posit a meaning that the filmmaker(s) could have intended. If it does not do so, then it would make sense to say that, while the *interpretation* is philosophy, the film is not, at least on that interpretation.

This is not to say that there can't be philosophically interesting audience-oriented interpretations of films, only that we need to be clear which type of interpretation we are giving. Only creator-oriented interpretations of a film can justify the claim that the film itself is philosophical.

In this chapter, I have shown that three purported objections to films doing philosophy fail. But although this justifies claiming that there are no a priori grounds for denying that films *can* do philosophy, it doesn't show that films actually have done philosophy. This positive argument remains to be made, and the question facing us is what method we should employ to establish that films actually screen philosophy.

There are two basic paths such a demonstration might take. The first is to argue that there is an inherent connection between film and philosophy, so that film by its very nature raises philosophical concerns. Most famously, Stanley Cavell has taken this route, arguing that film and philosophy are united by a common concern with skepticism (or, in his later work, moral perfectionism). Cavell's view has had a significant impact on other philosophers. A number of important scholars working in both the fields of philosophy and film studies have accepted Cavell's basic claim about the relationship between film and philosophy. Nonetheless, I think it is the wrong way to proceed in developing the philosophical significance of film. There are two basic reasons for this.

My first reservation about Cavell's view has to do with his narrow focus upon skepticism as the philosophical question that links film to philosophy. Skepticism about the reality of the external world and the existence of other minds – as the two traditional skeptical concerns are most widely characterized – are certainly important philosophical issues both historically and thematically. And Cavell has written extensively about the significance of this issue from his own unique philosophical point of view. I have no problem when he discusses this issue in regard to an individual film or a specific film genre – as he does both in *Pursuits of Happiness* and *Contesting Tears*. My concern is with his attempt to claim that film has an inherent connection to skepticism because of its very nature, a claim that he develops, for example, in a brief riff on the term "screen":

> The world of a moving picture is screened. The screen is not a support, not like a canvas; there is nothing to support, that way. It holds a projection, as light as light. A screen is a barrier. What does the silver screen screen? It screens me from the world it holds – that is, makes me invisible. And it screens that world from me – that is, screens its existence from me. That the projected world does not exist (now) is its only difference from reality.[34]

Cavell's claim is that the inaccessibility of the screen world to us and us to it makes it a "moving image of skepticism" (itself a Cavellean riff on Plato's claim that time is the moving image of eternity). Because of this, skepticism becomes for Cavell the inherent global link between film and philosophy.

What I am worried about is Cavell's limitation of the philosophical significance of film to its screening of skepticism.[35] As will become clear in the following chapters, I think that films discuss a much wider range of philosophical issues than simply that of skepticism, even in all its various forms. While I agree with Cavell that films do screen skepticism, I think that there are other issues that they also confront, such as *The Man Who Shot Liberty Valance*'s consideration of theories of history as necessarily progressive. It is a mistake to focus exclusively on one philosophical issue, no matter how significant, as the only one that films screen.

Cavell's claim about film and philosophy also suffers from a serious methodological problem. In so far as Cavell claims that the connection between film and philosophy is inherent, he is making an essentialist claim that relies on his view of what the essential features of each medium or field. In this respect, his view resembles that of the so-called grand theorists of film who attempted to articulate theories of film that explained what film was like in all places and at all times.[36]

The essentializing approach of the grand theorists has come under fire from many quarters. Here, I will only cite the essays in David Bordwell and Noël Carroll's anthology, *Post-Theory*, as an important instance of this attack on grand theory.[37] The theoretical basis for this critique is that the attempt to develop a unified theory of film's nature is at best premature and at worst ill-conceived. Carroll, for example, asserts that the academic study of film is not yet in a position to develop the over-arching theory about film's nature that the grand theorists have proposed. From his point of view, the discipline is still immature, in a state of formation, so it is not yet ready to coalesce into the unified approach required by grand theories. Others have claimed that the problem with grand theory is more basic, that it attempts to legislate a unified character to a diverse and differentiated field and that this attempt is illegitimate. My own view inclines towards the latter alternative. I see film as an evolving cultural presence whose nature cannot be fixed through a single theoretical paradigm.

Applying this view to the relationship between film and philosophy, we can see that we should eschew any approach that aims to specify an essential connection between them. Just as I have countered the a priori objections to screened philosophy, I think we need to reject any *global* – that is, *universal* and a priori – attempt to specify how film can raise philosophical issues, make philosophical claims, illustrate philosophical positions, develop philosophical arguments, etc. What I advocate is a more *local* – that is, *particular* and *empirical* – approach, one that investigates the question of film's relationship to philosophy by paying attention both to individual films and specific philosophical techniques.

In regard to specific films, the relevant questions to ask are "What philosophical question or issue does it raise?", and "How does it raise this question or issue, and what does it say about it?" In regard to specific philosophical techniques, the question becomes "How might a film *screen* that technique and what films, if any, have managed to do so?"

Still, an important question remains to be addressed: In order to claim that films should count as doing philosophy, isn't it necessary to understand what philosophy is? After all, if I am claiming that films can do philosophy, don't I need to make it clear what philosophy is, so we can assess the validity of my claim? But no sooner does one attempt to specify what philosophy is, than one finds oneself immersed in what seems to be an intractable problem.

For one thing, there is the question of who decides what counts as philosophy. And I don't just mean to raise the question of whether there is a contemporary school of philosophy – analytic, Continental, phenomenology, postmodernism, etc. – that deserves recognition as *the* correct way to do philosophy, so that its advocates are the ones to assess whether something counts as philosophy. I want to suggest that academic philosophers have a different understanding of philosophy than do many of those outside the academy.

This can be seen by comparing the reaction of non-academics to the question of whether film can philosophize to that of academic philosophers. The latter have a narrower conception of what philosophy is, so they tend to be more apprehensive than the former about characterizing films as doing philosophy. Whereas philosophers tend to be reluctant to grant film the ability to philosophize, most non-philosophers are intrigued by the idea and find it natural that films would raise the sorts of issues that they see as philosophical.

But even among academic philosophers, the concept of philosophy is contested. While there is broad agreement on a range of certain specific individuals whose works count as philosophy – Plato, Aristotle, Descartes, Kant, etc. – there are other names that raise questions about the philosophical nature of their works – Kierkegaard, Heidegger, Derrida, etc. And even among those enfranchised as truly philosophical, many would reject large portions of their writings as insufficiently rigorous by contemporary standards.

Despite these and many other concerns about specifying the nature of philosophy, I think there is a way out of the tangle for the purposes of this study. While not a completely adequate answer to the question of what philosophy is, it will allow us enough clarity to proceed with our inquiry.

So let me introduce three distinct conceptions of philosophy.[38] The first conceives of philosophy as a discipline that addresses a rather limited set of what are often termed "eternal questions." Examples of such specifically philosophical questions are: Do we possess knowledge of reality as it really is? What are the basic constituents of reality? What makes an action morally right? Must art be beautiful? Each of these questions address what might be thought of as a basic human concern. But what is also unique about them is that they are not addressed by any other academic discipline or intellectual pursuit. Psychologists, for example, worry about different styles of knowing, but they never address the question of whether the knowledge we do possess accurately characterizes the world as it actually is. The latter topic belongs exclusively to philosophy. Or, again, mathematicians are concerned about numbers, but they don't spend very much time asking about the existence of the entities that constitute the domain of their inquiry. They simply get on with their work of defining the properties that numbers have. The metaphysical question of whether numbers are real is the concern only of philosophers.

The second conception of philosophy treats it as a discipline that asks questions about the other disciplines. Those influenced by European terminology would characterize this as the "science of the positive sciences" or simply as "meta-science," indicating a field that takes the knowledge produced in other fields as its subject matter. From this point of view, there are as many specific fields of philosophy as there are independent intellectual pursuits. So alongside the philosophy of science and the philosophy of mathematics, we find the philosophy of film and the philosophy of economics. On this view, philosophy does not have any questions that are its exclusive provenance. Rather, each "positive science" includes questions that are so abstract and general that they are philosophical and can be addressed by a specific philosophical discipline focused on that science. Thus, a physicist might be interested in establishing laws of motion, but less so in the general concept of law, something that the philosopher of physics takes as a primary topic for her investigation.

The third and final conception of philosophy is methodological. Noting that virtually every philosophical issue has been addressed within some other field, this view rejects a specification of philosophy rooted in its subject matter in favor of one based on its form or method. The notion is that there are certain modes of discourse that count as specifically philosophical. Whereas literature, for example, essentially involves narrative, on this view philosophy consists of such specific discursive forms as the argument, the counterexample, and the thought experiment. Because each of these can be found to have been employed in canonical philosophical texts – I will, in fact, show this to be the case in the chapters that follow – this view treats philosophy less as a specific subject matter than as a set of specific ways of addressing topics that are also the concerns of other intellectual fields.

The problem with this conception of philosophy is that, although each of these modes of discourse may be characteristic of philosophy, none of them is limited to it. There are many academic disciplines, for example, that employ formal arguments as a mean of justifying their claims and positions, with mathematics being the prime example. Indeed, there have even been philosophers, such as Spinoza, who have modeled their philosophical methods on that of mathematics. His *Ethics*, for example, bears more resemblance to a geometry textbook than to more standard works of philosophy. So even if philosophy is characterized by a more determined use of argumentation than, say, sociology, it would be a mistake to assert that philosophy alone of all the intellectual disciplines proceeds by means of a logical argument. A sociologist can also present logical argumentation without thereby moving into philosophical territory.

Fortunately, in order to argue that films can do philosophy, I don't need to decide whether one or the other of these three conceptions of philosophy is the correct one. To do so would be to take an exclusivist approach in which only one of these three views was taken to be adequate. Instead, I will take an inclusive approach, seeing these three characterizations of philosophy as mutually supportive. Although this will not settle the question of philosophy's nature, it will allow us to employ a notion of philosophy adequate for the purposes for which we need it.

In particular, I will begin with the methodological characterization of philosophy as a way of structuring the argument of this book. That is, with one exception, each of the following chapters will focus upon a specific discursive technique that has actually been used by philosophers – such as the thought experiment, counterexample, and argument – in order to show how a film can provide a screening of each. (The one chapter that does not focus on a philosophical technique raises the question of whether a film can *illustrate* a philosophical theory and why being an illustration justifies my treatment of it as screening philosophy.) It is clear why I call this method "local," for it looks at specific discursive techniques used by philosophers. But this method is also empirical in that it relies on our understanding of the discursive techniques that philosophers have actually employed in their work that are generally accepted as genuinely philosophical. It is also inclusive in that it recognizes that none of these modes of discourse are the exclusive domain of philosophy. As a result, I will supplement this methodological view of philosophy with the two, more substantive characterizations of philosophy I have just explored – in which philosophy is specified by its unique concerns and, alternatively, as a meta-discourse – to provide the content that will justify seeing these non-exclusive discourse forms as raising philosophical concerns. So, to name just one example, my discussion of the possibility of a film screening a philosophical counterexample will rely not only on the counterexample as a specifically philosophical discursive technique, but will also apply that technique to a uniquely philosophical question, namely what makes an action morally right.

In this way, while not resolving the highly contentious question of what makes a work philosophical, I have a means of showing that some central examples of philosophical questions and techniques can be screened, that is to say, raised and discussed in films. This local, particular, and empirical approach to answering the question of what philosophy is relies on a general consensus among philosophers as to some of the basic elements of philosophy, both as a textual method of presentation and as a specific subject matter.

A central advantage of this approach to the question of whether films can do philosophy is that it shows a plurality of connections between the foremost artform of our time and the mode of reflection upon our condition with an ancient heritage. As C. S. Peirce pointed out long ago, cables that are made of many interlocking fibers are much stronger than a chain composed of only a series of links because a break in one of the multiple fibers will not affect the effectiveness of the cable.[39] I think of each of the following five chapters as developing one of those interlocking fibers through which film and philosophy are connected to one another.

3 Illustrating a philosophical theory
Modern Times

Some defenders of the philosophical significance of film have employed a dichotomy that undercuts their own efforts at showing film to be capable of philosophizing. In order to validate some films as making genuine contributions to philosophy, they have denigrated others as "mere illustrations" of philosophical theses or positions, asserting that these are not philosophically significant.

To begin my look at specific philosophical techniques that can qualify a film as a work of philosophy, I shall argue that films that illustrate previously articulated philosophical positions can, despite their status as illustrations, make a contribution to our understanding of the philosophical position that they illustrate. My example of such a philosophically significant film is Charlie Chaplin's 1935 masterpiece, *Modern Times*. Although the film is an illustration of Marx's theory of the alienation and exploitation of the worker in a capitalist society, I will show that the film is philosophically significant because it is the locus of serious thinking necessary for providing an interpretation of Marx's claims that is accessible and plausible to viewers. Because *Modern Times* presents a more concrete version of the abstract and highly metaphysical claims of Marx's theory, it counts as an instance of philosophy done on film.

I shall begin by examining two recent attempts to justify taking films seriously as sources of philosophical insight. My reason for doing so is to show not only that these attempts have serious deficiencies in their justification for claiming that films can philosophize, but also that they accept a problematic dichotomy between illustrating a philosophical claim and actually doing philosophy. Many philosophers of film other than the two whom I discuss here share this dichotomy.[1]

Christopher Falzon presents a defense of treating film as philosophy in his provocatively entitled book, *Philosophy Goes to the Movies: An Introduction to Philosophy*.[2] Falzon is aware that many philosophers are skeptical of his undertaking. Referencing Plato's Parable of the Cave, Falzon acknowledges that there has been "a deep philosophical prejudice against the visual image as an avenue to philosophical enlightenment,"[3] thereby admitting that his attempt to view film as a source of philosophical insight may be doomed from the start because of film's inherently visual nature. After all, many philosophers, from Plato onwards, have opposed philosophy – taken to be the paradigmatic source of rational conviction – to visual images – dismissed as beguiling viewers by appealing to their credulity via the emotions and/or desires. From such a point of view, it would seem that film lacks the capacity for philosophical thinking.

Falzon dismisses this objection because he believes that films are capable of providing genuine philosophical insights. To make his point, he distinguishes the use of films to "illustrate" philosophical positions from his own exploration of the philosophical "content" that he attributes to the films themselves. He explains that he does

> not only turn to films in order to help *illustrate or illuminate* philosophical themes. To identify philosophical positions, themes, or questions that are being presented or worked through in particular films is also to understand something important about what is going on within these films, to say something about *their intellectual and philosophical content.*[4]

Falzon's point is that films themselves, because they present philosophical ideas or views, have a genuine philosophical content.

My first reservation about Falzon's discussion is that he does not explain exactly how films have a philosophical content other than by simply illustrating philosophical themes that have already been articulated by philosophers in written texts. Although he clearly asserts that films make a larger contribution to philosophy than merely "illustrating or illuminating" philosophical ideas, he does no more than make the claim that films "present and work through ... philosophical positions, themes, or questions" and does not explain how films are able to do this or why it makes sense to attribute to them these capacities.

This is a problem because, while few would deny that at least some films have philosophical content, it is not clear that they would so readily accede to Falzon's claim that films develop philosophical views of their own. One could acknowledge, for example, that many of Woody Allen's films are vivid presentations of certain ideas from Sartre's philosophy without also holding that the films thereby are capable of actually doing philosophy and thus aptly characterized as "philosophy in action," to borrow Stephen Mulhall's useful if ambiguous phrase.[5] Falzon has provided us with a reason for thinking that the films themselves are, at most, presentations in visual form of already worked out philosophical ideas. But if this is so, by his own lights they won't count as themselves actively philosophizing.

Now Falzon does attempt to justify his attribution of philosophical content to films by citing what he takes to be an important commonality between film and philosophy: their mutual use of *images*. Central to his strategy in this regard is an acknowledgment of the presence of images within philosophy itself, for this allows him to dispute the claim that film's reliance on images undermines its potential for philosophy.

> Despite a lingering Platonic tendency to disparage the image in their "official" pronouncements, philosophers have always resorted to a multitude of arresting and vivid visions to illustrate or clarify their position, to formulate a problem or to provide some basis for discussion. Philosophy is full of strange and wonderful *images* and inventions of this sort.[6]

Although Falzon notes that one could argue that images are essential to the task of philosophy – despite philosophers' "official" pronouncements to the contrary – he does not wish to defend this claim. Rather, as he puts it in a clever turn of phrase, "my interest in images is not so much the role of the image in philosophy as in the philosophy we can discern in the image."[7]

Earlier, as we have seen, Falzon denied that films were merely illustrations of already worked out philosophical positions. But now, in linking film to philosophy, he focuses on the roles that images have in philosophical texts and, he tells us, among the things these images do is to *illustrate* a philosophical position. Are we now to take it that this counts as an instance of genuine philosophical thought whereas it was previously contrasted with it? Falzon seems not to notice this inconsistency in his position.

Even more importantly, Falzon does not provide an account of when the presence of an image in a philosophical text counts as an element in a philosophical argument or discussion and when it is merely a propaedeutic, an aid to our understanding. Although it may be true that some images, such as those contained in Plato's Parable of the Cave, play a necessary role in a philosophical argument, others do not.[8] After all, Kant's striking image of the understanding is generally not regarded as part of his argument for the a priori necessity of the categories, the central claim of the Analytic of the *Critique of Pure Reason*:

> We have now not merely explored the territory of pure understanding, and carefully surveyed every part of it, but have also measured its extent, and assigned to everything in it its rightful place. ... It is the land of truth – enchanting name! – surrounded by a wide and stormy ocean, the native home of illusion, where many a fog bank and many a swiftly melting iceberg give the deceptive appearance of farther shores, deluding the adventurous seafarer ever anew with empty hopes, and engaging him in enterprises which he can never abandon and yet is unable to carry to completion.[9]

Kant's imagery here, though quite graphic, does not make a philosophical contribution to his argument concerning the necessary limits of human understanding, even if it helps a reader comprehend his overall position.

Falzon has not supplied a criterion adequate for distinguishing such useful but dispensable images from the ones that should be deemed necessary to a philosopher's argument. So, the issue is whether there is a way to distinguish the non-essential imagery to be found in philosophical texts from those that play a necessary role in a philosophical argument.

To investigate this problem, I want to look more carefully at an example Falzon cites and that I discussed briefly in the last chapter: Plato's Parable of the Cave. In what sense is the Parable more than *merely* an illustration of Plato's metaphysics?

Plato presents the Parable of the Cave in *The Republic* (514a–517c). Because it is too long to quote in full, I will intersperse quotations from Plato's text with my own summary of his presentation. Throughout, we need to be careful to think about the Parable's contribution to Plato's overall argument in *The Republic*, for we want to see why it is more than just a handy way of illustrating his metaphysics.

Socrates begins by asking his interlocutors to "[i]magine men to be living in an underground cave-like dwelling. . . . Light is provided by a fire. . . . " One group holds the other captive.

> Between the fire and the prisoners . . . there is a path across the cave and along this a low wall has been built, like the screen at a puppet show. . . . See then also men carrying along that wall . . . all kinds of artifacts . . . some of the carriers are talking while others are silent.

These artifacts cast shadows on the cave's wall, shadows that the chained prisoners take to be real rather than the objects themselves.

There is justification for claiming that this much of the parable constitutes an illustration of Plato's metaphysics of Forms because of the analogy that he draws between the prisoners' mistaking of appearances for reality and our taking physical things to be real rather than mere appearances of the underlying reality of the Forms.[10] However, the parable does not stop there. Plato goes on to envision one of the prisoners escaping his bonds:

> Consider then what deliverance from their bonds and the curing of their ignorance would be. . . . Do you not think he [the freed prisoner] would . . . believe that the things which he saw earlier [the shadows on the cave wall] were truer than the things now pointed out to him [the physical things that cast the shadows that he now sees]?[11]

Plato goes on to discuss how difficult it would be for one unaccustomed to anything but firelight to see things in sunlight and how such a person would be regarded as mad when he returned to the cave to tell his fellow prisoners what he had seen.

This latter half of the parable is even more important to Plato's argument than the first, for it explains why someone who had attained knowledge would not desire to play a role in normal human life. Since Plato is concerned to show in *The Republic* that the just state will not be realized until philosophers become its rulers, an important step in his argument is his demonstration that philosophers do not want political offices.[12] The latter part of the Parable explains why this is so: After a person had seen the true nature of reality – a necessary condition of his or her becoming a philosopher – he or she would not desire to return to a focus upon the merely apparent objects that form the concerns of his fellow men:

> [Do] not be surprised that those who have reached this point are unwilling to occupy themselves with human affairs, and that their souls are always pressing upward to spend their time there [in the intelligible world], for this is natural if things are as our parable indicates.
>
> (517c–d.)

In this latter aspect, the Parable of the Cave is a *thought experiment*. A thought experiment functions in a philosophical argument by presenting readers with a hypothetical case. They are then asked to endorse a general principle on the basis of their reaction to this case. The thought experiment mobilizes people's intuitions about certain ideas or concepts, so that they can see why a general claim is true.[13]

I will discuss the nature of thought experiments – and films' embodiment of them – more fully in the following chapters. Here, I only want to point out that thought experiments are one example of the presence of a narrative in philosophy. Even though a thought experiment tells a particular story, the truth that it intends to validate is general, for it does not rely on the specific details of the narrative. Instead, the story is presented in order to persuade the reader of the truth of the general principle of which the thought experiment's narrative is but an instance.

What then emerges from our look at Plato's parable that is applicable to the question of whether cinematic illustrations of a philosophical theory or position can themselves count as doing philosophy? We have seen that the presence of (literary) images in philosophical texts does not automatically justify Falzon's claim that films can do philosophy because they too involve (visual) images. In particular, I argued that the philosophically distinctive use of an image was as a thought experiment, something that Falzon's own discussion obscures. Although this can help us think about the possibility of doing philosophy on/in/through film, Falzon has not provided us with an adequate rationale for accepting this possibility.

So let me turn now to Stephen Mulhall, another philosopher who explicitly endorses the claim that films can philosophize. His book, *On Film*, despite its very general title, is a study of the four films that make up the *Alien* tetralogy, supplemented by discussions of other films by each of the directors of those films. Mulhall claims that the *Alien* films actually philosophize. In explaining why he believes this, he cites what he sees as the general topic or focus of the films, namely "the relation of human identity to embodiment."[14] This issue, Mulhall claims, "has been central to philosophical reflection in the modern period since Descartes,"[15] an assertion that he takes to support his view of the films as engaging in philosophical reflection. The reason for this, he tells us, is that "the sophistication and self-awareness with which these films [in the *Alien* tetralogy] deploy and develop that issue ... suggest to me that they should themselves be taken as making *real contributions* to these [i.e. philosophy's] intellectual debates."[16]

Intriguing as this suggestion is, I also find it puzzling. There is no doubt that much of post-Cartesian philosophy in the West has been concerned with understanding what it is to be human and, in particular, what role our bodies play in structuring our sense of our own identity. But this concern may also be found in cultural forms besides philosophy, such as painting and literature. To choose but one example, there is a rich history in Western art of depictions of the Crucifixion. Given their subject matter, such depictions must generally involve the idea of human embodiment – as well as a great deal more, such as the relationship between suffering and redemption. But do they as a result of this concern also deal with human identity in a way that is specifically philosophical? And, even if they do, does this mean that they therefore should be seen as actively philosophizing and specifically in a manner that enriches the "properly" philosophical discussion of embodiment? I have no doubt that paintings and other artworks can have philosophical interest – and some may actually qualify as doing philosophy – but just because they focus upon aspects of our embodiment does not ensure that they have made "real contributions" to the specifically philosophical debates about that issue.

Consider, for example, any painting of the Crucifixion, such as Andrea Mantegna's *Calvary* (1457–60) located in the Louvre.[17] In this painting, Jesus is depicted flanked by the two others crucified with him, each of whom is shown screaming in agony in contrast to Jesus, whose placid expression may indicate that he is already dead. The three bodies rise above a crowd of onlookers who include Roman soldiers and Jesus' disciples. With its direct depiction of the bodies of three nearly naked males, there is no doubt that this painting is concerned with human embodiment and may even attempt to show that physical suffering can be mitigated by faith. But that does not justify the claim that the painting thereby *contributes* to the specifically philosophical discussion of the role of the body in constituting human identity. What Mulhall owes us, but fails to provide, is an explanation of how a cultural form other than philosophy itself – and, of course, it is film that is the real issue both for him and for us – can make a substantial contribution to the specifically philosophical discussion of an issue such as that of human embodiment.[18] Even though his discussion of the *Alien* films is insightful for showing how the monster itself, for example, raises issues about sexuality, reproduction, and gender, he never clarifies what he takes to be the film's specifically philosophical contribution.

In distinguishing his view of these films from alternatives that do not acknowledge their ability to do philosophy, Mulhall endorses a dichotomy similar to that we saw at work in Falzon: one between actually doing philosophy and merely illustrating philosophical ideas.

> I do not look to these films as handy or popular illustrations of views and arguments properly developed by philosophers; I see them rather as themselves *reflecting on and evaluating* such views and arguments, as thinking seriously and systematically about them *in just the way* that philosophers do. ... They [the films] are philosophical exercises, philosophy in action – film as philosophizing.[19]

There is much in this short passage that calls for comment, but I shall concentrate on only one issue here: the validity of Mulhall's dichotomy between "handy or popular illustrations" and "thinking seriously and systematically." This dichotomy suggests that there is a domain of serious and systematic philosophical thought – to which the films he is interested in belong – and one consisting of handy or popular illustrations of the views developed by philosophers – which contains films that Mulhall dismisses as lacking any serious and systematic thinking.

Each of the terms in Mulhall's dichotomy calls for discussion. To begin, consider his valorization of systematic thinking. Does Mulhall mean to identify philosophy with *systematic* thinking? If he does, he faces a serious problem. Although some philosophers, such as Immanuel Kant and G. W. F. Hegel, emphasized the systematic nature of their work, there is an alternative tradition of philosophizing that explicitly denies the possibility of systematic philosophy. I am thinking here of, among others, Søren Kierkegaard, Friedrich Nietzsche, and Ludwig Wittgenstein, all of whom opposed the systematic impulse. This signals a difficulty for Mulhall's emphasis upon the systematic nature of philosophical thought.

The other term in the dichotomy that he valorizes is no less problematic: *serious*. Again, it is not clear what Mulhall means when he characterizes thinking as serious. What would the alternative possibility be? Is there such a thing as non-serious thinking? In our post-Freudian era, it is clear that "non-serious" thoughts – dreams, jokes, slips of the tongue – can plausibly be seen as covers for serious ideas, e.g. that I love my mother and hate my father. Mulhall owes us a much more careful characterization of the dichotomy that lies at the heart of his claims about the possibility of films philosophizing.

So let's take it upon ourselves to supply the analysis, lacking in both Falzon and Mulhall, of the contrast between genuine philosophizing and merely illustrating a philosophical theory or claim. I know of no philosophic study of the role of illustrations and this is not the place to present one.[20] All I can hope to do here is make some initial steps towards a more complete study of what is involved in something being an illustration.

A first putative feature of illustrations is that they are always illustrations *of* something else, so that an illustration will always refer to something other than itself, that of which it is the illustration. If this is correct, then we can take "intentionality" to be a mark of illustrations, their reference to something beyond themselves.[21]

There are various different types of things that can serve as illustrations of other types of things. For example, we often tell stories to illustrate points that we have made, as when I tell my son about how I was a victim of teasing as a child in order to get him to see that the best way to handle such annoyances is by ignoring them. Also, as Falzon notes, philosophers often use imagery to illustrate their theories, as when Kant claimed that the understanding was an island surrounded by a threatening sea. But one especially prominent form of illustration is that of a picture illustrating a written text. Although this is clearly different from using a visual image to illustrate a philosophical theory, I want to look carefully at such pictorial illustrations in order to see whether this type of illustration can provide us with some insight into why the "mere illustration/serious and systematic thinking" dichotomy is problematic.

To begin, let's consider an illustrated version of a classic novel, such as Mark Twain's *The Adventures of Tom Sawyer* (see Figure 3).[22] Such illustrations are mere supplements to the text designed to make it more accessible to readers, especially those who are young. It keeps their interest in

Figure 3 The famous fence-painting scene from *The Adventures of Tom Sawyer.*

the story by showing them a rendering of what the text says and providing concrete images of the book's protagonists, here Tom Sawyer, and the various situations in which they find themselves, such as having to whitewash a fence. But the text itself is not substantially enriched by the illustration, which is, we might be inclined to say, *merely* an illustration of the pre-existing text. We do not think that our imagining of Tom is either constrained by or enhanced through this particular illustration of him.

But this is not the only type of illustration we find in children's books. Consider the case of *Alice's Adventures in Wonderland* by Lewis Carroll (see Figure 4).[23] John Tenniel's illustrations are more than simply "handy and popular illustrations" of the book, attempts to keep the attention of young readers or listeners. They were part of the book in its original publication and are an integral part of it. We can explain this fact by saying that these illustrations are *iconic* representations of the book's central characters.[24] Unlike the *Tom Sawyer* case, they don't just provide us with one example of how we might imagine the fictional characters of, say, Alice or the Mad Hatter. Rather, our imaginings of such characters are partially constituted by Tenniel's illustrations. It is even plausible to maintain that our imaginings of Alice and the Mad Hatter are as much the result of the illustrations that picture them as they are of the words that describe them. And, if this is true, Tenniel's illustrations are as essential a part of the book as Carroll's text.

Figure 4 Alice as illustrated by John Tenniel. From *Alice's Adventures in Wonderland*.

This suggests that we should be wary of assuming that illustrations are less important or significant than the texts they are designed to illustrate. In cases like that of the *Alice* books – the *Winnie-the-Pooh* and *Harry Potter* books might be other instances of this type – the illustrations are as integral to the work as the written text. The fictional world of the book is constituted by both the written text and its illustrations.[25]

Now someone might reply that the text still retains priority because the same text might have been published without illustrations or with different illustrations.[26] Since both of those books – the real one and its imagined counterpart with different illustrations – count as instances of *Alice's Adventures in Wonderland* by Lewis Carroll, this shows that the illustrations are really a supplement to the text proper.

But even though a book called *Alice's Adventures in Wonderland* might have had either no or other illustrations than those it does have, this does not show that the present book is not constituted as much by the illustrations as by the written text. Because the illustrations have become iconic for the various characters, the imaginative activity involved in reading the text-cum-illustrations is now simply part of what that book is. When we imagine a character like the Mad Hatter, we use both Tenniel's illustrations of him and Carroll's verbal descriptions of him to imagine him and the events in which he takes part. The illustrations are not – or, perhaps, no longer – dispensable as elements in our imaginative engagement with fictions such as this that involve iconic images.

Let's pause in our discussion of different types of pictorial illustrations in order to consider whether there are any pictorial illustrations of philosophical texts. There are a few, but a very few, that I can think of, and they are more diagrams than full-fledged illustrations. Edmund Husserl illustrates his theory of time as "running off" by means of a diagram whose meaning is even harder to grasp than the claims of the text it is meant to illustrate, difficult as that text is.[27] Arthur Danto also illustrates a number of different claims in his philosophy of art with diagrams. For example, in his influential article, "The Artworld," he uses a diagram to show how the properties taken to be necessary for something being a work of art change as new theories of art are developed.[28] In addition, some secondary works use pictorial illustrations in their attempt to render philosophical texts more accessible to students and others. A recent book on *The Matrix*, for example, includes an illustration of the Parable of the Cave – or, at least, the cave itself.[29] Illuminating as it might be to some readers, this illustration is more like the illustration of *Tom Sawyer* than *Alice's Adventures in Wonderland*, for its link to the text of which it is an illustration remains contingent. I, for one, prefer my own darker, more ambiguous imagined scene to the antiseptic and ordered one presented by this illustration. So philosophical texts are rarely illustrated pictorially and, when they are, the illustrations remain subordinate to the written text.

Returning to our general discussion of different types of pictorial illustration, I want to point to one domain in which pictorial illustrations, although still connected to the texts of which they are illustrations, are even more significant than that of the texts they illustrate or, to speak in a more tempered mode, equally important to their texts. What I have in mind are the illustrations in birding books, such as Florence Merriam Bailey's *Handbook of Birds of the Western United States*[30] (see Figure 5 below).

Birding books contain prose descriptions of individual bird species – including physical markings, vocal characteristics, and typical locations – together with illustrations of the relevant species. The goal of such books is to assist people in recognizing what species a bird they see belongs to. As such, the illustrations are integral to the books' purpose, for they convey a great deal of information that is not ascertainable from the written text alone. In particular, they give a sense of what the bird might look like when it is seen flying. The reason for this is that birders rely on the drawings to show them the aspects of the birds they need to use in order to recognize them in the field. I am told that most birds are recognized by their *jizz*, their appearance as they disappear from view. Drawings are sometimes able to depict this, but photographs cannot. The role of the illustrations in Bailey's *Handbook* is to present birders with accurate images of these jizzes, that is, illustrations of birds that birders can use to recognize the type to which the bird

Figure 5 Illustration of the Foster Tern. From *Handbook of Birds of the Western States*.

they are seeing belongs.[31] The presence of these illustrations is essential because they give birders the capacity to recognize a bird as being of a certain species or type.

So, without the presence of illustrations, birding guides would not achieve their purpose of helping people recognize birds with which they are not familiar. The illustrations of such texts are crucial to their fulfilling their purpose and, as a result, cannot be regarded as "a mere supplement" to the texts that they illustrate. Since the illustrations in such texts are integral to them, one cannot infer from the fact that something is an illustration that it is subordinate to the written text for which it is an illustration. Indeed, at least in the case of birding guides, illustrations are a fundamental element that allows the text to realize its purpose. This is because these illustrations play an essential role in our ability to recognize instances of the things of which they are illustrations.

Let me summarize the distinctions I have drawn to this point as follows: In the first case, our imagining of the characters and events in a work are not generally structured by the illustrations that may be found in it, but only by the written text; iconic illustrations – our second case – function together with the written text in our imaginings of the world of the work; and in the third case, we cannot recognize instances of the species described by the written text without the assistance of the work's illustrations.

Before proceeding, I want to acknowledge a fourth type of illustration very briefly. Here, an artist's illustration of a written text transcends the category of illustration and becomes a work of art in its own right. For example, Marc Chagall made a series of illustrations of Longus' story, *Daphne and Chloe*, in 1952. The illustrations are now treated as independent works of art, rather than as illustrations to be bound together in a book with the text of Longus' story. In cases such as this, the fact that something is an illustration does not preclude it from also being a work of art in its own right.[32] Such illustrations are generally more significant as artworks in their own right than they are as illustrations of the texts they illustrate. In this case, we standardly imagine the work's world without making recourse to the written text at all.

As an aside, it is worth remarking that a philosophical anticipation of this view can be found in Kant's claim, made in the "Aesthetic" of the first *Critique*, that constructions are an essential part of geometrical proofs. Whereas many modern accounts of geometry treat it as a purely axiomatic system, Kant thought that constructions – because of their stimulus to the imagination – play an essential role in the proof of geometrical truths. Clearly, this is not the occasion to decide whether Kant is right about geometry. Nonetheless, I want to mark that claim as related to the one I have been advancing: that certain "illustrations" are essential to the texts they illustrate.

Let me be clear on what I am *not* arguing by means of this categorization of different types of illustrations. I am not asserting that films that illustrate antecedently articulated philosophical theories should count as philosophizing because they are either iconic as in the case of *Alice*, necessary as in the case of the birding guide, or even because they are independent works. My point here is only that illustrations need *not* be subordinated to that of which they are the illustration, so that a work's status as an illustration cannot in itself justify denigrating it, treating it as subordinate to that which it illustrates, as merely an illustration.

This discussion of the nature of illustrations, then, shows that it is a mistake to conclude that, just because something is an illustration, it is not original or illuminating. Although I have focused on pictorial illustrations of written texts and this is only one type of illustration that a text can receive, my argument shows that one cannot without further support dismiss illustrations as simply accessible means for understanding the texts they illustrate.

If this is correct, then it is a mistake to conclude without providing additional argumentation, as Falzon and Mulhall do, that just because a film illustrates the view of a philosopher that it is not itself "philosophy in action," that is, a genuine instance of philosophy done on/in/through film. Although we are not yet in a position to assert that illustrations of philosophical positions on film can count as genuine instances of philosophizing, Falzon and Mulhall have not given us adequate grounds for rejecting the idea *tout court*.

To add more support to this idea, recall that most philosophers philosophize without making original contributions to the discipline. Philosophy journals are filled with essays that are clearly philosophical but few count as substantially advancing the discussion of the philosophical topics they address. Additionally, it is generally agreed that historians of philosophy are doing philosophy, even though their work is rarely taken to make an original contribution to philosophy itself rather than a contribution to our understanding of its history.[33] Haven't Falzon and Mulhall simply set the bar too high by claiming that films that illustrate philosophical theories in interesting and illuminating ways are not genuine instances of philosophy on/in/through film?

Does our reflection on the concept of illustration and, more specifically, on the relationship between visual illustrations and the texts they illustrate, shed any light on the question of whether films can philosophize? I think it does and, to show this, I want to consider a film that many might think of as "merely" an illustration of a philosophical text and, indeed, a comic rather than a serious illustration at that, Charlie Chaplin's 1936 masterpiece, *Modern Times*.[34] I will show that *Modern Times* illustrates Marx's theory of the exploitation and alienation or estrangement (*Entfremdung*) of the worker in a capitalist economic system, a view that forms the core of his philosophical critique of capitalism.[35]

Whether and how films can embody thoughts is an interesting philosophical question. *Modern Times* opens with an example of one way in which films can do so. After the title sequence – in which a clock face is shown with a relentlessly circling second hand – the film uses a skillful match cut in order to express the following thought: workers in a modern factory are like sheep being led to the slaughter. How does the film convey this assertion? By using a technique developed early in the history of cinema by Russian filmmakers such as Sergei Eisenstein: the juxtaposition of two seemingly unrelated images in a *symbolic montage*. The impact of such juxtaposition was theorized as the "Kuleshov effect," for the two images, when juxtaposed, it is claimed, acquire a meaning over and above that the two contain when each is considered in isolation from the other. The film's first shot is easily recognizable as one of sheep being forced up a chute that leads to a slaughterhouse (Figure 6). This shot dissolves into one of workers ascending a subway staircase – it is clear they are en route to a factory – in which the workers crowd one another in a way that presents a very similar visual image to that of the unfortunate sheep. Because of the structural similarity between the two shots despite their different contents, their juxtaposition produces a thought contained in neither: that the workers are like the sheep, that they too face an ignominious end.[36]

Although this opening sequence is not, or not yet, an illustration of a philosophical theory, I mention it to show that film's visual nature does not preclude it from being able to express a thought, to "think." The visual and the cognitive are not opposites, although many theorists have taken them to be.

But let's move ahead to the scenes from the film that follow and in which we see Charlie in the factory that the workers were entering in the opening shots, for these scenes provide a clear illustration of Marx's theory of the alienation and exploitation of the worker. Marx's theory depends upon a particular view of what is involved in human labor. For Marx, what constitutes human beings as a species is their ability to transform reality in accordance with their own plans of action. Following the Aristotelian tradition in which things are characterized by means of genus and species, Marx calls this ability the "species being of man" [sic]. However, in the capitalist economic system, according to Marx, workers are compelled to work for a wage and this results in what he calls *alienated* labor.

> [T]he object that labor produces, its product, stands opposed to it as *something alien*, as a *power independent* of the producer. The product of labor is labor embodied and made material in an object, it is the *objectification* of labor ... this realization of labor appears as a *loss of reality* for the worker, objectification as *loss of and bondage to the object*, and appropriation as *estrangement*, as *alienation*.[37]

Here, Marx claims that the worker interacts with objects by "embodying" his labor in them. This metaphysical terminology characterizes the workers' transformation of objects as the result of "mixing" their labor with them and thereby altering the objects, making them into commodities.

Figure 6 Modern Times asserts that factory workers are like sheep being led to the slaughter.

Source: *Modern Times* (Charlie Chaplin, 1936).

Although it is human nature to appropriate and transform objects in order to realize our goals and satisfy our desires, Marx thinks that under the capitalist system this natural relationship is inverted so that the worker, by working upon objects, satisfies a demand placed upon him by the object, so that his labor is not his own, but marshaled in service of an external demand. As a result, the object confronts the capitalist worker as if it had a life of its own to which his is subordinated.

> The externalization of the worker in his product means not only that his labor becomes an object, an *external* existence, but that it exists *outside him*, independently of him and alien to him, and begins to confront him as an autonomous power; that the life which he has bestowed on the object confronts him as hostile and alien.[38]

As we might expect, Chaplin uses humor to illustrate this aspect of Marx's theory. When we first see Charlie in the factory, he is working on an assembly line. The worker next to him is a huge man, Big Bill (Tiny Safford). As we shall see, this juxtaposition of two opposite body types – the diminutive Charlie with his enormous co-worker – opens up a range of comic possibilities that allow Chaplin to illustrate Marx's theory humorously.

Before seeing how he does this, it is worth recalling that the assembly line was an important innovation that made the modern factory possible. It was developed around 1913 by Henry Ford in Highland Park, Michigan. Marx's theory of alienated labor was developed with a different, less completely mechanized factory structure in mind. Although one could ask whether Marx's claims about the alienation of workers fit the new manufacturing structure of the modern assembly line, ironically it seems designed as a paradigm of Marx's view, as Chaplin certainly aimed to show.

The factory in which Charlie works in the film is hyper-modern. I characterize it in this way because Chaplin includes a range of advanced surveillance techniques that employ the newly deployed technology of television. They allow the president of the Electro Steel Corporation (Al Ernest Garcia) to observe his workers at all of their stations and even in the bathroom. Chaplin's imaginative depiction of the modern factory anticipates the deployment of technologies of observation that would only be realized decades later.

Charlie and his two co-workers work together on a conveyor belt. Each of them performs one single, routine operation after which the pieces they have worked on disappear down a chute into a series of gears whose actual function is not clear but which will allow Chaplin ample opportunity for a comic portrayal of Charlie's situation. Charlie's job is to tighten two bolts and his two co-workers then each hammer one of the bolts as they pass by on the conveyor belt before disappearing into the huge machine. This conveyor belt provides Chaplin with the context for illustrating Marx's claim that the objects that workers work on become an alien force that confronts the workers as independent of their control. This first becomes apparent when Charlie has to scratch an itch – and then has to rush to tighten the pieces that have moved by without him tightening their bolts, causing him to push into his co-workers and nearly getting the belt shut down, an event that would bring disciplinary action. Chaplin's humorous depiction of the production process as making demands on the workers shows that humans have become, as Marx puts it, appendages of the machines, for the workers must accommodate their own needs – to scratch an itch, sneeze, relieve themselves, etc. – to the pace of the machines and demands of production.

Funny as this routine is, it pales in comparison to another in which Charlie uses his recognition of the alien power exhibited by objects to control his fellow workers. This occurs right after Charlie has caused a shut down on the line because he was swatting a fly and therefore failed to tighten the bolts as required by the pace of the assembly line. When a manager comes by to upbraid him, he gestures towards Big Bill, explaining that he had hit Charlie's hand with his hammer and this is what caused him to miss tightening the objects that passed by him. When the manager upbraids Big Bill and then leaves, Big Bill kicks Charlie in the pants, to which Charlie responds in kind. As the huge man threatens to hit Charlie again, Charlie cleverly points towards the restarted assembly line, getting Big Bill to rush to his post lest he cause yet another work stoppage.[39] These humorous events on the assembly line have a serious message to convey: that the objects upon which the workers labor control the laborers rather than vice-versa, precisely as Marx claimed. *Modern Times* here conveys this idea to its audience with a deft, light touch.

Objects do not acquire their power over the workers magically. They do so, Marx tells us, because of the separation between labor and capital, that is to say, as a result of the control by the owners over the means of the workers' subsistence, their ability to survive.

> If, therefore, he [the worker] regards the product of his labor, his objectified labor, as an *alien, hostile,* and powerful object which is independent of him, then his relationship to that object is such that another man – alien, hostile, powerful, and independent of him – is its master. If he relates to his own activity as unfree activity, then he relates to it as activity in the service, under the rule, coercion, and yoke of another man.[40]

Marx here points out that the alienated nature of the workers' labor can only be understood if we recognize that there are human beings who stand opposed to the workers – the capitalists – and who control the workers' activity.

Again, this is a feature that the film emphasizes in its early scenes. We first see the steel company's president sitting in his office, trying to solve a jigsaw puzzle and then perusing a newspaper. In other early scenes, he is also shown observing the workers with televisual surveillance – most notably Charlie when he goes to the bathroom to enjoy an illicit smoke – and demanding repeated speed-ups on the assembly line. But perhaps his most memorable scene comes when he agrees to test the Billows Feeding Machine. This machine has been touted as a means to increase production and keep the factory ahead of its competitors by eliminating the need for a lunch hour for the workers. This fantastic machine feeds the worker his lunch – soup, a main dish, corn on the cob – while also periodically wiping his mouth so as to avoid getting stains on his clothing.

The Billows Feeding Machine exemplifies what Marx calls "the commodification of the worker." The term "commodity" refers to the structure of the goods produced by a factory: In a capitalist economy, the goods that are produced are treated simply as something to be sold, to produce revenue, without consideration of what needs they actually satisfy for human beings. When workers are commodified, they are also treated simply as sources of profit, with no concern for their welfare. But this is exactly what this feeding technology does: It treats the worker as an aspect of the production process that must be utilized in a profit-maximizing manner. Why not rationalize their human needs – such as that for nourishment – so as to maximize their contribution to profits?

But, as any viewer can anticipate, things go awry with this technology. The Billows Feeding Machine becomes an excuse for a range of slapstick routines that are enacted upon the body of the unfortunate Charlie, who is belted into position to be fed. Everything that can go wrong does: A corncob rotates wildly, mashing Charlie's face as it wildly spins out of control; the soup spills onto his lap and then is thrown in his face by the machine; it feeds him bolts in addition to his main course when an engineer carelessly places them onto his feeding tray; Charlie even gets a pie in the face in homage to the traditions of slapstick; and the electric napkin repeatedly bashes him in the face instead of wiping his lips.

One could make much of the way Charlie is treated by this feeding machine, for rather than serving his need for food and drink, the machine assaults his body, using each of its features to beat and humiliate him. This could be, on its own, a metaphoric picture of how the human being is transformed under capitalism from a potentially creative being into what Marx calls an "appendage of the machine."

This comes out even more clearly after the lunch break when the president orders that the speed of the assembly line be increased "to the limit" in a scene I will examine in a moment. To fully appreciate this scene, we first need to examine another aspect of the alienation of the workers: their transformation into *machines*.

> What constitutes the alienation of labor? ... The fact that labor is *external* to the worker, i.e. does not belong to his essential being; that

he therefore does not confirm himself in his work but denies himself, feels miserable and not happy, does not develop free mental and physical energy, but mortifies his flesh and ruins his mind. ... The machine accommodates itself to man's *weakness*, in order to turn *weak* man into a machine.[41]

Although we all have an intuitive sense of what Marx's metaphor of a person being turned into a machine means, the use of a metaphor seems to render this claim poetic rather than it being a literal claim made about the conditions of the working class. What would it mean, after all, for a person quite literally to become a machine?

I want to suggest that one instance of the philosophical thinking embodied in *Modern Times* involves a complete visualization of Marx's metaphor, one that makes it more concrete. That is, my claim for the film as an instance of philosophy on film is supported by its providing a specific interpretation of the mechanization of the human being that Marx attributes to capitalism. This is achieved by showing Charlie's arms continuing to rotate in the tightening motion he is required to perform even when the assembly line has been shut down. One example occurs at lunchtime. Charlie nearly sits on a bowl of soup that Big Bill has poured and, so, has to pass the soup to him. But his arms and entire upper body continue to twitch in that tightening motion, causing him to spill the soup on his massive co-worker.

Although this scene is funny, it is much more than that. Although Marx claimed that workers' bodies became machines, he did not provide a detailed account of what about factories do this, nor how such mechanization is registered on and by the human body and the human mind. Clearly, one factor is the repetitive nature of the work required in modern manufacturing. In even the earliest factories, the division of labor meant that workers no longer did everything necessary to produce an object, as they generally did in the older guild system, but performed only one (or, perhaps, a limited number of) operation(s) necessary for the production of a commodity such as a shirt or a shoe. In so far as a worker was now merely doing one (or a few) repetitive task(s), his activity resembled that of a machine that can only do the specific thing(s) it is designed to do.

Is this all there is to the mechanization of the human being under the factory system? Not according to the film. The mechanization of Charlie's body – now presented in tandem with the destruction of his mind – is vividly dramatized in the film by his continuing to use his wrenches on objects other than those he is supposed to. Especially as a result of a speed-up on the line, Charlie cannot control his own arms, nor can he maintain an awareness of the distinction between the line and the balance of his life-world, as he suffers a mental breakdown as a result of the speed-up. As a result, he mistakes other patterns in the world that are similar to those of the two nuts he has been tightening and, with his ever-twitching, wrench-laden arms, tries to tighten those "nuts" as well – even when they are buttons on a woman's dress or the noses of the factory bosses. Neither a verbal description nor a still photograph can convey the humor in these routines, even as a serious point emerges: it is not just the repetitiveness of the work Charlie is forced to do but more specifically its *pace* – a fact determined by the assembly line and the commands of the boss – that turns him into a veritable bolt-tightening machine, whose arms continue their bolt-tightening movements even when there are no bolts to tighten and whose mind is so fixated on bolts that he assimilates all the visual information he receives to the pattern they form, finding it in unexpected, and hence humorous, places (see Figure 7).

It is worth emphasizing that the film's depiction of human mechanization has two elements to it. To the more obvious idea of a body becoming mechanical, *Modern Times* adds the notion of a mind so rigidified by routine that it also becomes a mere mechanism, seeing only evidence of patterns it has been required to search for and recognize. Both of these elements in the portrayal of the mechanized human being are very creative and, I think, philosophically significant.

So far, I have examined a few elements of the film's opening sequence in the Electro Steel factory in order to show how they illustrate, apply, and extend Marx's theory of alienation. Let me now briefly indicate how the rest of the film exemplifies other aspects of Marx's claims.

Figure 7 Charlie tightening bolts wherever he finds them. From *Modern Times*.
Source: Chaplin/United Artists/The Kobal Collection.

An important feature of the balance of the film is the relationship that develops between Charlie and a nameless "gamin" or street urchin (Paulette Goddard) (see Figure 8). I shall comment on only two features of this part of the film. The first is a very funny scene that occurs when Charlie is hired as a night watchman by a department store. Letting the gamin into the store after hours, Charlie skates around the store's balcony blindfolded, unaware that he is repeatedly coming within inches of the end of the floor and a long drop.

Although the scene is very funny, it also makes an important point by depicting Charlie as a skilled skater, for Charlie is here shown as realizing what Marx calls his "species being" by engaging in free conscious activity, the antithesis to the "forced" labor in the factory. His efforts here are a source of pride to Charlie, as opposed to his various attempts to evade the demands of factory labor by shirking.

Another feature of Marx's theory is illustrated by Charlie and the gamin's attempt to live a normal life as a married couple in a home of their own. Seeing a young wife bidding her husband goodbye as he heads to work, the two create the fantasy of being able to live such a life together. Their attempt to do so recalls Marx's claim that contrasts the dwellings of the rich and the poor:

Figure 8 Charlie and the gamin. From *Modern Times*.
Source: Chaplin/United Artists/The Kobal Collection.

It is true that labor produces marvels for the rich, but it produces privation for the worker. It produces palaces, but hovels for the worker. It produces beauty, but deformity for the worker.[42]

Their repeated attempts to create a "normal" life for themselves are constantly frustrated, usually by the police, who arrest both Charlie and the gamin at different times. As the two are shown marching down a highway into the rising sun in the film's final shot, we wonder if there exists a place where they will be able to realize their domestic dream.

My all too brief discussion of this aspect of the film – there are many comic elements here that deserve separate treatment – is meant to gesture towards another aspect of Marx's theory that the film embodies. Against the stereotype that the poor are lazy, the film, following Marx, shows that their best efforts to live a more fulfilling life are frustrated by a system that turns those efforts against them.

Thus, we can see how *Modern Times* illustrates Marx's conception of the ills of a capitalist society. Focusing on both the workplace and the personal sphere, the film uses Chaplin's comic skills to show a variety of ways in which workers are victimized by a capitalist economic structure.

But does this mean that the film is really *doing* philosophy? I answer this question affirmatively because it provides its viewers with concrete illustrations of Marx's abstract claims, illustrations that show the film's audience the human significance of those abstractions. Viewers of the film are presented with the result of a great deal of thinking about how to convey many of Marx's claims in a clear, understandable, and – because humorous – highly palatable manner. While, for example, the notion that the human being under capitalism is alienated from its species-being is a difficult one to grasp and explicate – witness the disagreement among philosophers about its significance and validity[43] – the difference between Charlie working on the factory floor and skating on the balcony of the department store is easy to comprehend and thus allows a central tenet of Marx's theory to remain etched in a viewer's mind. The film enhances the persuasive force of certain elements of Marx's theory of alienation and exploitation under capitalism by providing accessible interpretations of key elements of that theory.[44]

There are many philosophical articles that seek to explain the meaning of a difficult and obscure philosophical theory. They often do so by presenting a more detailed and worked out account of the claims at issue. While such explications may not often rise to the level of being original contributions to the discipline, they are quite necessary to the ongoing dialectic that is philosophy. My suggestion is that we treat cinematic illustrations of philosophical theories such as *Modern Times* in a similar way. Such cinematic illustrations of philosophical theories play an important role in transmitting the ideas developed by philosophical theories to a wide audience.

Up to now, I have kept one issue submerged, namely that of what accounts for a work being an illustration of something else. Although I claimed that intentionality was a mark of illustrations, I did not stress that this meant that it was possible for something to fail to be an illustration of the thing it was intended to illustrate when, for example, it was so poorly executed that no one could recognize it as one. I mention this only to say that illustrating a text – either pictorially or via a parable or some other technique – takes skill and intelligence. As such, these illustrations deserve to be seen, in certain specific cases, as capable of doing philosophy.

Still, I can imagine someone objecting to my account of *Modern Times* by saying that viewers don't watch the Chaplin film for its philosophical insights, but for its humor. Although a philosophically inclined critic like myself might be able to squeeze some philosophy out of its portrayal of the factory and the lives of the workers, we aren't interested in the film for its philosophical acumen, but rather for Charlie's amazing antics.[45]

Here, I can only agree that Charlie's comic riffs are an important source of our interest in *Modern Times*. But I would go on to point out that the humor of the sequences I have been discussing is intimately bound up with their serving as accessible illustrations of Marx's claims about the evils of capitalism. So the objector's distinction between Charlie's antics and the film's illustration of Marx's theory will not stand up, for the two are intrinsically bound together in this film. As I see it, you can't separate the film's philosophical thinking about alienation and exploitation from its comic portrayal in order to deny that the film ought to count as doing philosophy.

In this chapter, I have critically examined two recent attempts to justify the claim that films can make a significant contribution to contemporary philosophy. I found those accounts to be flawed because of their reliance on an inadequately theorized dichotomy between doing philosophy and merely illustrating it. After an initial investigation into the notion of pictorial illustration, one that undercut the validity of the thinking/illustrating dichotomy, I showed how *Modern Times* could be both an illustration of a philosophical theory and yet also a site of deep thinking about the evils of capitalism. This, taken together with my earlier discussion of *The Man Who Shot Liberty Valance* as an illustration of Nietzsche's critique of Hegel's view of history as progressive, should make it clear that films have the ability to illustrate philosophical theories and that, when they do, they count as themselves doing philosophy. Although being such an illustration does not exhaust the various ways in which films can philosophize, I think that it lays to rest some skeptical doubts about the validity of seeing philosophy in the moving image.

This chapter is thus a first step in my investigation of different techniques that films employ in order to philosophize. In the next chapter, I will begin an exploration of how films can do philosophy by focusing on one important philosophical technique embodied in film that I touched upon earlier in this chapter, namely the thought experiment.

4   A skeptical thought experiment
The Matrix

It is tempting to credit the Wachowski Brothers' film, *The Matrix* (1999), with ushering in an era of brisk philosophical activity focused on film. And, indeed, this film has engendered more philosophical discussion than any other film I know of – including such perplexing art film masterpieces as Alain Resnais' *Last Year at Marienbad* (1961) that seem to cry out for a philosopher's help in understanding them. At last count, there were three anthologies containing philosophical essays explicating *The Matrix* as well as at least one single-authored book by a philosopher about it.[1] But even if attributing an "epistemological break" to this film would be an exaggeration, we should remain blind neither to its extraordinary impact on philosophers nor to the interest they have manifested about it. The question I want to pursue is why this is so: What is it about *The Matrix* that has made it so stimulating to philosophers?

There can be no doubt that philosophers' fascination with *The Matrix* has to do with the film's relationship to Descartes' claim in the first of his *Meditations on First Philosophy* that all of our beliefs about reality might be false.[2] Let's call this "the deception hypothesis" to indicate that it posits our being radically deceived about the nature of the world we inhabit. Descartes' endorsement of the deception hypothesis in the first Meditation signals the beginning of modern philosophy, in which concern about the mind's access to reality replaces the more traditional view that the structure of reality is the fundamental issue of theoretical philosophy.

Over the centuries, there have been various attempts to lie to rest the ghost of the deception hypothesis. Immanuel Kant attempted to provide a proof of the reality of the external world that would expose the folly of the Cartesian privileging of the inner realm of our thoughts and feelings over the outer world of people and things. American pragmatists took exception to the metaphysical doubt at the heart of Descartes' program – more on this soon – seeking to sink Descartes' ship with an account of doubt that made it more specific and contextual than Descartes thought it was. And if Kant had proclaimed it a scandal of philosophy that the reality of external things had not yet been proven conclusively, the twentieth-century German philosopher Martin Heidegger retorted that the *real* scandal was that such a proof had even been attempted, for the key was to resist Descartes' view of the mental and the physical as two separate domains, since only if this claim was accepted could the deception hypothesis even be framed coherently. Wittgenstein's argument against the possibility of a private language is my final example of an attempt to undermine the coherence of Descartes' theory. Its central claim is the denial of Descartes' assumption that our ideas could be intelligible to us in the absence of a community of other language users. What Wittgenstein is purported to have shown is that the intelligibility of our own thoughts requires a set of public criteria for correct usage that the Cartesian skeptic implicitly relies upon but fails to acknowledge.

Given the centrality of the deception hypothesis to modern philosophy – this quick sketch touches only on some of the highlights of the debates it inaugurated in epistemology and metaphysics – if *The Matrix* were somehow able to renew the plausibility of that hypothesis, it would be no wonder that it would excite philosophers, for it would then represent an intervention into a more than 350-year-old debate. But could it really be the case that this film could genuinely make a contribution to that debate? And, if it could, in what way?

The central aim of this chapter is to establish that *The Matrix* is a philosophically significant film in that it *updates* Descartes' deception hypothesis albeit in a new and very contemporary context. It does so by means of a *thought experiment* involving universal deception that has an analogue in Descartes' own evil demon thought experiment in the first Meditation.[3] *The Matrix*'s unique Cartesian thought experiment qualifies it as our second example of a film that actually philosophizes.

In the last chapter, although I brought up the subject of thought experiments in the context of Plato's Parable of the Cave, I could not pursue that topic further then. Now, however, the time is ripe for a more extended discussion of thought experiments and their role in philosophy.

At this point it should be clear that characterizing philosophy accurately is such a difficult task that it would be foolhardy to think that we could do it, let alone in short compass here. Nonetheless, I would like to make a few quick points about philosophy to guide our inquiry into the nature of thought experiments.

You will recall that in **Chapter 2** I introduced three competing characterizations of philosophy as a form of thinking or reflection. At that point, I introduced two substantive and one methodological characterizations of philosophy: The first claimed that philosophy was concerned with "the eternal questions" such as whether or not there is a purpose to our existence; the second focused upon the relationship between philosophy and specific disciplines, claiming that there were abstract questions in each discipline that were the province of the philosopher, rather than the discipline's practitioners; and, finally, I cited an attempt to specify philosophy's nature by delimiting what we might call "rhetorical strategies" characteristic of philosophy, such as the argument, thought experiment, and counterexample. At that time, I asserted that none of these conceptions was a fully adequate means of capturing the nature of philosophy but that employing them jointly would allow us to characterize philosophy in a manner that was sufficiently precise for our undertaking.

In this chapter, I will investigate one philosophical rhetorical structure that I already singled out for its affinities to fiction film: the thought experiment. Although thought experiments are not the exclusive domain of the philosopher, as we shall see, they have played a central role in many philosophical arguments going all the way back to Plato at least. This would by itself justify our investigating how they might provide a link between philosophy and film.

But there is an additional reason for thinking that thought experiments would provide one of the links between film and philosophy that we are seeking: their reliance on hypothetical – i.e. fictional – scenarios. Since one of the questions we are pursuing concerns fiction film's ability to do philosophy, it seems natural to focus on this aspect of philosophy precisely for its use of fictional narratives.

The term "thought experiment" is a translation of the German word *Gedankenexperiment*, used by, among others, Ernst Mach who claimed that a great deal of "instinctive knowledge" could be made explicit by its use.[4] For Mach, physics was an important arena for the use of thought experiments. Nonetheless, the technique that Mach conceptualizes by this term is one that extends back much further in the history of philosophy, reaching, as I have said, back to Plato.

But what exactly is a thought experiment? Roy A. Sorenson defines it as "an experiment ... that purports to achieve its aim without the benefit of execution."[5] More helpful is Tamar Szabó Gendler's attempt: "To perform a thought experiment is to reason about an imaginary scenario with the aim of confirming or disconfirming some hypothesis or theory."[6] There are two elements present in Gendler's proposed definition. The first is the imaginary scenario or, as I shall call it, the thought experiment proper. The philosopher – or, more carefully, the narrator of the philosophical text – asks his reader to imagine a certain fictional narrative – "Imagine that you were driving a trolley and ... " But to be a thought experiment, the imagined scenario – the thought experiment proper – needs to play a role in a broader argument about a philosophical claim, principle, or theory, adding or withdrawing support to the item in question. As we shall see, it will be important to bear these two aspects of thought experiments in mind as we explore the question of whether they can be screened.

Now, there is no single role that all thought experiments play in philosophical argumentation. In fact, their roles are as variable as the arguments in which they are to be found. So, it will be useful to survey a few different types of the thought experiments found in the central texts – both recent and old – of the Western philosophical tradition. Doing so will not only show that these traditional texts are ripe with thought experiments, but will also open us up to some of the possible uses of thought experiments in films.[7]

Thought experiments as counterexamples

Plato's dialogues contain numerous examples of thought experiments that function as counterexamples to philosophical claims, usually those proposed by his interlocutors. Since I have already looked at one in the last chapter and will consider another in depth in the following one, I won't give an example of one here but turn instead to more contemporary instances of this philosophical technique.

Contemporary analytic philosophy is replete with thought experiments that function as counterexamples. Probably the most famous is known as the Gettier counterexample after its author, Edmund Gettier. The philosophical principle to which the counterexample is offered is the definition of knowledge as justified true belief, a view of knowledge dating back to Plato. Gettier asks us to imagine a situation like the following: Suppose I am at a party and I see John conniving with the bartender to bring Mary a spiked drink. When I see Mary with a drink in her hand, I not only believe that her drink is spiked but I think that I have knowledge of that fact. But suppose that John was merely joking, so the bartender did not spike Mary's drink, but that, unbeknownst to John, Fred dropped a drug into the drink John was bringing Mary. In this case, although my belief about Mary's drink is true and I have justification for it, I do not possess knowledge since I am wrong about how Mary's drink came to be spiked. The thought experiment is a counterexample to the Platonic conception of knowledge as justified true belief.

Epistemology is not the only field in which there are well known thought experiments that function as counterexamples. Another renowned one belongs to ethics. Judith Jarvis Thomson thinks that abortion is morally permissible. In order to demonstrate this, she proposes a counterexample to the claim that women have a moral obligation to carry their fetuses to term. She thinks that this principle can only be justified on the basis of a more general principle to the effect that, if one finds oneself in a situation in which some other being requires the use of one's body for a relatively short period of time in order to live, then morality requires one to do so. She then asks us to imagine waking up one morning to find a famous violinist plugged into our body in conditions much like that of carrying a fetus: the hook-up is only needed for nine months, it will allow the violinist not to perish, it will provide him or her with all that he needs to exist for those months, etc.[8] But even though the violinist will die if we refuse to remain hooked up to him for the requisite nine months, we do not think that we are morally obligated to remain connected to him. It might seem peevish or small to refuse, but it would not be morally wrong to do so. This means, according to Thomson, that we do not have an obligation to remain connected to a being who depends upon us simply because not remaining so connected would result in the death of the dependent being. But in order for abortion to be considered to be morally wrong, some such principle must hold and she claims this counterexample shows that it does not. So abortion cannot be wrong since people do not have an obligation to support a life simply because that life can only exist through a dependent relationship with them.

Counterexamples are also prominent in metaphysics and the philosophy of mind. Frank Jackson developed a well known thought experiment that functions as a counterexample to physicalism.[9] Physicalism asserts that physical facts are the only basic facts that exist. Jackson asks us to consider Mary, a brilliant scientist who had been confined from birth to a laboratory in which the only colors that she saw were black and white. However, being a scientist, she learned all of the scientific facts about perception. When she leaves the laboratory one day, she experiences colors for the first time, learning, among other things, what it is like to experience *red*. According to Jackson, Mary learns something new when she learns this. But, since she already knew all the physical facts, Mary must have learned a non-physical fact when she learned what it was like to see *red*. But this means that physicalism must be wrong.

In each case, the counterexample targets an important philosophical principle: Knowledge is justified true belief, abortion is morally wrong, or physical facts are all the facts there are. What the thought experiment does is to present a fictional scenario in which we think that the principles do not hold. We are supposed to deny that John has knowledge that Mary's drink is spiked, that the person hooked up to the violinist has an obligation to remain hooked up to him, and that Mary's experience of color can be accounted for by physicalism. The thought experiments show that the purported universal principles do not apply in all circumstances and so must be rejected.

All of these counterexamples have been disputed by other philosophers. There has even been debate about whether counterexamples are a defensible philosophical method.[10] So I am not claiming that they definitively establish the claims that they purport to. I am only interested in showing that a prominent use of thought experiments is that of developing counterexamples to philosophical claims.

Thought experiments as establishing possibility

An epistemological thought experiment has pride of place in the history of modern Western philosophy. As I have said, in his *Meditations on First Philosophy*, Descartes attempts to persuade his readers that they have no good reasons to suppose that their current beliefs about reality are true. This skeptical conclusion is only a step on the way to Descartes' articulation of his own metaphysical vision of the world, which includes a more adequate grounding for those of our beliefs that we take to be true. So let us look in some detail at one of the most famous thought experiments in the history of Western philosophy, Descartes' invocation of the evil demon hypothesis in the first Meditation.[11] (Later, I will show how *The Matrix* presents an analogous thought experiment and so, in my view, needs to be thought of as screening skepticism.)

One central concern of Descartes is the widely accepted belief that common sense gives us an accurate picture of the world. Most of us believe, for example, that when we see a book in front of us under normal viewing conditions, we can generally conclude that there really is a book there. In so doing, we accept the senses as accurate guides for determining the structure of reality. Descartes, as is well known, thought that reason, and not the senses, was the only reliable guide to the nature of reality. As part of his argument for this conclusion, he articulates the skeptical project of the first Meditation: to "withhold my assent no less carefully from things which are not plainly certain and indubitable than I would to what is patently false."[12] It turns out, however, that "withholding assent" from one's customary ideas, i.e. not endorsing them as true, is not as easy for Descartes as it might seem, for the sway of habit makes it difficult for him not to accept the truth of ideas that "keep coming back again and again, almost against my will." Indeed, Descartes tells us, these ideas "seize upon my credulity," i.e. compel his assent even as he resolves to withhold it.[13]

Given this fact – the tenacity of the habitual – how can Descartes succeed at his task of dislodging the hold of received ways of thinking? Descartes thinks his famous thought experiment involving an evil demon will do the trick:

> Thus I will suppose not a supremely good God, the source of truth, but rather an evil demon, as clever and deceitful as he is powerful, who has directed his entire effort to misleading me. I will regard the heavens, the air, the earth, colors, shapes, sounds, and all external things as nothing but the deceptive games of my dreams, with which he lays snares for my credulity.[14]

Descartes' supposition that this evil demon exists provides him with the necessary means for actualizing his project of withholding assent to all the ideas that he finds flooding his consciousness for whose adequacy there is some element of doubt. It does so because it provides him with an imaginary scenario in which those ideas do not provide accurate guidance about the nature of reality. The hypothesis that there is an evil demon deceiving him at every moment, despite being entertained as a fiction, enables Descartes to fulfill his intention of withholding belief from all his dubitable ideas because it fills in this abstract intention with a concrete scenario in which it is realized. This thought experiment is thus a crucial step in his philosophical argument.[15]

Of course, later in the *Meditations*, Descartes goes on to show that what he had presented as possible – the truth of the deception hypothesis – is not really, since rational argumentation establishes the existence of God and his not being a deceiver. Still, Descartes' use of a thought experiment to establish possibility illustrates a distinct philosophical employment of it. First, a certain state of affairs is presented as conceivable, something we are to imagine. Once this is done, we are to conclude that such a state of affairs is actually possible, so that beliefs that contradict it are inadequately grounded.

Failed thought experiments as demonstrating impossibility

A related use of a thought experiment occurs in Bishop Berkeley's *Principles of Human Knowledge*. The target of Berkeley's thought experiment is John Locke's claim that there are abstract ideas. An essential element of Locke's *empiricist* program was to show that all of our ideas could be traced back to their origins in our experience, either sensory or introspective.

Although there is initial plausibility to thinking that our concept of red is some type of imprint caused by red things – their "idea" – this view is less plausible in relation to abstract ideas, ideas for which there is no single empirical instance to count as its cause. Take, for example, the idea of a triangle. All we ever see are individual triangles: this one isosceles, that one equilateral, another one scalene. How, then, Locke asks, since we have never seen an example of the general idea of a triangle, do we come by the idea itself? He answers, proposing a thought example of his own, that we develop the abstract idea "triangle" by inspecting its individual instances, i.e. looking at specific triangles, and then abstracting from the specific features that each has – whether they are isosceles, equilateral, or scalene – to arrive at the general idea "triangle."

In order to reject Locke's purported genealogy of our idea of triangle, Berkeley reports a failure. He tries to do what Locke has asked: to imagine the abstract idea of triangle. He claims that he has failed to be able to do so: No matter how hard he tries to imagine a triangle without a specific length of side and size of angle, he cannot, for he always finds himself imagining a specific triangle. Hence, Berkeley concludes, there are no abstract ideas.

From his inability to successfully imagine an abstract idea, Berkeley concludes that abstract ideas are an impossibility. This is sort of the inverse of Descartes' use of a thought experiment. Whereas Descartes argued from the conceivability of a hypothetical situation to its possibility, Berkeley is arguing from the inconceivability of one to its impossibility.

A similar strategy animates a thought experiment that grounds one of the most important theses of twentieth-century analytic philosophy: that of the indeterminacy of translation. In *Word and Object*, W. V. O. Quine argues against the traditional notion of meaning. The crucial step in his argument involves the following thought experiment: Imagine a linguistic anthropologist confronting a native tribe with the task of creating a dictionary that correctly and uniquely translates the terms of "Native" into English. Can he do this? Quine argues not, for there is no way to decide on objective grounds what the tribe's ontology is, what types of things they take to be the basic constituents of reality. When the tribe's members respond, for example, to the presence of a rabbit with the native expression *gavagai*, Quine argues there is no way for the linguist to tell whether they are referring to whole rabbits, temporally distinct rabbit stages, or, even, undetached rabbit parts, that we can imagine equally good dictionaries based on competing ontologies as translations of Native terms. The ontology of the natives, Quine concludes, is underdetermined by their linguistic behavior, so there can be multiple English–Native dictionaries that are equally valid despite their having different English translations of Native terms. There is no unique meaning of the word *gavagai* in English, to return to Quine's example, so that multiple dictionaries are possible with incompatible ontologies.

Quine intended his thought experiment to justify the rejection of the traditional notion of meaning. Translation is generally understood to involve taking the meaning of a word or expression in one language and providing the term in another with the same meaning. What Quine took his thought experiment to show was that meaning was not completely determined by people's linguistic behavior. As a result, Quine argued, the traditional notion of meaning had to be abandoned.

Many have questioned the validity of Quine's argument, myself included.[16] His argument nonetheless has been incredibly influential on analytic philosophers as well as the development of analytic philosophy during the last half of the twentieth century. And, as we have just seen, the thought experiment involving a tribe and a linguist plays a crucial role in establishing his thesis. Like Berkeley, Quine uses a thought experiment to reject an important philosophical concept.

Thought experiments as establishing necessary connections

In an article that attempts to explain thought experiments as transforming conceptual abilities into propositional knowledge, C. Mason Meyers points out another role thought experiments have played in philosophical argumentation. "An analytical thought experiment," he explains, "is a procedure for revealing conceptual relationships of an *a priori* nature."[17] What Meyers means by this is that thought experiments establish what I would call "necessary connections." To understand this, consider one of his examples: In book II, chapter xxvii, section 15 of his *Essay Concerning Human Understanding*, Locke asks us to consider the case of a prince whose mind, complete with all of its memories, enters the body of a cobbler that has had all of its mental contents removed. The question Locke poses is who we think the new composite being *is*. Is he the prince, despite having the body of the cobbler? Or is he, perhaps, the cobbler, with the mind of the prince?

Locke uses this thought experiment to make a distinction between the *person* and the *man*. He takes it as obvious that his readers would all agree that the resulting *person* was the prince, but that the *man* would be, to everyone but the person himself, the cobbler. We need not dwell on Locke's peculiar distinction, but should turn our attention to the more interesting claim about personal identity, for Locke has claimed that personal identity is established by the identity of the mind regardless of what happens to the body. This is a contentious but very influential claim, one that Locke thinks is important, given his religious concerns.

The important feature that thought experiments of this type share is the attempt to justify a conceptual or necessary connection by means of an imaginary example. They assume that we can draw general conclusions about conceptual relationships from single, imaginary instances.

Locke's argument was taken up by the analytic philosopher Derek Parfit, who proposed a thought experiment of his own that challenges Locke's conclusions about personal identity.[18] He imagines a situation in which I have two brothers who have suffered brain damage and in which each of my brain hemispheres is identical to the other. If each hemisphere were transplanted into one of the two brothers, it would appear that each of the resulting beings would have an equally valid claim to be me, even though they are obviously not identical with each other. Parfit takes this to show that identity cannot be the concept at issue in questions of survival, thereby challenging Locke's account.

Thought experiments as confirming a theory

Another type of thought experiment is based upon principles used in scientific reasoning. Philosophers in the Western tradition have often taken natural science to be a good model for their own theorizing. One basic feature of the scientific method is its use of experiments to justify a theory.

What exactly is an experiment? In order to understand this concept, we need to consider a related notion. A *theory* is a generalization that is made on the basis of a certain body of evidence. If we look around and see five white swans, we could develop a (very low level) theory consisting only of a single generalization: "All swans are white." There are always consequences of a theory that exceed its evidential base; in this case, all the actual swans that we have not examined constitute this excess. A (simple) *experiment* occurs when one such consequence predicted by the theory is used to test whether the theory is true. When the experiment succeeds and the theory's prediction holds, we take the theory to gain added confirmation. So if we go out, hunt for and find a swan, and note its white color, we have per-formed an experiment that adds confirmation to the theory.

Just finding another instance of a law or theory is the limit case of an experiment.[19] A more robust example is Galileo's supposed dropping of objects of different weights off the Leaning Tower of Pisa and his discovery that, *contra* Aristotle, they fall at the same rates. His own theory of motion – that the rate of fall of falling bodies was independent of their mass – was therefore confirmed by this experiment and led to the rejection of Aristotelian physics.[20]

It might seem odd to think that philosophy contains similar experiments and, of course, philosophical experiments are different from scientific experiments. Indeed, they are *thought* experiments, experiments you can do in your own study. A nice example of this use of a thought experiment is to be found in Arthur Danto's philosophy of art. Danto asks us to consider the case of Testadura, who mistakes a sculpture or assemblage made from an actual bed – Robert Rauschenberg's *Bed* (1955) – for an actual bed and sleeps in it. What sort of mistake, Danto asks, is this, since it involves nothing more than mistaking a bed for a bed?

Danto had previously argued that there is a *sui generis* sense of "is" – the "is" of artistic identification – that explains why we think that certain things are art even though they are perceptually indistinguishable from what he calls "mere things." Andy Warhol's *Brillo Box* (1964) is one example of such a work, since it looks exactly like the Brillo cartons that are to be found in the stockrooms of grocery stores. Danto had claimed that only one who understands the "is" of artistic identification is able to understand why the Warhol piece is a work of art rather than a mere thing.

Danto's thought experiment adds confirmation to his theory, just as an actual experiment does to a scientific theory. The idea is that, only on the supposition that there is an "is" of artistic identification, can we explain Testadura's mistake. Once we accept a special use of "is" in which it designates artistic rather than "mere" empirical properties and things, we can understand that Rauschenberg's *Bed* is a bed in two different senses: As well as being made out of a "mere" bed, it is an artistic representation of a bed. Testadura fails to see the ontological complexity of the artwork by taking it to be *only* a physical bed. Danto thus uses this thought experiment to give added confirmation to this theory concerning the "is" of artistic identification. Formulated in relation to *Brillo Box*, the theory gains confirmation through its explanation of the artistic status of Rauschenberg's *Bed*.

Theory building through idealization thought experiments

Thought experiments themselves play another important role in natural science. Some scientific theories are themselves elaborate thought experiments in which an idealized model of the real world is created. It is argued that the idealization should be taken as an approximation to the real world that only adds more complexity to the idealized model.

Consider, for example, the kinetic theory of gases. In order to develop an account of the behavior of gases like air, molecules were treated as point masses, an obvious idealization of the fact that molecules are spatially extended entities. This idealization allowed for the development of laws governing the behavior of ideal gasses, laws that actual gases only adhere to roughly. The imagined reality of the ideal gas is a thought experiment that allowed for scientific progress.

Philosophers also use thought experiments in this way. They construct an idealized version of reality and then ask us to accept reality as an approximation of the idealization they have introduced. An excellent example of such a thought experiment is Plato's *Republic*. The bulk of that dialogue is nothing but an elaborate thought experiment in which an ideal state is set up. The task that Socrates has set for himself in this dialogue is to define justice (or acting morally) as a trait of individuals. In order to do so, he suggests that it will be easier to see what justice is in a state, for he regards the state as "the individual writ large." Most of the dialogue consists of Socrates and his interlocutors describing in great detail the structure of such a state. The description of this ideal state is an extended thought experiment, an imagining of how such a state should be structured. But once it has been completed, Socrates extracts his principle of justice – each part fulfilling its function – by abstracting it from the structure of the imaginary state he and his interlocutors have developed.

Socrates' procedure here is much like that involved in creating the gas laws. In both cases, an idealized version of reality is created that is then taken to have normative force in regard to the real world, albeit only approximately. Even though things in reality do not behave precisely in the way the idealization predicts, the laws or principles established in these thought experiments are taken to have validity as idealizations of a messy empirical reality.

This type of thought experiment continues to play a central role in social and political philosophy. John Rawls' momentous book, *A Theory of Justice*, contains a thought experiment as complex as Plato's. In order to legitimate his two principles of justice, Rawls invokes what he calls "the original position." Readers are asked to imagine themselves to be deciding on what principles of justice to accept for a society to which they will belong. For the purposes of the decision-making, they are ignorant of the specific positions they will themselves occupy in the society whose rules they are attempting to construct. Rawls argues that rational agents operating under the conditions of ignorance he has outlined would choose the principles of justice he favors.

So both philosophy and natural science use idealization thought experiments in order to derive principles or laws that are then taken to hold, at least in first approximation, of reality itself. This is a complex use of thought experiments that shows how widespread their use is within both the sciences and the humanities.

This cursory examination of some of the uses to which thought experiments have been put within the texts of the Western philosophical tradition is not intended to be either systematic or complete. Rather, I take it to establish two things: first, that thought experiments play a crucial role in a wide range of philosophical argumentation; and second, that there is no single way in which thought experiments function. Even if we can say that all thought experiments involve imagining a non-actual or hypothetical situation, this does not provide us with an understanding of the precise manner in which any one of them functions in a philosophical argument.

An awareness of the diverse roles that thought experiments have in philosophical argumentation provides a model for thinking about how films function analogously. Although I will assert that films can philosophize in so far as they contain thought experiments, I also maintain that the specific way in which a cinematic thought experiment is to be understood will depend upon a careful examination of an individual film. Thought experiments are a diverse lot – and so, too, are their uses in film.[21]

Why does it make sense to think of fiction films as thought experiments? As a first step towards answering this question, consider what we have just learned. In a thought experiment, a philosopher asks his readers to envision an imaginary situation, one that often includes some rather bizarre or unusual elements, say by asking them to suppose that there is an evil demon who is constantly deceiving them about the truth of their beliefs. From this act of imagining, the philosopher then draws a conclusion that she claims follows from her readers' ability to entertain the imagined scenario.

Fiction films share an important characteristic with such philosophical thought experiments, for their audiences have to imagine the reality of a certain non-actual state of affairs.[22] When watching *King Kong* (Merian C. Cooper and Ernest B. Schoedsack), for example, the audience imagines that a monstrous ape is on the loose in New York City in 1933, the year of the film's making, something that did not actually take place. This requires the film's audience to perform a mental operation analogous to that of imagining that there is an evil demon deceiving us about whether our thoughts are accurate guides to reality. In both cases, there is an imaginative activity going on in which a fictive hypothesis about reality is entertained.

This similarity makes it plausible to interpret some fiction films as thought experiments. Like philosophical thought experiments, fiction films present non-existent events and/or worlds to their audiences. The hypothetical examples of philosophical thought experiments – "Consider, for example, a person who ... " – have a marked similarity to the fictional worlds presented by films, some of which are even presented in similar ways – "Once upon a time, in a galaxy far, far away ... " It therefore seems reasonable to assume that some fiction films function as thought experiments. All that is required is that the imaginative activity that an audience experiences in watching a film yield the sort of conclusion that philosophical thought experiments do. One way to establish that films can do this would be to show that a particular fiction film works in one of the ways we have identified as characteristic of philosophical thought experiments: as a counter-example to a philosophic thesis; as a demonstration of the possibility of a world; as a proof of a certain impossibility; as a confirmatory instance of a theory; as an idealized model of the real world; or in some other, standard role that philosophical thought experiments play.

What would be required to support my contention that some fiction films work in ways that philosophical thought experiments do? A careful examination of specific films that explains their function as philosophical thought experiments. So far, I have only established that there are reasons to think that fiction films *can* play this role, not that they actually do.

In this chapter and the following one, I will look at films that function as thought experiments of the sort we have examined. I will begin, as promised, with a look at *The Matrix* and its screening of the deception hypothesis.

My claim is that the Wachowski Brothers' 1999 film, *The Matrix*,[23] screens Descartes' skeptical deception hypothesis by showing us a fictional world of which the deception hypothesis is true.[24] It accomplishes this by means of a narrative that updates Descartes' evil demon thought experiment by substituting a vast array of malevolent computers for that hypothetical being. After exploring how the film does this, I will return to a more general consideration of film as screening philosophical thought experiments.

The conceit of *The Matrix* is that what the characters experience as reality – and their reality is pretty much the world that its audience would have inhabited in 1999, the year of the film's release, although the film supposedly takes place some 200 years later – is actually a huge, interactive perceptual illusion – the Matrix – that is created and maintained by the computers that have taken over the world.[25] According to the film, this situation is the result of the computers' victory over human beings in a devastating war. The triumphant computers "farm" human beings in a manner analogous to how we humans now farm animals for food. According to the film, the human body actually produces more energy than it consumes, so, in a bizarre analogy to Marx's theory of the role of surplus labor in structuring capitalism, the computers breed humans and keep their bodies alive in huge skyscraper-like complexes for their surplus energy. Since the film never provides a complete rationale for this, viewers are left to presume that the reason for the existence of the Matrix is that humans need to have their minds distracted while their bodies produce the required surplus of electrical energy.

With this scenario, *The Matrix* presents what I call a *screening* of the deception hypothesis. That is, upon viewing *The Matrix*, a viewer must confront the question of whether it might not be the case that all of *her* perceptual experience could be what it now is without there being a world that resembles those perceptions. This raises a number of questions. How does the film raise the skeptical question about a viewer's experience? Does its doing so amount to a real screening of a philosophical claim? Does the screened version of Descartes' claim carry the same conviction as the written one? What, if anything, does this tell us about the nature of film?

In order to answer these questions, we have to look more closely at the film's narrative. *The Matrix*'s protagonist is Neo (Keanu Reeves) and, early in the film, he is contacted by Trinity (Carrie Anne Moss) who, we later learn, is part of an underground war against the dominance of the computers. Throughout the early scenes of the film, although he is clearly bothered by something about his world and trying to get to the bottom of his worries, Neo is not convinced that the world that he believes to be real is anything but that. Only as the result of the intervention of Trinity and her cohorts does he come to realize that the world that he had taken to be real is in fact merely an apparent one.[26]

Neo's revelation occurs after he swallows a pill offered to him by Morpheus (Laurence Fishburne), the leader of the rebels.[27] Morpheus offers him a choice between two pills, with the assurance that one – the blue one – will allow him to return to his former life as if nothing had happened while the other – the red one – will let him see the reality of his situation and learn what the Matrix really is. After taking the red pill, Neo is led into a large room filled with computer and video equipment operated by a number of people all clad, like Morpheus and Trinity, in black leather. He is placed in a chair and electrodes are taped to his chest and inserted into his ear. Morpheus explains that the pill Neo has taken is part of a trace program that will help him and his associates find Neo's location. Although neither Neo nor the film's viewers know enough to understand Morpheus' explanation at the time, it turns out that Neo's body is actually located within the complex in which the computers have housed people's bodies. (Later in the sequence, Neo and the film's viewers get to see this structure and Neo's location within it.) The rebels have the equipment to pierce through the apparent world of the Matrix and determine where Neo really is located. Once they have done so, they will be able to rescue him by unplugging him from the electronic network and then bringing him aboard their ship. At that point, Neo will be able to see reality as it truly is for the first time.

After a quip by Cypher (Joe Pantoliano) comparing Neo's impending journey to Dorothy's in *The Wizard of Oz*,[28] Neo sees his own image in a mirror. Suddenly, the image fractures, lights appear in it, and it seems to move as if it were a liquid. Neo reaches out to touch the mirror and his finger goes into it, as if it were a liquid metal, like mercury. When he withdraws his finger, the liquid mirror is pulled with it, though eventually it pulls back into its original shape. As this is going on, Morpheus asks Neo if he has ever had a dream that he was sure was real. He then invokes a quasi-Cartesian puzzle: Once you awoke, how would you know the difference between the dream world and the real world? As the mirror-like substance begins to move up his arm and onto the rest of his body, Neo begins to fibrillate and go into cardiac arrest. At this exact moment, the rebels locate his body and the screen momentarily goes black.

Although the scene continues, let me pause it at this frame in order to consider what has happened so far. I claim that the film provides its viewers with a visual experience that is analogous to Neo's, an experience in which the world that they take to be real – and here I'm talking about the imaginary world that the film projects – begins to exhibit irregularities that suggest that one's perceptual experience is not an accurate guide to the nature of that reality. After all, as we have been looking at the screen, we have been assuming that the images we are seeing provide us with accurate information about the fictional world of the film. That is, all along we have been interpreting the images that we see projected on the movie screen as images of objects and persons that are real in the film's fictional world. But as Neo begins to experience disruptions to the regularities of his world, the filmmakers disrupt our experience of the film world as well, providing us viewers with an actual experience (albeit of a fictional world) in which we recognize that our senses have been deceiving us about the nature of reality.[29]

In so doing, the film transforms our awareness of the screen as opening up a fictional world to us into an awareness of the screen as screening that world from us through representations for which there are no corresponding objects in its fictional world (or only objects whose natures differ from the manner in which they are presented). This realization is an exact parallel of the one that Neo has, although his realization has to do with a world that is real for him. The film accomplishes this by making us aware that it has similar abilities to those it attributes to the giant computers that simulate the Matrix, for *The Matrix* also presents its viewers with a world that is not real even in a fictional sense.

But I paused the film in mid-scene, so let's hit play. When the blank screen fills, we are introduced to the film's actual reality, that from which both we and Neo had been screened. Neo surfaces in a large, womb-like tank in which his body has been kept submerged. His body is coated with a thick, amniotic-type fluid and has electrical umbilical cords attached to the arms, chest, and the back of the head.[30] As he looks around, seeing reality for the first time, he sees many similar "wombs" electronically connected into huge skyscraper-like structures that frequently emit lightning (see Figure 9).

This is the reality underlying the Matrix, the human body farm that produces the electricity that keeps the computers powered. A bug-like creature descends on Neo and disconnects one of the cords. All the other cords then pop off of his body and he goes down a long water-slide into a pool of water. He sees a light and trapdoor in the ceiling of the room he is in. Suddenly, a large claw descends, capturing him and pulling him through the door into the light. Neo then finds himself aboard the rebel ship, *Nebuchadnezzar*. The crew now wears much less trendy clothes and the whole environment is much less glitzy than it appeared as presented in the apparent world of the Matrix. The scene ends as Morpheus intones, "Welcome to the real world."

The film has here depicted a situation analogous to that envisioned in Descartes' evil demon thought experiment. That is, what Descartes contemplates as a possibility and what he later denies could actually obtain – that we are systematically deluded about the nature of reality – the film reveals

Figure 9 Neo discovers the real world. From *The Matrix*.

Source: Warner Bros/The Kobal Collection.

to be the actual situation of humans in its fictional world. So what most of the Matrix's inhabitants had taken to be real – and what we viewers had accepted as the film's fictional reality – is shown to be no more than an appearance generated by an interactive computer program, just as Descartes hypothesized that reality might be nothing but an appearance generated by a malign demon.

Viewers generally do not immediately grasp the full significance of what they have seen, for it all goes by very quickly in the film. Later scenes help viewers understand the metaphysics of what they have seen by including shots in which the characters exist as they do within the Matrix intercut with scenes of the reality behind this orchestrated illusion. This helps viewers "see" that the Matrix is a world that is merely apparent (see Figure 10).

One example involves a fight between Neo and Morpheus. As Morpheus repeatedly instructs Neo to reject his belief that the world of the Matrix is the real world so that he can realize his true power and ability, the film cuts to the other members of the ship's crew who are watching Neo and Morpheus on CRT screens.

This juxtaposition of the apparent world of the Matrix with the reality that grounds it not only ensures that the film's viewers understand (to some extent) how the Matrix is supposed to work but allows them to see the *Nebuchadnezzar*'s crew as a group of viewers analogous to themselves who are able to see the illusion of the Matrix while recognizing it for what it is.

Figure 10 Trinity holds Neo in the "real world" as she gazes at him on screen in the Matrix. From *The Matrix*.

Source: Warner Bros/The Kobal Collection/Boland, Jasin.

More is going on in these scenes and others like them than simply the revelation that the world of the Matrix is merely apparent. *The Matrix* achieves something with film that had never happened before, at least to this extent and with this technological sophistication. Beginning with our sense of film as a medium that reveals a (fictional) world to us, the film shows us that the world that we were taking to be (fictionally) real was merely apparent, a projection. Of course, there is a history of self-reflexive films that ask us to think about the nature of film itself, a history that goes back, at least, to Buster Keaton's 1924 masterpiece, *Sherlock Junior*. In that film, the Keaton character actually enters the projected world of a film, albeit in a dream, allowing Keaton to pose questions about the relationship between the film world and the real world. The difference is that *Sherlock Junior*'s audience is always itself aware of the difference between the real and film worlds as depicted within Keaton's film. But as we experience *The Matrix*, we initially believe in the (fictional) reality of the world that is depicted by the film. As Neo comes to see that the world he had believed to be real was only a computer simulation, *so do we*. That is, we have an experience analogous to his of coming to see that the "real world" of the film is only a computer projection – the Matrix – and, hence, merely apparent, and that there is an underlying (fictional) reality that differs in marked ways from this apparent one. But what we see is that what we had taken to be the "real" world of the film was merely a projected one.

What I am suggesting is that *The Matrix*, by means of its ability to get its viewers to see the world of the Matrix as (fictionally) real when it is (fictionally) only apparent, puts a new twist on Descartes' deception hypothesis. By substituting a vast network of rebellious computers for the evil demon, the film shows itself to be capable of a deception of its viewers analogous to that which Descartes imagines the evil demon to be capable of in relation to himself. So viewers come to acknowledge that *The Matrix* itself has the power to deceive *them* about (fictional) reality. The film has thus done to us what the computers do to Neo and the other inhabitants of the Matrix: cause us/them to mistake a generated and merely apparent world for the real world.

Films are not unique in their ability to get readers to draw false inferences about the nature of their fictional worlds. A novel like Ian McEwan's *Atonement* has a "twist" ending in which the "author" of the fiction is revealed to be a character within the fiction and not an omniscient narrator as had seemed to be the case. This requires that readers need to reassess the truth of many of the novel's statements, for we now recognize them to have been made by a character who has a particular slant on what took place. What's unique about *The Matrix*, however, is that it deceives viewers about their *perceptual beliefs*, for, while watching the initial segment of the film, they believe themselves to be perceiving a real, albeit fictional, world when all they are perceiving is the illusory world of the Matrix. As such, the film's deception takes place in an even more immediate manner than that of the novel.

There is an earlier sequence in which the film already establishes its power to deceive and manipulate not only its own characters (much as Keaton does in a famous series of jump cuts that takes place when Buster first "enters" the film world of *Sherlock Junior*) but the members of its audience as well.[31] The sequence begins after Neo is arrested and interrogated by the computer forces known as agents. It is a scary experience for him, one that ends with the agents injecting a bug-like creature into him through his belly button. As this rather horrifying event ends, Neo is shown to be awakening from a nightmare and we – along with him – experience a first shift in our interpretation of the previous scene, assuming that what we had seen was just the content of a nightmare he had had. Here, the film has relied on a technical possibility that has been exploited by films for some time: They are able to frame a sequence in such a way that what the audience took to be part of the fictional world of the film was really just the subjective experience of one of that world's characters.

Not content with a single twist to our understanding of what has transpired, the film reveals that Neo was not just dreaming shortly thereafter, when he is literally debugged by Trinity prior to his being taken to Morpheus aboard the *Nebuchadnezzar*. When we see the very bug that had been injected through his belly button being sucked out, we experience a reversal of the earlier reversal, as we (and Neo) are forced to return to our earlier belief that Neo's arrest and questioning were not just events in his nightmare. But we are left puzzled by elements of what takes place during Neo's questioning that seem impossible, such as the literal erasure of his mouth to keep him quiet. While we can retrospectively understand this as a manipulation of the Matrix by the computers, we do not yet have sufficient knowledge of the film's actual (fictional) world to successfully interpret what transpires here.

In this sequence, *The Matrix* had already toyed with our understanding of the reality of what we were seeing on the screen, albeit in ways that were not revolutionary. In so doing, the filmmakers played on the analogy between film and the Matrix. Our belief in the "reality" of the (fictional) world that we see on the screen is created and controlled by the filmmakers in an analogous manner to how the experience of the inhabitants of the Matrix is determined by the computers. Our understanding of reality as of a completely different order of being than dreams is undermined by these reversals.

But only with its revelation of the (fictional) reality of the human-computer array through which the (fictional) appearance of the Matrix is actually generated does the film complete its philosophical thought: that the real world might be no more than a projection. Viewers are led to this thought through their experience of their own credulity, for the film has succeeded in manipulating their beliefs about its (fictional) world as easily and successfully as Descartes' hypothetical evil demon could deceive Descartes about his. Given the increasing presence of screen mediations of reality in our everyday experience, the film pushes its audience to ask: "How do we know what the real world is like?" Morpheus is addressing *us* as well as Neo when he asks how one can tell the real world from the dream.

In the last chapter, I argued that a film that illustrated a philosophical view could thereby actually be doing philosophy. I now want to argue that *The Matrix* is doing philosophy, but not only by being an illustration of the deception hypothesis. What more, then, does the film do?

Let's begin by considering a film – let's call it *The Matron* – identical to *The Matrix* except that viewers are always aware that Neo and his ilk are deceived about reality, say by our sharing the epistemic perspective of the crew of the *Nebuchadnezzar* who watch the Matrix world on their TV screens. *The Matron* would illustrate the deception hypothesis by showing viewers a world in which it is true. The difference is that in *The Matrix*, because we share Neo's epistemic limitations, we actually are taken in by the deceptive world of the Matrix as fully as he – only we are deceived about the nature of a fictional world while, within the fiction, he is deceived about his real world. We thus participate not only in the deception, but also its subsequent removal.

It is the experience that viewers of *The Matrix* have watching the film that distinguishes it from its more pedestrian counterpart, *The Matron*. This is because *The Matrix* places viewers in an epistemic position where they are faced with the question of what justifies their belief that they are not in an analogous situation to that of the Matrix's inhabitants. It does this, as I have said, by actually deceiving them about their perceptions of the film's fictional world. They have to admit that the deception hypothesis is true, not only in the fictional world of the film but in the real world in which they have been deceived about the world of the film they have been watching. They are thus left with a skeptical doubt about their own experience – How do I know that I am not trapped in a Matrix-like situation? – a doubt that is caused by their being deceived about their perceptual experience by *The Matrix*.

Placing a person in an epistemic situation where they are made to question the justification of a certain belief or action is, of course, one of the characteristic moves of philosophy. What better way to characterize the practice of Socrates in the early dialogues of Plato than to say that he made his interlocutors skeptical about the validity of certain key concepts or beliefs that structured their world? If *The Matrix* is able to engender a similar perplexity in its audience, doesn't it make sense to see it as actually philosophizing?

But why doesn't this only mean that *The Matrix* is a really good illustration of Descartes' philosophy? After all, I have only argued that the film does something similar to what Descartes' text does: It renders problematic the assumption that our ordinary beliefs are reliable guides to the nature of reality. How does this qualify the film as a work of philosophy rather than simply an illustration of a philosophic view?

One avenue of response open to me would be to claim, using the terminology developed in the last chapter, that *The Matrix* has become an iconic illustration of the deception hypothesis of the first Meditation, so that it has achieved a greater degree of importance than that which arbitrary illustrations of texts have. As evidence, I could cite my own classes, where students immediately understand the issues Descartes raises once I have simply directed their attention to the film. On this account, the film would have achieved a broad recognition of the skeptical dilemma that Descartes first pointed out.

But I am not satisfied with this account, for I think that *The Matrix* has achieved even more than this: In my view, the film raises skeptical doubts in its audience for a purpose quite different from that of Descartes. The great philosopher was attempting to overthrow our faith in our senses in order to secure reason pride of place as the mental faculty that determines metaphysical truth. The film not only raises the possibility of deception, but actually deceives us, its viewers, for a very different purpose: to get us to think about the role that computers and other devices with screens – films, video and DVD players, etc. – have come to play in our lives. By getting audiences to take seriously the possibility that what we take to be the real world is nothing but a projection of a different reality, the film is asking us to think about how such devices may have screened us from the world rather than allowed the world to be visible on their screens.

It is the presence of a complex thought experiment within the broader narrative of *The Matrix*, then, that qualifies it as genuinely doing philosophy. The film not only shows viewers a situation in which skepticism about the external world is justified, it actually deceives them in a way that engenders their own skeptical doubts. This thought experiment not only updates Descartes' own evil demon thought experiment for an audience more worried about their own susceptibility to virtual realities than the truth of modern science, it also demonstrates its own ability, as a technology for screening reality, to get us to take its own projections to be real.

5 Arguing against utilitarianism
Eternal Sunshine of the Spotless Mind

In previous chapters, I have explored two ways in which films can qualify as doing philosophy. First, I argued that a film that illustrates a philosophical theory can make a contribution to that theory. Second, I showed that films can present thought experiments, an important philosophical technique that has flourished within analytic philosophy.

Still, there is one philosophical technique that many philosophers see as essential to philosophy and that it might be thought lies outside the range of film's capabilities, viz. presenting an argument. For many contemporary philosophers, especially those working within the analytic tradition, logical argumentation is the hallmark of philosophy. If film cannot be shown to have the capacity to present arguments, then it might be thought that there can only be a tenuous connection between film and philosophy.

In this chapter, I will demonstrate that films can indeed present arguments by showing that there is one type of argument – the presentation of a counterexample to a philosophical thesis by means of a thought experiment – that films are well-suited to make. After clearing the way for this view with some general considerations, I will develop an interpretation of Michel Gondry's 2004 film, *Eternal Sunshine of the Spotless Mind*, that shows how the film presents a counterexample to the ethical theory of utilitarianism.

To begin, I shall consider an important objection to the idea that films can present arguments that I discussed briefly in **Chapter 2** but postponed addressing fully. The *generality objection* relied on the fact that the film that I am concerned with in this chapter, and those that have been of great interest to recent philosophers, involve fictional narratives. Although there certainly are non-narrative films that qualify as meriting philosophical interest, such as those in the structuralist tradition of avant-garde film,[1] I am concerned for the moment primarily with narrative fiction films – especially popular ones – for the issue is whether such films can present arguments. The objection to this possibility relies on the fact that the stories that such films impart involve specific individuals and circumstances. In so far as they do so, the objection maintains, they are incapable of employing the discursive form of an argument, for arguments involve universal claims while narratives are inherently particular. Because a fiction film like Orson Welles' *Citizen Kane* (1941) tells the story of the specific fictional individual, Charles Foster Kane, this objection maintains there is no way that it can result in our accepting on logical grounds the validity of a general claim that would qualify it as making a philosophical argument. [2] While our sympathy for the fates of certain characters might encourage us to accept a general truth, the objection concludes, this is not the same thing as our acquiring rational conviction through an argument.

In response, let me first admit that written philosophy has only rarely employed a narrative structure. While it is true that Hegel's *Phenomenology of Spirit* is an extended narrative, it can be regarded as the exception that proves the rule, for its central character is *consciousness* – hardly the sort of entity one would expect to be the star of a popular film – and its story is of the tragic road consciousness faces in attaining self-consciousness – not exactly suitable material for the Hollywood "dream machine." And though Nietzsche's *Thus Spoke Zarathustra* does tell a story – that of the mythic Zarathustra's trials and tribulations – it can be maintained that its philosophy resides in the argument-like speeches that Zarathustra gives about the eternal recurrence and other matters, rather than in the story of his ascent and descent. Even if we grant that Nietzsche's narrative has philosophical significance, his unique text would also seem to support the more general contention that philosophic argumentation stands at odds with narrative structure.

Despite the paucity of narratives in written philosophy, recent analytic philosophy has begun to acknowledge their philosophical significance. The recent emphasis on narrative began with Alasdair MacIntyre's *After Virtue*.[3] Although most accounts of personal identity had pointed to some feature such as bodily continuity or the continuity of memory as the ground for taking ourselves to be unified beings, it has been recently argued, taking off from MacIntyre's view, that we see ourselves as unified beings because of a story that we narrate about ourselves.[4]

It is important not to confuse the claim that narrative has become a newly discussed topic *within* philosophy – and the idea has flourished in a variety of contexts – with the assertion that philosophy itself can *proceed* narratively. This latter claim receives no support from the former and is widely rejected by philosophers. So despite attention paid to the notion of narrative in recent philosophy, the fact that fiction films proceed narratively marks them as having a different structure from that putatively necessary for philosophy itself.

To respond to the generality objection, it is important to recognize that films can – and sometimes do – contain *explicit* arguments, although this fact will prove less interesting to our investigation than it might first seem. To see why, consider a hypothetical film – perhaps just a recording of a class or a lecture – that shows an actual philosopher making an argument. You might think here of the late John Rawls, the influential twentieth-century social and political philosopher, presenting a lecture in which he argues that the difference principle would be agreed upon by individuals in the original position, that is, under the veil of ignorance, an idea I introduced in the last chapter.[5] Let's call this hypothetical film, *Justifying Difference*. Certainly films can, in virtue of their ability to record reality – a fact made much of by the Bazanian tradition in film studies – present material like this. And, in so far as they can record a philosopher making an argument, such films might seem to themselves qualify as instances of philosophy.[6]

It would be possible to enter into a long discussion of whether it is the film rather than the philosopher that makes the philosophical argument here, but I don't think that is necessary. The issue of whether films can screen a philosophical argument would not be resolved by the existence of such a documentary, even were we inclined to say that it should be counted as developing Rawls' argument. The reason for this is that, in *Justifying Difference*, the film merely functions as a device for recording Rawls' talk. As far as capturing the content of what he is saying, a tape recorder would have done as well, and I take it that no one would assert that audiotapes have some special connection to philosophy. In such uses, these media – films, audiotapes – are simply means for recording work that was actually done in another medium. As a result, they don't themselves produce independent works, functioning instead simply as records or duplicates of previously existing works. So while the hypothetical *Justifying Difference* does present the argument made by Rawls, its doing so does not qualify it as the maker of the argument, for it merely reproduces in a non-standard medium the argument that Rawls himself presents to an actual audience.[7]

We can find support for my assessment of this hypothetical film by turning to the actual case of a PBS *Great Performances* show in which actual stage plays are broadcast. It is generally agreed that, because the PBS show involves recordings of specific performances of stage plays – say, to cite one real example, the recording of the October 7, 2000, performance by the Roundabout Theater Company of Moss Hart and George S. Kaufman's play, *The Man Who Came to Dinner* – the film here is not an independent work of art but only a means of transmitting the stage performance, the actual work, to a wider audience than was able to see it live, say on Broadway. And just as the PBS recording of *The Man Who Came to Dinner* is not an independent work of art but only a recording of one, *Justifying Difference* would not itself count as making a screen version of a philosophical argument, but only recording a person actually making one at a specific place and time.[8]

I don't want to be taken as claiming here that there is no way for a recording of a lecture (or a play) to become an independent work of philosophy (or art). Were illustrations and new points added, it might be possible to make a film of a philosophy class or lecture that was itself a work of philosophy.[9] My only point is that *merely* recording a lecture on film, while it would succeed in presenting philosophy on film, does not solve the problem we began with of whether a film can independently screen an argument that is philosophically significant.

Our discussion of fiction films' ability to "screen" philosophical arguments will be assisted by a more general discussion of documentary films.[10] And, indeed, some readers may think it high time for me to discuss them, for they are the most obvious candidates for films that are capable of doing philosophy. So, one might hold that such films provide one instance in which it is possible to answer the question of whether films can present arguments in the affirmative, for documentaries often do make explicit arguments by means of their narratives. Consider Carl Plantinga's claim that what distinguishes the documentary from the fiction film is precisely the assumption that documentary films are making assertions about the world. Even if not all documentaries involve explicit argumentation, there are many that do use their soundtracks in conjunction with their imagetracks in order to present arguments. Plantinga cites the *CBS Reports* documentary *Harvest of Shame* (1960) as an example of such a film. He states that the film "documents the degrading plight [of] the nation's migrant farm workers, placing the blame squarely on the landowners/farmers, and advocating specific legislation to alleviate the problem."[11] If Plantinga is right about this film – he points to a range of different claims that the film justifies argumentatively to support his view – then we have to admit that some films do present arguments, even if not yet ones that are clearly philosophical in nature.

But this obviously does not settle the issue of whether fiction films can present arguments. Although the case of documentary films does show that the visual nature of films does not preclude them from presenting arguments, such films usually rely on the explicit linguistic statements, made on the soundtrack, with intertitles, or in subtitles, to present at least some of the claims that constitute their argument. Often the balance of the film, including much of the visual material, functions only as evidence for the claims that are explicitly made linguistically.

Still, that documentary films can screen philosophy is an important claim to acknowledge. Indeed, it may seem odd that I have not devoted more space to a discussion of documentary films, for they seem to provide a clear means of establishing my thesis that films can screen philosophy. Consider, for example, John Berger's 1972 BBC television documentary, *Ways of Seeing*. One of the philosophical claims the film attempts to prove is Walter Benjamin's assertion that the aura of paintings and other works of art has been changed by the prevalence of techniques of mechanical reproduction. One strategy Berger employs is asking viewers to look at "a landscape of a cornfield with birds flying out of it" as it appears on the screen. He gives them a moment to do so and then explains, "This is the last painting that Van Gogh painted before he killed himself." After another pause, he states his understanding of how this information changes their way of looking at the picture. He claims that "the image now illustrates the sentence" and thus becomes a piece of information that has to compete with "all the other information being continually transmitted" to us, thereby confirming Benjamin's thesis about the transformed ontological status of works of art.[12] What this example illustrates is that, as in the case of *Harvest of Shame*, a documentary can present a philosophical argument through the creative use of the imagetrack to confirm, illustrate, and/or support claims made in the soundtrack. This is certainly an important example of philosophy being done in/on/through film.

However, the case of documentaries ironically leads us to another difficulty faced in affirming the possibility that fiction films can present arguments, for the question is not whether fiction films can present arguments of any type, but whether they can present specifically *philosophical* arguments. In a documentary like *Harvest of Shame*, parts of the film can be used to provide evidence for claims made about, for example, the awful working conditions the laborers had to endure by showing what those conditions actually were like. But philosophical arguments rarely involve empirical evidence that can be presented without verbal language. So the question of whether fiction films can present philosophical arguments is not only not answered by an appeal of documentary films, but even made to seem less likely of receiving affirmation.[13]

There is yet a further wrinkle to the issue, for many of the films that have attracted philosophers' attention as sources of philosophical insight are *popular* narrative films, films like Ridley Scott's 1982 sci-fi action classic, *Blade Runner*, Harold Ramis' 1993 comedy, *Groundhog Day*, or Christopher Nolan's 2000 twist film, *Memento*.[14] Such films are often deemed to be vehicles of popular entertainment, so it is hard to see what could justify their being taken to be works of philosophy. Such "ephemera" seem the polar opposite of philosophy, with its concern for eternal questions.

The crux of the issue facing us, then, is whether a film can present a philosophical argument through a fictional narrative that involves dialogue and images, a soundtrack and an imagetrack.[15] Some philosophers have taken the obvious course and denied this possibility. For example, Noël Carroll asserts quite baldly "narrative films are not arguments."[16] And while I would not disagree with the literal assertion made by this claim, I want to affirm that narrative films can, in addition to doing many other things, present arguments, a possibility Carroll denies. Similarly, Seymour Chatman offers little support for my case when he affirms that films are only able to present arguments "in the loose sense," while denying that they can present the more formal arguments he identifies as constitutive of philosophical texts.[17]

We can, however, find support for my claim in unexpected quarters. In the very article in which he denies that narrative films are arguments, Carroll does affirm that films often attempt to convince of us something, only the method they use, he claims, is not that of a formal argument. To establish that films exhibit this intention, Carroll cites approvingly Andre Bazin's claim that *Citizen Kane* establishes the universal truth that "there is no profit in gaining the whole world if one has lost one's own childhood."[18] And while this is not specifically a philosophical claim, it does point in a direction that leads towards our desired conclusion.

Carroll's discussion relies upon the view of argumentation Aristotle develops in his *Rhetoric*. There, Aristotle is interested in explaining the different ways in which language can be used as a means of persuasion. The example that he discusses that is relevant here is that of the fable. A fable is a made-up story, often featuring talking animals, that is intended to establish a general conclusion or moral that can, but need not be, explicitly stated. Aesop's well-known fable of the tortoise and the hare tells the story of a speedy but overconfident hare who is literally caught napping by a plodding tortoise who, despite his slowness, perseveres and beats his flashy competitor to the finish line. The fable is intended to establish the moral truth, "Slow and steady wins the race," or, in less metaphorical terms, that perseverance and tenacity are moral virtues, while flashiness is not. And, indeed, the story provides an instance of this general truth.

Now, there are films that, at least on the surface, conform to this model. One is Merian C. Cooper and Ernest B. Schoedsack's 1933 horror-adventure film, *King Kong*. After the opening credits, an intertitle displays what it claims to be an "old Arabian proverb": "And lo, the beast looked upon the face of beauty. And it stayed its hand from killing. And from that day, it was as one dead." The film thus presents itself as a fable that will demonstrate the intertitle's claim that beauty has the power to tame, and even kill, a beast. And as if to ensure that we get the point, the film concludes with Kong's captor, Carl Denham (Robert Armstrong), reiterating this idea by saying that it was beauty, rather than bullets, that killed "the beast."[19]

However, neither Aristotle nor Carroll credits a fable's attempt to establish a moral as presenting a legitimate argument, although both acknowledge its persuasive power. Carroll dubs it the "argument by example," for a single instance – the story presented by the fable – is cited as evidence for the general truth it seeks to vindicate. From a formal point of view, it is obvious why the argument by example is an invalid form of argumentation, one that philosophers discuss under the rubric of inductive inference. Inductive inferences are ones in which one attempts to use empirical evidence to justify a general conclusion. An example of a successful induction would be Kepler's supporting his law about the orbits of the planets – that they are elliptical – with extensive observation and data gathering that showed specific planets moving around the sun in elliptical paths.

It is generally agreed that generalizing from a single case to a universal proposition is invalid. To do so would be to commit the fallacy of composition by assuming that the character of a class of objects can be determined from an examination of just one of them. While a particular lion may be friendly – say one trained for a circus – it would be a mistake to make an inductive inference from the case of this one affectionate beast to the general claim that all lions are friendly. In formal terms, this fallacy can be characterized as involving the following invalid inference pattern:

A_1 is F
Therefore, All A's are F.

This is an invalid inductive inference because there is no guarantee that A_1 might not just happen to be F, so that there would be many other things that are A's while not being F's. Our friendly lion is a very special case of lionhood. One could jeopardize one's health, as well as one's logical credentials, by generalizing about lions on the basis of the nature of this one, very unusual beast.

At this point, even the most sympathetic of my readers might think that my attempt to show that fictions films can present philosophical arguments is doomed to failure. After all, in addition to the general arguments against this possibility, hasn't my examination of the "argument by example" definitively shown that fiction films cannot present arguments, let alone philosophical ones? Since fiction films generally present stories about specific individuals, wouldn't the attempt to move from a story about a particular character – such as Charles Foster Kane – to a general claim – such as the one about childhood proffered by Bazin – involve the sorts of illicit induction we have just seen in the case of the fallacious reasoning concerning lions?

Our situation is not, however, as desperate as this. After all, in the last chapter we already discovered a type of thought experiment that plays a role in philosophical argumentation: the counterexample. Perhaps a more careful examination of this classical philosophical technique can provide us with a route out of our present quandary.

Thought experiments can provide *counterexamples* to philosophical theses. How exactly do they do this in a way that contributes to a philosophical argument? As we have seen, an important component in the articulation of a philosophic vision is the establishment of universal claims or even definitions. Equally important is the testing of those general assertions to see whether there are any situations or circumstances in which they do not hold. This is where counterexamples come in. A counterexample to a universal claim is a single instance that contradicts the universal claim. Thus, to use a trite example, if we asserted that all crows are black, the existence of an albino crow would be a counterexample to that general claim, for it would show that there is at least one crow that does not have the color specified by the generalization. Similarly, if I claim that all politicians are liars and you can show me one politician who always tells the truth, then that unique politician would function as a counterexample to my general claim about politicians.

Developing counterexamples to philosophical claims is an important aspect of philosophy, but, since most philosophical claims are not empirical generalizations like those we have just considered about crows and politicians, normally philosophical counterexamples cannot employ actual examples of things that violate the generalization. So instead of relying on actual exceptions to a proposed rule or definition – such as that provided by the albino crow and the honest politician – philosophical counterexamples are generally provided by *thought experiments*: imaginary narratives that present cases that do not accord with the principle in question. What a philosopher does is to present a story that she has invented and that she claims is a counterexample to the proposed general truth.

I now want to explore the logic of counterexamples more carefully than I did in the last chapter. Consider the following well-known counterexample involving a thought experiment from the first book of Plato's *Republic*. The overall aim of this dialogue is to develop an adequate definition of morality or justice.[20] At an early stage of the dialogue (331c), "telling the truth and paying one's debts" has been proposed as such a definition. In order to show that it is inadequate, Socrates asks his interlocutors to imagine the following situation: Suppose someone has leant you a weapon and subsequently, having lost his mind and become a threat to himself and others, asks you to return what you have borrowed. Certainly, although we all believe that we ought to return what we have borrowed, we also think it would be a mistake to give the weapon back to the insane menace. But this means that, in at least one case – that specified by the story of the insane weapon owner – the formula "paying one's debts" does not indicate what the right thing to do is, since the formula would require returning the gun to its now untrustworthy owner. So the proposed definition of justice or morality fails. And the reason it fails is that this imaginary case provides a counterexample to the general claim that justice or morality (i.e. the right way to act) is simply telling the truth and paying one's debts.

Despite the brevity of Socrates' thought experiment, only an extended analysis can explain exactly how it functions as a counterexample to the proposed definition of justice. There are two elements involved in any counterexample to a philosophical thesis. The first is what I have called the counterexample proper: here, the imaginary scenario involving the insane weapon owner. But equally important is the reasoning process that shows why this scenario is a counterexample to the general philosophical thesis, one that involves deductive reasoning of the following sort: Assume a general proposition of the form, "All A's are B", is true, here, "All acts in which one tells the truth or pays one's debts are moral." The counterexample furnishes a case of an A – an act of paying one's debt, i.e., returning the borrowed weapon to its owner – that is not an instance of B – a moral action. Through the reasoning process, we conclude that the general proposition is false, that is, we deny that all acts of telling the truth or paying one's debts are moral, so the proposed definition fails.

In the last chapter, I said that contemporary analytic philosophy is replete with thought experiments that function in philosophical arguments as counterexamples to universal claims. Indeed, I claimed that these were the most basic type of thought experiment. So here I will look at only one other counterexample because it will play a role in my subsequent discussion. John Rawls discusses a counterexample that claims to expose a problem in the conceptual foundations of utilitarianism. Utilitarians take the principle of utility – the claim that a social institution is justified if it contributes more than any alternative to the general welfare – to be the supreme principle of morality. Rawls presents his own version of a widely accepted objection to utilitarianism through a thought experiment involving the hypothetical social institution of telishment.[21]

> Try to imagine, then, an institution (which we may call "telishment") which is such that the officials set up by it have authority to arrange a trial for the condemnation of an innocent man [sic] whenever they are of the opinion that doing so would be in the best interests of society. The discretion of officials is limited, however, by the rule that they may not condemn an innocent man to undergo such an ordeal unless there is, at the time, a wave of offenses similar to that with which they charge him and telish him for.[22]

Telishment is designed to be exactly like our present practice of punishment except that, in extreme circumstances of social unrest, it allows an innocent person to be penalized. The idea behind making this exception is as follows: In such extreme situations, such as when there is a series of violent crimes that has led to general fear and anxiety, the social order will be served by "telishing" an innocent person, for then everyone else will be reassured – albeit falsely – that the threat has been extinguished.

Telishment was taken to be a counterexample to the utilitarian theory of institutional justification because the following two things appear to be true:

1. The principle of utility justifies telishment. That is, because telishment provides a means of establishing calm is situations of major social unrest, it is a social institution that contributes more to the social welfare than the alternative of our normal practice of punishment in which, at least conceptually, innocent people are not punished.
2. Our moral intuitions tell us that there is something wrong with telishment. The idea is that we resist accepting a social practice that harms innocent people, no matter how greatly society as a whole would benefit from so doing.

Utilitarianism cannot be the correct moral theory, the argument goes, because it justifies a social institution we believe is illegitimate.

Rawls actually thinks that telishment does not provide a counterexample to utilitarianism. This is because, once it is acknowledged that utilitarianism should be taken as a principle that applies not to individual actions but to the social practices that legitimate them, the utilitarian justification of telishment will not succeed. Specifically, there will be no way to make the argument in support of telishment if one accepts the idea that the rules of the practice must be publicly known.

But we need not worry about the validity of telishment as a counter-example to utilitarianism because we are now in a position to argue for the following important claim: Films can present arguments when they are thought experiments that function as counterexamples to philosophical theses. In order to make this plausible, I will turn to Michel Gondry's 2004 film, *Eternal Sunshine of the Spotless Mind*.[23]

As was the case with the purported counterexample of telishment, the target of the counterexample presented by the film is utilitarianism, only the practice that constitutes the film's counterexample is quite different: selective memory erasure. Although this practice appears to be justifiable in the case of severely troubled individuals on utilitarian grounds, *Eternal Sunshine* argues that it is problematic nonetheless, so that consideration of this procedure provides a counterexample to utilitarianism.

Eternal Sunshine focuses upon a fictional procedure for selective memory erasure developed by Dr. Howard Mierzwiak (Tom Wilkinson). Using a non-linear narrative, the film shows us two young people – Joel Barish (Jim Carrey) and Clementine Kruczynski (Kate Winslet) – who

Figure 11 The Doctor and his helpers erasing Joel's memories of Clem. From *Eternal Sunshine of the Spotless Mind*.

Source: Focus Features/The Kobal Collection/Lee, David.

appear to have a chance meeting on a beach in the Hamptons. As the narrative continues, it goes back in time to reveal that the two had been lovers previously and had chosen to have their memories of each other erased: Clementine because she was so unhappy about their break-up and Joel because he couldn't bear the realization that Clementine had erased all of her memories of him. The film tells the story of the demise of the first relationship between these two through a variety of techniques, most interestingly by presenting what we are to take as the contents of Joel's consciousness as his memories of Clementine are erased. In the end, despite having found out from pre-erasure audiotapes of their dissatisfactions with each other how unsuited to each other they really were, the two decide to pursue a relationship for a second time.

The first question that we need to ask is how *Eternal Sunshine* presents an initial justification for this remarkable technology. At one level, the film takes the justification to be self-evident: People who are experiencing a great deal of psychological pain choose to undergo selective memory erasure because it promises them relief from that pain. In addition to the lovers who choose to erase their painful memories of each other, we see an oriental woman who appears to be so distressed over the death of her cat that she is going to erase all her memories of her feline companion. We also hear a woman who has called the clinic being told that she cannot schedule yet a third memory erasure in a short time period. The film presents the

Figure 12 Joel listens to Clem's tape about him. From *Eternal Sunshine of the Spotless Mind.*

Source: Focus Features/The Kobal Collection/Lee, David.

technique as popular, with the doctor having an always-crowded waiting room. So, on the surface at least, the procedure seems justified because it produces so much happiness for those upon whom it is used.

But there is more to the film's justification of the technology than this. When Joel confronts Dr Mierzwiak about Clementine having erased all of her memories of him, the doctor replies: "Miss Kruczynski was not happy and wanted to move on." The implication is clearly that Clementine needed to erase her memories of Joel in order to be able to get on with her life. We are meant to conclude that she will be happier for having done so, or at least that she thinks she will be.

By itself, this would not indicate that the film was justifying selective memory erasure through the ethical theory of utilitarianism rather than a view such as psychological hedonism, according to which individuals act to promote their own well-being or happiness.

That the film is initially proposing a utilitarian justification for memory erasure becomes evident as a result of Mary's (Kirsten Dunst) glowing description of what the procedure achieves. While visiting the technicians during the night on which they erase Joel's memories, she says:

> It's amazing. What Howard [Dr Mierzwiak] gives the world. To let people begin again. It's beautiful. You look at a baby and it's so pure and so free and so clean. Adults are like this mess of sadness and phobias. And Howard just makes it all go away.

In drawing a contrast between babies and adults, Mary suggests that people are made happier by having a memory-erasure procedure because it makes them more like babies, freeing them from all the grief associated with adulthood and that she admires the technology – and its inventor – for this reason: What it does is a tremendous benefit for humankind. That is, Mary presents a utilitarian justification of the procedure. The argument is not just that people are made better off if, when they were having extremely painful memories that disrupt their lives and keep them from "moving on," they can have those memories erased. It asserts that the procedure should be valued precisely because it makes this contribution to the general welfare of human beings.

So let's formulate the film's presentation of the justification for the employment of this technology as follows: People who have had a traumatic experience suffer a great deal of pain because of the memory of that experience. Eliminating the memory of that experience would increase the welfare of such people without adversely affecting others. Therefore, from a utilitarian point of view the practice of selective memory erasure in the case of severely traumatized individuals is justified.

It's clear, however, that *Eternal Sunshine* views the technology of selective memory erasure as a failure. The central aspect of the film's narrative that supports this claim is that all of the people we know to have had the

procedure – Mary, Joel, and Clementine – wind up pursuing the very relationship whose memory they attempted to erase. The question is how these
repetitions can function as a criticism of the utilitarian justification of the
practice/technology.

As we have seen, from the point of view of the technology of selective
memory erasure, memories are either good or bad, pleasant or unpleasant.
When there is a huge preponderance of bad memories surrounding a particular
event or person – enough to view that event or person as traumatizing the
person who has those memories – that person's life will be enhanced, the
utilitarian justification of this practice goes, if those memories and all
others related to that person or event are simply erased. Of course, there are
many practical questions one could ask about the feasibility of such a technology and whether one could coherently eliminate a set of memories without
altering a person's identity in a deep sense, but we need not worry about
them here. What we might call *the recidivism problem* – the fact that each
repeats the behavior that lead to the offensive memories – indicates the
problem with the technology pinpointed by the film: Eliminating a person's
memory of a traumatic experience leaves them vulnerable to repeat it.

One of the ways in which children learn is by doing things they want to
and suffering painful or otherwise negative consequences as a result. My
slightly pyromaniacal son is attracted to fires of all sorts. He even appears
to have a desire to touch fire, attracted as he is to it. When, at age 4, he did
so – placing his hand on a burning match – he not surprisingly got burned.
The memory of that event has had an educative function for him. He has
learned that he has certain desires – like that to touch a flame – that are
best left unfulfilled, because the negative consequences of fulfilling them
are simply too large to warrant so doing. I call this the *educative function
of memory in relation to desire*. This is essentially a label that captures the
fact that remembering what it was like to have fulfilled a desire has an
effect on whether we continue to be interested in fulfilling it.

So it is important that we realize, as the film's narrative gets us to, that
having one's memories of a disastrous love affair, say, selectively erased
leaves one prey to the recidivism problem because of the erasure of the
memory of what effect the fulfilling of one's desire had. The narrative of
Eternal Sunshine is structured to allow us to realize that the technology of
selective memory erasure that it portrays is problematic because it ignores
the educative function that memory has in relation to desire. Each of the
lovers in the film has a desire to be involved with their respective partner.
When the negative memories resulting from pursuing their desires are
erased, the education their desires had undergone is also erased along with
the memories. It is for this reason that they become subject to the recidivism problem: Their desires are given full rein without the education they
would have received from the memory of the results of their fulfillment.

Now this amounts to a philosophical argument made by *Eternal Sunshine* against the employment of such a technology should it ever become

available and should such problems as I mentioned earlier in its use be overcome. The argument is that this technology not only eliminates unproblematic memories, it also eliminates the learning processes that are dependent on them, more specifically what I have called the education of desire. Mary's comment that people become like babies after they have undergone the process can now be seen to have a sinister side to it that might not have been visible before we fully realized some of the consequences of employing the technology: If adults are turned into babies – a fact that she takes to recommend the technology – it may well cure any cynicism that they have acquired over the years, but it will also wipe out whatever knowledge about life and their desires that they have gained from their experiences. As a result, they won't know which desires they have are worth fulfilling and which not. Rather than freeing them to live their lives without the burden of their painful memories, the technology of selective memory erasure creates adults whose lives are dictated to them by their desires.

A skeptical reader might well wonder what the philosophical payoff is to introducing an imaginary technology and showing that there are moral problems with its acceptance. What use could such a thought experiment have philosophically? My answer is that it provides a very clear and, to my mind, impressive brief in favor of the thesis that memory has an *educative function* in relation to desire. This is a claim about the significance of memory, what important role it plays in human life. While no one would deny, I think, that memory has an educational function, the specific role that the film attributes to memory in relationship to desire is one that I think is worth extended philosophical discussion. The film has not only formulated this as a philosophically meaningful thesis, but it has provided a thought experiment to show how important it is.

Still, impressive as this argument may be, it does not show that *Eternal Sunshine* presents a counterexample to utilitarianism. In order to do so, it cannot simply claim that the social welfare is not actually increased when a person's painful memories are erased, for this would only show that use of the technology was not sanctioned by utilitarianism. The recidivism problem shows us that there is a reason to reject this technology on utilitarian grounds: It does not actually increase the welfare of those upon whom it is exercised. But is this the only reason presented by the film as a reason for rejecting it? That is, say that the recidivism problem could be eliminated, so that those who underwent the procedure of selective memory erasure would not simply reenter the very relationships of whose memories they had desired to be free, perhaps, we may imagine, by another procedure that dulled the offending desire. Would we still find the procedure problematic?

I think we can find the answer to this question by focusing on Joel's experience of the erasure of his memories of Clementine. A good deal of the film – other than the framing device of Joel and Clem's re-meeting, this time made problematic by Mary's intrusion via the mailing of the tapes of their pre-erasure complaints about each other – takes place literally in

Joel's mind. That is, what we are seeing and hearing is basically the contents of his mind as he is experiencing the erasure of all of the memories he has of his relationship with Clementine. What quickly becomes apparent to him is that he does not want to go through with the procedure, but, because he has been immobilized by some drugs given to him, he cannot tell those doing the memory erasure to stop what they are doing. Instead, we witness a whole series of antics in which Joel, often with Clementine's help – it is actually his memory-image of Clementine that becomes an agent in his own mental life in these scenes – seeks to evade the probing of the erasers, thus allowing at least some of his memories of his relationship to Clementine to remain. But all of these frantic efforts come to naught as the good doctor finds the last of the offending memories and wipes the slate of Joel's mind clean of any traces of Clementine.

Although the comic inventiveness of these scenes makes it hard for the audience to reflect on *why* Joel wants to stop the erasure of all of his memories of Clementine, it is important that we do so. Although it may at first appear difficult to figure out what the reason for Joel's change of mind is, there is one feature of his experience that strikes viewers forcefully: He has lost control over his own mind. As the doctor and his two inept assistants go after Joel's memories of Clem, it becomes clear to viewers how deeply troubling a technology that takes over control of our mind really is.

Dr Mierzwiak's assistants, Stan (Mark Ruffalo) and Patrick (Elijah Woods) are both bumbling and irresponsible. Although we laugh at their disregard for Joel's welfare as they drink and, in Stan's case, have sex on the bed where Joel is lying comatose, we are also aware that Joel has made a very dangerous decision when he has decided to have the memory erasure, for he has given over control of his mind to some quite irresponsible people. And even if we admit that their irresponsibility need not be a feature of the practice, the film thereby signals its deepest concern about the practice: that it is problematic for us to cede control over our minds to others, for we then lack the means to regain control. It is the highly heteronymous nature of this practice for the one undergoing it that marks it as so problematic for the film. And in so doing, the film uses the practice as a counterexample to utilitarianism, for that moral theory lacks the means to explain why heteronymy is a bad thing.

Now a utilitarian will of course object that there is a way for that theory to accommodate our sense that heteronymy is a bad thing. But the point is only that, within the terms set up by the film, there is an objection to selective memory erasure that is presented on non-utilitarian grounds. That objection is that one has ceded too much control over one's mental life to others, for there can be no way to guarantee that they will not misuse one's trust.

On this interpretation, then, *Eternal Sunshine* involves a thought experiment that functions as a counterexample to utilitarianism. The hypothetical technology that we see in the film is one (i) whose use could be justified, at least initially, by considerations of utility and yet (ii) the film asserts that there is something wrong with it being implemented in addition to the fact that it cannot really be justified on utilitarian grounds. Hence, the film presents a counterexample to utilitarianism.

Structurally, the film's presentation of a procedure for memory erasure and of the thought experiment involving the social practice of telishment are similar. Both of them present purported counterexamples to utilitarianism. The film, like the written philosophical text, incorporates an argument involving a thought experiment that functions as a counterexample to the principle of utility.

But now the imposition objection recurs. This objection to films doing philosophy begins by noting that, whereas Rawls explicitly argues that many have taken thought experiments like the one he puts forward as counterexamples to utilitarianism, the film makes no such assertion. In fact, the objection claims, it is the philosophical interpreter – in this case, myself – who *uses* the film *as* a counterexample to the philosophical theory. Without my *imposition* of utilitarianism as a philosophical theory, the film would not itself be a counterexample to it.

But I have tried to show in some details that the film itself presents this technology as at least initially attractive on utilitarian grounds. For this reason, I think that it is the film – and, of course, its makers are the real agents here – that presents utilitarianism as the subject its wishes to discuss. Indeed, its subsequent criticism of the technology for failing to provide the benefits that it would have to in order to be justified from a utilitarian point of view suggest to me that the film cannot fully be understood without recourse to the idea of utilitarian justification of social practices.

Still, I can imagine a critic wondering whether it really makes sense to understand the film as targeting so abstract a philosophical theory as utilitarianism. In the first chapter of this book, I introduced a distinction between creator- and audience-oriented interpretations of works of art and claimed that creator-oriented ones had to present interpretations that a work's creator could have intended it to have. But I also later added that this did not mean that the creator had to have direct acquaintance with the philosophical position that the creator-oriented interpretation presented as the focus of the work, only that it had to be plausible that he might be responding to the positions or ideas contained in that work. Although philosophical texts are the origins of many ideas, theories, and positions, they acquire a life of their own within a culture and all that is necessary for a creator-oriented interpretation to be acceptable in this regard is that the creator might have been acquainted with the philosophical ideas, etc., because of, for example, their general circulation within a culture.

Utilitarianism is a philosophical theory that has gained wide-ranging recognition within American culture in general. The slogan "the greatest good for the greatest number" is known by many more people than have read the texts from which it springs. It therefore seems plausible to me that a contemporary film might target such a view precisely because it has gained widespread attention and acceptance. It is also important not to ignore the film's explicit invocation of Nietzsche by Mary who repeats his sarcastic parodying of Jesus' Sermon on the Mount in *Beyond Good and Evil*, "Blessed are the forgetful for they get the better even of their blunders." Since one of the targets of Nietzsche's philosophical critique is utilitarianism, my claim that the film could be targeting that theory receives added confirmation from its allusion to the famous German philosopher.

So in relation to the charge that my interpretation of *Eternal Sunshine imposes* the context of utilitarian ethical theory on the film, I simply reject it. My interpretation shows that the film very clearly presents the procedure for memory erasure as initially supported by a utilitarian justification and that this is the view that the film takes as its target for criticism. One element in the film's more general argument against the procedure is its rejection of utilitarianism as an adequate moral theory, for such a theory provides a *prima facie* justification for memory erasure. In its attempt to convince its audience that selective memory erasure is immoral, the film does not simply contest its utilitarian justification, though it does do that. It shows that there are other moral grounds for rejecting this practice, so that it should be rejected *even if it promoted social utility*. It is in this specific context that the film presents a philosophical counterexample.

Additional support for my rejection of the imposition objection is the fact that memory erasure is not simply an issue that the filmmakers have invented whole cloth. In fact, there is a growing debate about memory erasure that involves the drug, Propranolol.[24] The fanciful technology for memory erasure presented by the film can be thought of as an imaginative means for getting audiences to think about a complex issue that is becoming significant in the mental health field. Is it too far fetched to think of the film as a timely intervention into the ethics of memory erasure? I think not. And it is precisely because the use of drugs such as Propranolol has been justified as nearly self-evident because of the improvement in patients' sense of their well being that it makes sense to see this film as, among things, contesting the validity of a utilitarian justification of the practice of memory erasure that it sees as so problematic.

It is true, however, that the meaning of the film is not reducible to its providing a counterexample to utilitarianism. That the film is also interested in exploring what in the human psyche makes us wish for a world free of the torments of passion. The film's title is taken from Alexander Pope's poem, "Eloise to Abelard," which is his reconstruction of Héloïse's actual letters to Abelard in which she talks about the conflict she feels between her desire to love God and the passion she feels for her lover, Abelard. At one point, she writes:

How happy is the blameless vestal's lot!
The world forgetting, by the world forgot.

Eternal sunshine of the spotless mind!
Each pray'r accepted, and each wish resign'd;

Eloise is here manifesting the same desire as Clementine, to be free of a passion that causes her torment. But the illusory nature of this desire is shown in the following stanza, where Eloise acknowledges the importance her love for Abelard has for her:

Far other dreams my erring soul employ,
Far other raptures, of unholy joy:
When at the close of each sad, sorrowing day,
Fancy restores what vengeance snatch'd away,
Then conscience sleeps, and leaving nature free,
All my loose soul unbounded springs to thee.
Oh curs'd, dear horrors of all-conscious night!
How glowing guilt exalts the keen delight! ...

The torture of her unrequitable love for Abelard is apparent in this stanza, in which Eloise curses the pleasure that wracks her with guilt. The film's invocation of a technique for selective memory erasure provides it with a means of investigating this psychological terrain.

In this chapter, I have not attempted to provide a complete analysis of *Eternal Sunshine*.[25] What I have tried to show is that, despite a range of serious objections to the possibility that fiction films can present philosophical arguments, they sometimes do just that. We have seen that one film – *Eternal Sunshine of the Spotless Mind* – presents a counterexample to utilitarianism and thus actually *does* philosophy. Although there is a lot more to be said both about the example I have used and the more general question of whether and how films can present arguments, I hope to have convinced you at this point that, counter-intuitive as it might seem to film scholars and philosophers alike, fiction films can present arguments through their narratives because they screen thought experiments that play a crucial role in providing counterexamples to philosophical theses.

6 Moral intelligence and the limits of loyalty
The Third Man

In previous chapters, I have proposed two ways whereby films can do philosophy: by illustrating a philosophical theory in a perspicuous manner and by presenting a philosophical thought experiment. In this chapter, I consider a film that does both: Carol Reed's masterpiece *The Third Man* (1945). Its presentation of a pulp fiction writer's difficulties upon arriving in Vienna only to find that the friend who has brought him there is dead makes two distinct philosophical contributions. First, its depiction of the novelist's refusal to believe that his friend could be a notorious criminal develops an account of what I shall call "the vicissitudes of moral intelligence." Moral intelligence (or practical wisdom, *phronesis*) is a notion that Aristotle develops in his *Nichomachean Ethics*. The film pinpoints two obstacles to its unproblematic employment in our lives: prior commitments and the influence of pulp fictions. This is an important contribution that the film makes to Aristotelian ethics.

But the film also illustrates some important aspects of Aristotle's account of friendship, a topic he also discusses in the *Nichomachean Ethics*. Two of the issues that Aristotle raises are when it is legitimate to dissolve a friendship and how the dissolution of a friendship should impact our loyalty to our (former) friend. *The Third Man*'s narrative of the novelist's growing realization that his friend is a hardened criminal and not the friend he thought he was illustrates Aristotle's claims in this regard. By using its narrative to unify disparate elements of Aristotle's account of friendship, the film demonstrates their systematic relationship and, in so doing, justifies our attribution to it of a second philosophical contribution.

Before presenting my view of the film, I want to briefly consider a very different interpretation of the film's philosophical content. I do so less to show the superiority of my interpretation than to provide an example of the sort of interpretation that might be used to support the contention that films can only present trivial and obvious philosophical truths, what has been called the *banality objection* to films doing philosophy.[1] Although I have not previously discussed this objection, it is an important one, for if films can only make trivial philosophical claims, there would not be much significance to the idea of films doing philosophy.

In his Presidential Address to the American Society for Aesthetics, "The Wheel of Virtue," Noël Carroll claims that *The Third Man* does philosophy by presenting a counterexample to a general claim implicit in E. M. Forster's well-known remark: "if I had to choose between betraying my country and betraying a friend, I hope I should have the guts to betray my country."[2] ("The Wheel of Virtue," p. 9.) Carroll extracts the following ethical principle from Forster's remark: "When loyalty to a friend conflicts with loyalty to a cause, one ought to choose in favor of the friend." ("The Wheel of Virtue," p.10.) Let's call this Principle F, for friendship. According to Carroll, *The Third Man* is the story of a man who comes to realize that Principle F is mistaken and that, at least in the circumstances in which he finds himself, morality requires him to betray his friend rather than his country. Carroll claims that, by telling a story in which the ethical principle attributed to Forster is shown to yield an inappropriate consequence, *The Third Man* provides a counterexample to it.

There are a number of serious problems with Carroll's interpretation of the *Third Man*.[3] To begin with, Principle F is not an important principle of moral philosophy. I doubt that such a principle could be found in any book about ethics, even one that discussed specific ethical norms. In part, this is because the principle is formulated very vaguely. The notion of a cause is not one that is generally found in ethical discussions. It's also not clear why Carroll has used it, given that Forster's original claim had to do with patriotism, loyalty to one's country. So I'm just not convinced that anyone would endorse Principle F. If the philosophical interest of *The Third Man* depends upon its being a counterexample to a dubious moral principle, then its contribution to philosophy will be banal at best, thereby confirming the banality objection.

I also have another, related concern about Carroll's example: If all that the film were doing philosophically was presenting a counterexample to Principle F, we would not need a story as complex and involved as *The Third Man*. Suppose that I'm really concerned to show that Principle F is misguided – that friendship cannot be elevated to the status given it by Principle F. Rather than turning to *The Third Man* in order to justify rejecting it, I could develop my own imaginary story or thought experiment that would equally well be a counterexample to the claim, or I could argue against it on general grounds that it misunderstands the nature of friendship. In fact, a mini-narration of the sort more common to philosophical thought experiments would do the trick of providing a counterexample more directly and with less ambiguity than the film. For example, say that the cause I endorse is world peace and that, if I just work hard for another day, it will become a reality. Suppose, further, that a friend asks me to help him move on the day I need to work to bring about world peace. It's pretty clear that being loyal to my friend by helping him move would not be a good idea, for its cost – world peace – would be too great.

If this story works as I intend, then it would do the job of showing the falsity of Principle F at least as well as *The Third Man* does. Even if the film could be used to develop a counterexample to Principle F, it seems arbitrary and even ill advised to do so, since a thought experiment like this one, specifically devised for just that purpose, does the job more efficiently and effectively because it is very clear that it targets Principle F.

So Carroll's interpretation of *The Third Man* makes it difficult to see why we should characterize the film as actually doing philosophy. The contribution the film might make to philosophy is, at best, so banal that it is unlikely to strike anyone as significant. On the other hand, Carroll's interpretation seems to impose his own view onto the film, since it is hard to see how the film raises the question of Principle F's validity. It is precisely this sort of interpretation that supports skepticism about film's philosophical potential.[4] But rather than accept such a conclusion, we would do better to see if the film does not actually make a more significant contribution to philosophy than that attributed to it by Carroll.

Since I am claiming that one part of *The Third Man*'s philosophical contribution is its supplementation of Aristotle's concept of practical intelligence with an account of what I am calling its vicissitudes, we need a preliminary account of Aristotle's notion. As I mentioned, moral or practical intelligence (*phronesis*) is a notion developed by Aristotle in the *Nichomachean Ethics*. Intelligence might not leap to mind as an important ethical virtue, but rather such traditional virtues as courage, loyalty, modesty, integrity, and truthfulness. But Aristotle thinks that, in addition to exhibiting *moral* virtues, the ethical individual needs to manifest *intellectual* virtues, for these are as important to her ability to act morally as the moral virtues themselves. The reason for this is that moral intelligence allows one to make good moral judgments: "For the agent they would call intelligent is the one who studies well each question about his own [good]."[5]

So what exactly is moral intelligence, practical wisdom? One feature of moral intelligence is knowing what one's moral commitments are. A person who did not know, for example, that, in general, telling the truth is a good thing to do would lack moral intelligence in this regard. But Aristotle argues that having moral intelligence requires more than simply knowing what one's commitments are; it entails knowing how to assess their applicability in concrete situations. The example he gives involves the moral commitment to promoting one's own health. He points out that knowledge of universals by itself is inadequate for realizing this commitment:

> Nor is intelligence about universals only. It also must come to know particulars, since it is concerned with action and action is about particulars . . . For someone who knows that light meats are digestible and healthy, but not which sorts of meats are light, will not produce health; the one who knows that bird meats are healthy will be better at producing health.[6]

Aristotle's point is that a morally intelligent person needs to know how to apply his general moral commitments in particular situations. Rather than discussing his example, his point will be clearer if we focus on one's commitment to tell the truth. Knowing that one has this commitment would be useless morally speaking if one could not apply it correctly in specific situations. There can be various reasons why one might have difficulty applying one's general commitment to truth telling in particular circumstances. One could be wrong, for example, about what the truth is and so tell a falsehood even when she tried to tell the truth. But one also might fail to realize that there are circumstances in which this commitment should be overridden by one's other moral commitments. This would happen, for example, if one revealed the location of one's child to a savage child molester who asked where he was on the grounds that one is committed to telling the truth, for doing so would violate one's commitment to care for one's child(ren), a commitment that should override truth telling in this context.

Although the notion of moral intelligence did not receive a great deal of attention from those moral philosophers concerned with the question of whether utilitarianism or Kantianism was the more correct ethical theory, it has lately been discussed by Iris Murdoch, Martha Nussbaum, and Lawrence A. Blum, among others. They have argued for the importance of this notion in ethical theory, thereby correcting its neglect within contemporary ethics.[7] Given this renewed attention to the notion, what could *The Third Man* possibly contribute to our understanding of it?

From my discussion, it might seem that exercising moral intelligence is a simple matter, for it only involves getting one's facts straight and being clear about one's moral priorities. But this is not true. Life is full of highly complex moral situations. If I consider my own situation as an example, there are a variety of different commitments that I could plausibly be said to have. Some accrue to me as a father, others as a husband. But I'm also a citizen and a professor, not to say a friend and a colleague. Each of these roles brings putative commitments with it, and there are also the general ethical commitments I have simply in virtue of my humanity. So when it comes to acting, how do I decide what I actually should be doing? Should I spend my time furthering my own intellectual projects? Or should I be helping my son do well in school or succeed in sports? And what about fighting for the social order I deem just? These represent real choices that I must make. Is there any way for me to achieve what we might call "a morally perspicuous understanding of my situation" that will allow me to balance these competing demands?

The Third Man is engaged in thinking about the complexity of our ethical lives and, in particular, certain difficulties we have in acting in a morally intelligent manner. Specifically, the film isolates two factors that make it hard for us to act with moral intelligence: the distorting effect that prior commitments have on our assessment of new situations and the impact of mass art on our imaginations.

What my account of the film will show, then, is that *The Third Man* supplements our ethical theorizing in a way that philosophers' normal examples – such as my thought experiment about truth telling and the child molester (or Thomson's of the violinist) – cannot, for such examples are designed to elicit specific intuitions and thus need to simplify the complexity of our moral lives. One philosophically significant task that a film – as well as works of narrative fiction – can do is to allow us to see the complexity of our moral lives in a manner that allows us to more fully grasp morally significant aspects of it. *The Third Man* does this in regard to the notion of moral intelligence, for its central character – the pulp novelist – has a great deal of trouble managing his situation with moral intelligence.

The Third Man begins by throwing us willy-nilly into the milieu of post-World War II Vienna, presenting a series of newsreel-like clips accompanied by a voiceover in which a self-acknowledged black marketeer attempts to insinuate himself into our good graces. These clips depict post-war Vienna as a world in which things are not what they seem. People have to get by as best they can, and one cannot always judge accurately by appearances. The anonymous narrator tells us what the city is like "now," i.e., after the war, claiming he had not seen it before. Now is the "classic period of the black market," he says, identifying himself as one of its players. "We'd run anything if people wanted it enough and had the money to pay." (*The Third Man*, pp. 3–4.)[8] He also explains the geo-political realities of the city, describing how the four Allies had divided it into different zones but that the center of the city – where the action of the film takes place – remains shared by all of them and so policed by an international force. He comments: "Wonderful! What a hope they had. All strangers to the place … and none of them could speak the same language … Except of course a smattering of German. Good fellows on the whole. Did their best, you know." (*The Third Man*, pp. 5–6.)

This unusual opening scene is unsettling because an unidentified voice speaks to us in what can only be called a confidential and confiding tone that suggests an intimacy for which there is no basis: It seems to presume that we were conspirators in some deed whose nature we know nothing of. It is difficult to know exactly how we are to take the narrator's assertions.[9] Since he identifies himself as a black marketeer, he speaks with cynicism about the aims of the Allies, as if they did the best they could given their lack of knowledge of the city they were trying to control and their inability to even talk with one another. He characterizes the resulting situation in Vienna as one in which ethical principles have to take a back seat to necessity. In this context, people needed to do whatever it took for them to survive, he avers.

The film thereby raises the skeptical question that forms one of its foci: In a situation in which we lack any basis for knowing whom to trust, how can we decide when someone is telling the truth and how do we then settle on an adequate perspective for understanding what is taking place? When the narrator condescendingly judges that the Allies were "good fellows on the whole. Did their best, you know," what is the basis for that judgment? How should we assess it? In doing their best, what did they let happen that they shouldn't have? Or is he just being ironic and, if so, how should we then interpret his claim? These are all questions that create an atmosphere of ambiguity and give some urgency to the film's philosophic investigation of how one can achieve the correct moral perspective for viewing a situation, especially in complex moral situations when it appears that the usual ethical rules do not apply.

This atmosphere of pervasive uncertainty continues throughout the body of the film and is achieved through a variety of cinematic techniques. Among the film's many superb expressionist elements is the use of a slightly tilted camera to record many scenes, especially those involving conversations. By having us look at its world slightly askance, the film not only registers its central character's distrust, but also it distances us from the conversations it so depicts, keeping us a little off balance and dubious about the veracity of some of the characters. The film here achieves a cinematic equivalent of skepticism, deploying a visual analogue of doubt.[10]

This sense of uncertainty, the lack of a secure perspective from which to assess competing claims about what the truth is, is not something that exclusively affects the film's audience, for its main character, at least in the sense of the one with whom we are aligned for most of the film – Hollis Martins (Joseph Cotton) – also suffers serious confusion.[11] Martins is the penniless writer of cheap western novelettes who has come to Vienna because his old friend Harry Lime (Orson Welles) has offered him a job and sent him a plane ticket for the flight. The film follows Martins as he arrives in Vienna and goes to Lime's apartment only to discover he has just missed his friend's funeral service. Clearly taken aback, Martins has to figure out exactly what to do now, for here he is, nearly broke and in a foreign city, brought there by a friend who has unexpectedly died, with no clear agenda other than understanding what's going on.

Things will get worse for Martins before they get better, for he will find his friend suspected of being a criminal. But even now, the film has created an atmosphere of doubt and uncertainty both for Martins and its audience about what is really going on in Vienna. This sets the appropriate context for its investigation into the question of how to act with moral intelligence, for this is a situation in which it is difficult to know what the truth is.

Martins achieves his first settled assessment of his situation – albeit on the basis of what we later come to recognize as mistaken inferences – as a result of his encounter with Major Calloway (Trevor Howard), the British officer in charge of the British military police in Vienna. Calloway gives Martins a lift back into town after Lime's burial and suggests they go for a drink. As Martins gets drunk, he tells Calloway how much Lime meant to him: "Best friend I ever had," he slurs. (*The Third Man*, p. 17.) Lime had, it seems, filled an important void in his life: "Never so lonesome in my life till he showed up." (*The Third Man*, p. 17.) Calloway's response – "that sounds like a cheap novelette" (*The Third Man*, p. 18) – is rude and unsympathetic. After all, Martins has received a real shock and we therefore have sympathy for him and his plight, especially because the film is structured so that our access to the events in its narrative is nearly always through

Figure 13 *The Third Man*'s tilted camera.

Source: London Films/The Kobal Collection.

following him around. Although we will come to see Martins as a gullible and incurable romantic, at this point we lack sufficient reason to make such judgments about him.

We are therefore taken aback by Calloway's repeated baiting of him. When Martins opines that Lime's dying by being hit by a car was "a shame," Calloway retorts, "Best thing that ever happened to him." He goes on to explain why: "He was the worst racketeer who ever made a dirty living in this city." (*The Third Man*, p. 19.) When Martins responds by conceding that Lime could have been involved in minor black marketeering – an admission the film's initial newsreel-like sequence prepares us for – Calloway counters that Lime's illicit dealings involved murder and not just the petty racketeering Martins has in mind. When he then dismisses Martins as a "scribbler with too much to drink," Martins responds by accusing Calloway of not taking Lime's death seriously but only using it to provide solutions for crimes he is too lazy to investigate. Once again, Calloway's contemptuous response emphasizes Martins' profession as an author of popular fiction: "Going to find me the real criminal? It sounds like one of your stories." (*The Third Man*, p. 22.)

Although we may only realize it retrospectively – or, more likely, in subsequent viewings – Calloway has been sizing up Martins and already dismissed him as innocent of knowledge of Lime's crimes. Because we don't yet know whom to believe about Lime – Was he a good person or a wicked criminal? – we remain uncertain about how to assess Calloway's accusations against him, a doubt the tilted camera accentuates. (See Figure 13.) Martins' excessive drinking, cloying self-pity, and precipitous but ineffectual attempt to slug Calloway all undercut our initial sympathy for him. Still, we lack sufficient grounds for deciding whether this means Calloway's view of Lime is mistaken.

During this scene Martins has also sized up Calloway. Annoyed by Calloway's suspicions of Lime, he questions Calloway's motives, accusing him of trying to save himself work by using Lime as the patsy for his unsolved cases: "Pin it on a dead man." (*The Third Man*, p. 20.) And when Calloway continues on in the same vein, Martins steps up his aggressive response to Calloway's comments: "Why don't you catch a few murderers for a change?" (*The Third Man*, p. 21.) Aside from the obvious antagonism that Martins has for Calloway, these remarks establish an important if very ordinary moral commitment that Martins has: He believes that murderers should be caught and punished, and he is contemptuous of Calloway because he believes that he has shirked his moral responsibility to do so. What we can recognize as an investigator's strategy for determining the guilt or innocence of a suspect, Martins takes at face value. At the same time, Martins also reveals another important moral commitment he has: his loyalty to his friend Lime. Faced with accusations about Lime's conduct and despite a lack of any specific knowledge of what Lime has been doing in recent years, Martins defends him and is even willing to try to hit Calloway to defend his friend's honor.

How does this scene establish the parameters for the film's investigation of moral intelligence? To see this, we first need to consider Aristotle's presentation of the moral dimensions of friendship in Books VIII and IX of his *Nichomachean Ethics*. The relevant idea is Aristotle's claim that one of the advantages of friendship is that friends do not believe lies told about their friends. Whereas others might believe malicious rumors, one's friends will not, Aristotle tells us:

> Furthermore, it is only the friendship of good people that is immune to slander. For it is hard to trust anyone speaking against someone whom we ourselves found reliable for a long time; and among good people there is trust, the belief that he would never do injustice, and all the other things expected in a true friendship.
>
> (1157a21ff.)[12]

Because a true friendship can only exist between moral people for Aristotle, a friend will never believe that his friend could act immorally. As a result, one's friends will be immune to slanders made against one.

But not everything that appears to a friend to be slander actually is. As a result, a true friend's loyalty, although treated by Aristotle as an unmixed benefit, can be a detriment, specifically to the friend's ability to act with moral intelligence. How can this be? Well, that's exactly what *The Third Man* has just shown us. Martins does not act with moral intelligence in his interaction with Calloway in the bar because his friendship with Lime blinds him to the possibility that Lime could be the evil person Calloway thinks he is. Martins' friendship with Lime is a prior allegiance that filters Calloway's assertions and causes Martins to dismiss them without granting them a fair hearing. *The Third Man* thus shows one set of circumstances in which loyalty to a friend can be a bad thing, leading one to ignore facts about one's friend that one might be able to recognize if that person were not one to whom one was loyal antecedently.

I call the presence of the prior commitment of friendship one of the vicissitudes of moral intelligence. I do so to indicate that friendships are one factor that can hamper a person's ability to act with the moral intelligence they do possess. True friendships do this because they prefilter one's assessment of information as a result of one's commitment to being loyal to one's friends. This is an aspect of friendship that Aristotle does not discuss in his account of a friend's loyalty but that the film expressly foregrounds. So this is one instance of *The Third Man*'s contribution to the theory of moral intelligence.

It is worth explicitly pointing out that viewers can only come to this awareness retrospectively, once they realize that Lime is in fact the awful criminal that Calloway has said that he is. At the point in the film when we actually view this scene, we are not ourselves in a position to "objectively" assess the information we are being presented because of our alignment with Martins. In a sense, the film is getting its viewers to make the very error that Martins makes – for they allow their already constituted relationship with him to structure their response to what Calloway says.

This scene depicts another important feature of the film's account of moral intelligence's vicissitudes. Even taking account of his loyalty to Lime, Martins seems incredibly inept at interpreting what is taking place between him and Calloway. The film is quick to suggest why: He uses the plots of his own "cheap fictions" to provide him with the stock roles and trite narrative into which he inserts both Calloway, Lime, and himself. As Noël Carroll has pointed out, a fictional work of art can provide a variety of moral roles that function as templates for interpreting one's experience[13] and this is precisely how *The Third Man* shows Martins handling the uncertainties he faces: He perceives his world through a tableau of fictional characters and scenarios articulated in his own "cheap novelettes." But, unlike Carroll, the film sees this as a problem, at least in certain circumstances, for it can lead one to misunderstanding the nature of his situation.[14]

This all emerges clearly when, a moment later, Martins addresses Calloway's assistant, Sergeant Paine (Bernard Lee), a fan of Martins' writing. "Did you ever read a book of mine called *The Lone Rider of Santa Fe*?" he queries. When Paine says that he hasn't, Martins tells him, "It's a story of a man who hunted down a sheriff who was victimizing his best friend. ... I'm gunning just the same way for your Major Callaghan," misremembering Calloway's name for the second time (*The Third Man*, p. 31). Because one of his pulp novels involves roles that allow him to maintain a view of Lime as his friend while explaining Calloway's negative view of him and apparent failure to pursue his killers – corrupt cop, innocent but persecuted best friend, lone crusader for justice – Martins finds relief from his confusion by adopting the novel's perspective and thereby gaining a settled view of his very perplexing situation.

But how does the film show that using popular literature as a way of understanding one's life hinders the use of moral intelligence? By showing that Martin's bungling investigation into Lime's death – in which he takes on the role of righteous defender of his friend – results in the death of an innocent person. Martins, who has precipitously gone off to discover Lime's murderer on his own, finds inconsistencies in the testimony of the eyewitnesses to the event. His persistent questioning induces the porter of Lime's building (Paul Hoerbiger) to admit that he saw a *third man* carrying Lime's body from the middle of the road, despite the testimony of Lime's associates Popescu (Siegfried Bauer) and Baron Kurtz (Ernst Deutsch) that they were the only ones present. When Martins reveals the porter's testimony to Popescu, we suspect Martins of making a grave error, for Popescu is clearly part of a plot to obscure the truth about Lime's death – a suspicion confirmed by the porter's subsequent murder. And when Martins himself is suspected of being the murderer, it also becomes apparent that he has unleashed forces that he is ill-equipped to deal with, portending dire consequences for himself and others.

At this point, the problems that the film sees with a certain type of popular fiction become clearer. It is critical of such works for presenting a romanticized worldview that hampers its aficionados' exercise of moral intelligence because they rely on simplistic and stereotyped moral schemes to make moral assessments of their situations. This is more than simply a problem for those people, according to the film, for their misjudgments can result in real harm being done to others. Because "cheap fictions" hinder their readers' ability to act with moral intelligence and this can lead to harm others, the film takes a dim view of popular fiction.[15]

The second of moral intelligence's vicissitudes, then, is caused by the pulp fictions. The film shows that the tendency people have of using the stereotypes recycled by mass artworks as a way of interpreting their own lives is a second factor that hinders them from employing their moral intelligence. In Martins' case, reliance on the plots and character types of his own "cheap fictions" spares him the effort of using his moral intelligence to sort through all the confusing and contradictory information that he has received since his arrival in Vienna.

The Third Man has thus already made an important contribution to Aristotle's account of moral intelligence by suggesting that there are two factors that undermine our ability to employ this faculty: prior allegiances and pulp fictions. The balance of the film will depict the process by which such hindrances can be removed so that a person can employ his moral intelligence in an adequate manner.

The balance of the film presents Martins' dawning acknowledgment that Lime was never a true friend and his resulting willingness to aid in Lime's apprehension. In so doing, the film illustrates a number of features of Aristotle's account of the morality of dissolving a friendship. My claim for the film's doing philosophy in this part of its narrative is that, by presenting these disparate elements of Aristotle's theory in a *unified* narrative, it allows us to see the *systematic interconnections* of Aristotle's discussion.

To begin this part of my account, I first turn to Aristotle's discussion of whether friendships can be dissolved. Why is this an ethical problem? One way to think of it is as follows: If I am truly your friend, you have a right to count on me. You can expect me to do various things, because, as a friend, I take your welfare as one of my concerns, according to Aristotle. But, if this is so, then it seems like I can't just dissolve our friendship when I feel like it. Because by being your friend I have created legitimate expectations in you about how I will behave, I cannot simply decide on my own no longer to be your friend. The ethical relationship of friendship brings with it a commitment not to summarily dissolve it without adequate reason.

Things are different with the two other, more limited types of friendship that Aristotle considers, friendships of utility and pleasure, for dissolving these presents no problem. In such cases, Aristotle tells us, "there is nothing absurd in dissolving the friendship whenever they are no longer

pleasant or useful." (1165b4.) Such friendships are based on specific benefits that accrue to the friends – utility or pleasure – and where there is no
such benefit, there is no reason to maintain the friendship.

The dissolution problem, then, occurs only for true friendships, for these
are based upon our concern for the welfare of our friends. So if we accept
the idea that these cannot ordinarily be summarily dissolved, we can ask
whether there nonetheless are any circumstances in which they could be
dissolved unilaterally. Aristotle thinks that there are two sets of circumstances in which they could be: (1) when one has been deceived about the
nature of one's friendship with another and (2) when the ethical character
of one's friend changes. Let's consider each of these possibilities.

The first ground for the unilateral dissolution of a friendship is that the
friend has deceived us about the nature of the friendship. Although Aristotle
adds some qualifications that I will skip over, here is what he says:[16]

> However, we might accuse a friend if he really liked us for utility or
> pleasure, and pretended to like us for our character. ... If we are
> deceived by his pretence [of being a true friend], we are justified in
> accusing him – even more justified than in accusing debasers of the
> currency, to the extent that his evildoing debases something more pre-
> cious [i.e. the friendship or virtue].
>
> (1165b5ff.)

Although Aristotle here speaks of "accusing" the friend, that is, of making
a moral criticism of him or her, the context of this discussion makes it clear
that he thinks such criticism provides a legitimate ground for dissolving the
friendship.

The other ground that Aristotle mentions for legitimating the dissolution
of a friendship is when a friend's character actually changes:

> But if we accept a friend as a good person, and then he becomes
> vicious, and seems to, should we still love him? Surely we cannot, if
> not everything, but only what is good, is lovable. What is bad is not
> lovable, and must not be loved. ...
>
> (1165b12ff.)

Here, Aristotle uses a different terminology, referring to our "love" or
concern for a friend. What he asserts is that it is impossible to maintain a
true friendship with someone who has become vicious or evil, for such
friendships can only exist between people who are virtuous, for a virtuous
person cannot love an evil one. While this might seem a questionable assertion,
it follows from Aristotle's notion of friendship. When the other has a bad
character, he cannot be a true friend, for he cannot maintain real concern
about our welfare. That's just what it is to be a bad person. So in this case,
it is even clearer why it is all right to dissolve the friendship, for there is a

sense in which the friendship self-destructs: If a true friendship requires two virtuous people in order to exist, the fact that one person has become bad means that this necessary condition is not met and the friendship dissolves on its own. As a result, there is evident justification for dissolving the friendship:

> [So] the friend who dissolves the friendship seems to be doing nothing absurd. For he was not the friend of a person of this sort; hence, if the friend has altered, and he cannot save him, he leaves him.
>
> (1165b17ff.)

We are now in a position to see how *The Third Man* illustrates Aristotle's claims about the dissolution of a friendship. Martins' presence has become more than a mere nuisance for Calloway, who has been trying unsuccessfully to get him to leave Vienna. The film includes the running joke of Martins repeatedly failing to catch the plane for which Calloway repeatedly provides him with a ticket. Because Martins' bumbling has now caused the death of an innocent bystander, it is imperative that Calloway get him out of harm's way before he precipitates further disasters. The problem is that Martins won't leave so long as his understanding of his situation remains unaltered and he feels that he needs to defend his friend's reputation. Calloway therefore has the task of getting Martins to see the reality of his situation. And this can only happen if Martins rejects the adequacy of the judgments he has made about his situation through the lens of his own fiction. Only then will he be able to revise his judgments of both Lime and Calloway, seeing neither the former as an innocent victim nor the latter as a corrupt cop.

For this reason, Calloway shows Martins exactly what Lime has done, what crimes he is guilty of, thinking that this will get Martins to see the validity of Calloway's contempt for Lime as well as to reject his unquestioned loyalty to his friend. At the same time, it marks a crucial element of the film's depiction of the process that results in Martins being able to legitimately dissolve his friendship with Lime.

Calloway explains to Martins that Lime has committed the crime of selling diluted tubes of penicillin on the black market for huge profits. At first, Martins doesn't see the significance of Calloway's revelation, dominated as he is by a pulp-fiction-induced suspicion of both the Major and also his loyalty to his friend. As a result, he dismisses this new information, reiterating his disgust at Calloway for his supposed failure to even try to apprehend Lime's murderers: "Are you too busy chasing a few tubes of penicillin to investigate a murder?" Calloway patiently explains that, while there is a murder here, Lime is its perpetrator, not its victim. Many people were treated with the doctored drug – "Men with gangrene legs ... women in child birth ... and there were children, too," Calloway tells Martins. He continues, "They used some of this diluted penicillin against meningitis. The lucky children died ... The unlucky ones went off their heads. You can see them now in the mental wards." (*The Third Man*, p. 132.) When Martins counters that Calloway has still not shown him any *evidence* of Lime's crimes, Calloway resorts to "a magic lantern show." (*The Third Man*, p. 133.) He has his assistant, Sergeant Paine, project photographic slides onto a screen, slides that include, among other things, pictures of Lime with his collaborator, Joseph Harbin, a medical orderly who, we later learn, Lime has killed and substituted for himself in his coffin to prevent the man from being a witness against him. These images, together with some actual physical evidence, convince Martins of Lime's guilt: "How could he have done it?" he asks incredulously, to which Calloway cynically replies, "Seventy pounds a tube."

How does viewing the evidence of Lime's guilt affect Martins? First of all, it radically alters his view of Lime, for he can no longer maintain his preconceived image of his former friend. Seeing what Lime has done – for that is how the show impacts Martins; it lets him see *with his own eyes* evidence of Lime's guilt – diminishes the hold of the pulp-fiction-induced judgment that Lime is a good friend who deserves his loyalty especially since he is being persecuted by a corrupt cop. This allows Martins to have some sympathy for Calloway's perspective, for Martins now knows that Lime is a murderer as well as a black marketeer. Seeing the actual evidence of Lime's treachery forces Martins to reassess Lime's actions and character, no longer trusting the array of characters derived from his own pulp fiction.

I italicized the words "with his own eyes" in the last paragraph to emphasize the film's presentation of a series of photographs as able to constitute evidence of Lime's treacherous actions. The film thus juxtaposes photography and popular fiction as alternative sources of moral conviction. But whereas the film presents pulp fiction as lacking the means to provide a morally perspicuous assessment of Martins' situation, it characterizes Calloway's slideshow in very different terms: Its use of photographs provides the evidence of Lime's crimes that Martins demands and that play a role in his dawning acknowledgment that Lime was not really his friend and thus might not deserve his loyalty.

But how does the slideshow have the power to provide Martins with the evidence he requires? Calloway's role here is similar to that of a film director. That is, he has carefully arranged a series of visual images to produce a specific effect in its beholder, Martins. And that – together with the fact that "magic lantern show" is an oddly appropriate way to describe film itself – suggests that *The Third Man* is presenting film as a photographic medium that can serve as an alternative to pulp fiction as a determiner of a person's moral outlook. The reason that film is superior to pulp fiction is that it allows us to see the evidence that supports a particular perspective in close up and with attention to detail, to foreshadow the terms that I will introduce more circumspectly in a moment.

The film emphasizes the beneficial effects of Calloway's magic lantern show in the following scene when Martins appears – resorting to alcohol once more when his view of the world has been undermined – at the apartment of Anna Schmidt (Alida Valli), Lime's former lover. Self-pity has overwhelmed him again, although this time it is also fueled by his unrequited love for Schmidt.[17] What's important for us, however, is his reassessment of Lime. He tells Schmidt, whom Calloway has also told of Lime's treachery, that he is no longer so sure of who Lime is: "I knew him for twenty years – at least I thought I knew him. I suppose he was laughing at fools like us all the time." (*The Third Man*, p. 145.) Schmidt grows impatient with Martins for saying that Lime might have brought him to Vienna to enhance the profitability of his illegal penicillin sales: "Oh, please, for heaven's sake, stop making him in your image. Harry was real. He wasn't just your friend and my lover. He was Harry." (*The Third Man*, p. 145.) Martins is not really listening to her but continuing his own line of thought. He tells her that he now sees Lime's death as in some way righting the wrongs he had done: "Whoever killed him, there was some kind of justice. Maybe I'd have killed him myself." (*The Third Man*, p. 146.) Once more, Schmidt counters, this time telling Martins that Calloway's information shouldn't affect their sense of who Lime was: "A person doesn't change because you find out more." (*The Third Man*, p. 146.)

The film's presentation of Schmidt and Martins as having different reactions to Calloway's revelations begins its depiction of an alternative to the moral characteristics that Martins has used to think about his situation. In particular, the film will present Schmidt, Martins, and Lime – we will be introduced to him in a moment – as three characters with different ideas about how being a friend commits one to being loyal to one's friend.[18]

In his discussion of friendship, Aristotle claims that having friends is one of the components of a good life. More recently, Lawrence Blum has argued that friendship entails a concern for the good of the friend.[19] Surprisingly, however, there has been little philosophical discussion of the extent to which a friend is committed to being loyal to his or her friends. This is an issue about which *The Third Man* makes important suggestions through its depiction of characters who exhibit this virtue to different degrees.

As we have already seen, the film presents Martins as totally loyal to Lime in the face of Calloway's initial jibes at Lime's character. Now, however, the information he has received from Calloway causes him to reassess that loyalty. In particular, the brutal murders that Lime has committed cause Martins to doubt that his supposed friend deserves his loyalty. In fact, in a foreshadowing of the film's dramatic penultimate scene, he even envisions himself as the agent of Lime's death. Schmidt, on the other hand, remains completely loyal to Lime despite the new information she has received.[20] She appears the embodiment of the old saw "love is blind," for she refuses to change her assessment of Lime even after being informed of his evil deeds.[21]

Even though Martins has begun to acknowledge the limitations of his earlier judgment of Lime and his activities, he is not yet ready to accept all the implications of what Calloway has told him. Schmidt's unquestioned loyalty to her ex-lover still attracts Martins – he remains in love with her even at the film's conclusion as she impassively walks by his forlorn figure. Yet he has also shown a strong vulnerability to the idea that evildoers should get what they deserve, as he showed in his initial criticisms of Calloway as well as in his own fictions.

To complete its tableau of characters with differing commitments to the amount of loyalty that is due friends, *The Third Man* needs to have someone who shows no loyalty to those whom he considers his friends. Harry Lime is such a person. But how can the film show us his character when he is dead?

The films resolves this problem by demonstrating that, at the very moment when our uncertainties appear to have been resolved, neither Martins nor we really understand the significance of what has taken place.[22] When Martins leaves Schmidt, he thinks that Calloway is tailing him. To his surprise, and ours, the figure that emerges from the shadows is that of his friend Harry Lime, now seen by us for the first time, some two-thirds of the way through the film. Lime is revealed only because Martins has made such a racket that a woman in a neighboring building opens the shutters of her window to yell at Martins to keep quiet and, in so doing, the light from her window coincidentally illuminates Lime's enigmatically smiling face. When she has finished her tirade, she closes the shutters and Lime's face is once again covered in shadows and, when a car blocks Martins' access to him, he makes a run for it. Although Martins gives chase, Lime seems to vanish into thin air. Only later does Calloway figure out the secret to Lime's disappearance: He has descended into the vast sewer network that runs beneath the streets of Vienna and that gives him access to the entire city without attracting the attention of the police.

At this point, Calloway has Lime's coffin disinterred, revealing the murder of Joseph Harbin, the medical orderly who actually procured the penicillin Lime sold on the black market. If Calloway hadn't already convinced Martins that Lime was an evil person, Lime's strategic and apparently cold-blooded killing of his own associate should give Martins pause. Here is a man who is willing to murder one of his co-workers in order to save his own skin. But for Martins' bumbling expose, the clever plot might have succeeded.

However, rather than shy away from the chase, Martins continues blithely on his way, demanding that Lime meet with him. Lime attempts to placate him in a scene that is one of the highlights of the film, for the two talk on the Ferris wheel of the famous Prater Amusement Park in Vienna.

They are alone in a cabin that slowly ascends over the city. As they do so, Martins confronts his friend. He begins by telling Lime that the police have arrested Schmidt. Lime's seeming indifference upsets the love-struck Martins, while Lime's response recalls the film's earlier portrayal of Martins as a victim of his own fictions. After quoting from the famous ending

Figure 14 The Ferris wheel at the Prater Amusement Park. From *The Third Man*.
Source: London Films/The Kobal Collection.

of *A Tale of Two Cities* – "It is a far better thing I do. . . . " – Lime responds
in a manner that emphasizes the limitations of Martins' pulp fictional perspective: "Holly, you and I aren't heroes, the world doesn't make heroes . . .
Outside of your stories . . . I've got to be careful." (*The Third Man*, p. 171.)
Lime then lets slip that his safety depends on his usefulness to the Russians,
thereby tipping Martins off that Lime has betrayed Schmidt to save his
own skin.

With its presentation of Lime, *The Third Man* completes its array of characters with different conceptions of the relationship between loyalty and friendship. At one pole stands Schmidt. She represents a view of friendship as demanding absolute loyalty to one's friends. Nothing that a friend has done can undermine the commitment a person has to being loyal to her friend. At the opposite pole stands Lime. The only person he is loyal to is himself. His willingness to kill Harbin and betray Schmidt to the Russians are evidence that he does "not see friendship as requiring one to override one's own self-interest. Because loyalty plays no role in his conception of the ethical commitments he has to his friends, Aristotle would claim Lime is not a true friend, but only one whose friendships depend upon their utility to him. Occupying a position between these two is Martins. Neither an unwaveringly loyal friend nor merely a participant in friendships of convenience, Martins recognizes that friends need to *deserve* one's loyalty. If one has a true friend, one should be loyal to him, but, if one does not, there is no such need. *The Third Man*'s array of characters and roles thus functions as an alternative to that derived from Martins' own novel. In place of the corrupt cop, best friend, and crusading avenger of injustice, the film presents three friends with different conceptions of what friendship entails. These character types not only are less stereotyped than those Martins employs in his novel, they actually represent the virtue of friendship quite accurately.

Martins' realization that Lime is not a true friend allows him to reassess their relationship, resulting in the sort of insight characteristic of psychotherapy: Once he is able to see that Lime is not the loyal friend he believed him to be, a repressed memory floods his consciousness and confirms that view. Remembering an incident from their youth, he tells Lime, "I remember when they raided the gambling joint – you know a safe way out. ... Yes, safe for you ... not safe for me." (*The Third Man*, pp. 172–73.)

The film here depicts an important step that will eventually lead to Martins' dissolution of his friendship with Lime. With overwhelming evidence of Lime's callousness to those closest to him literally staring him in the face – he notices Lime drawing on the fogged window of their cabin a heart with "Anna" inside – Martins is able to reject the idealized image he has had of him and to entertain the thought that he is an evil man. As a result, he can rethink the nature of their "friendship." What he discovers is that his own perspective on the past – "Best friend I ever had" – is radically mistaken, for his "best friend" displayed a willingness to sacrifice him to save his own skin.

Armed with this more realistic assessment of Lime, Martins asks him if he has ever seen one of the victims of his crimes. Lime responds with a speech that reveals the moral perspective that allows him to commit evil deeds. Moving to the cabin door, Lime opens it, glances down, and asks Martins to look at the people far below.

They are so small that they appear to be nothing but *dots*.[23] "Would you feel any pity, " Lime asks Martins, "if one of those dots stopped moving forever?" (*The Third Man*, p. 173.) This rhetorical question conveys Lime's ethical perspective. When viewed from such a distance, Lime implies, people appear so insignificant that it is difficult to be concerned about their fate, so that any moral regard for them fails to carry conviction. If one benefits from harming them – and Lime now admits that he has – there is no reason not to go ahead and do so.

This equation of an evil moral perspective with a physically distant one reinforces the metaphoric structure the film uses to present its under-standing of how an adequate moral perspective on one's situation is achieved. In this framework, physically seeing something up close and in detail results in the mobilization of one's moral intelligence. On the other hand, when one maintains a great physical distance between oneself and others, it becomes easy to resort to stock ideas that enable one to harm others without second thoughts, for they lose their humanity when looked at from afar. On this model, physical distance breeds psychical distance. But even as it presents Lime's view, the film criticizes it, for it comes on the heels of Martins' realization that Lime has kept his distance, and hence his detachment, from those who care for him: Martins himself as well as Schmidt.

The conversation between the two friends now takes a more sinister turn. Upset that Martins has informed the police that he is alive, Lime

Figure 15 Lime and Martins look at the dots. From *The Third Man*.

Source: London Films/The Kobal Collection.

threatens to kill him since he appears to be the only witness against him. Martins informs him, however, that his grave has been dug up by the police and Harbin's body found. As he digests this information, Lime's tone changes from threatening to solicitous – Welles' performance here is masterful – as he tells Martins that he still wants to give him a cut of the action. In a fateful admission that will prove to be his undoing, Lime tells Martins that he will meet with him "any place, any time" only not with the police present (*The Third Man*, p. 178).

Even though the evidence of Lime's treachery is now overwhelming, Martins still retains traces of his romantic, pulp-fiction-inspired perspective. Earlier in the film, Martins had upbraided Calloway for his failure to pursue Lime's killers and had even taken it upon himself to bring them to justice. Doesn't this commitment now require him to help apprehend a murderer, even if it happens that the murderer is his friend? How could he justify not doing so?

The answer is that he still thinks that his friendship with Lime requires him to be loyal. When Calloway asks him to help set a trap to capture Lime, Martins initially demurs: "Calloway, you expect too much. I know he deserves to hang, you proved your stuff. But twenty years is a long time – don't ask me to tie the rope." (*The Third Man*, p. 179.) Martins here uses his loyalty to his "friend" to excuse himself from assisting in his capture. He does so even though he believes that Lime deserves to die for the crimes he has committed.

Here, the film illustrates the claims that Aristotle makes about the morality of dissolving a friendship. Aristotle asserts that there is a reason for us to act differently to people who were once our friends even though we have dissolved the friendship because the friend has turned out to be someone different from the person we thought they were:

> Then should the better person regard the other as though he had never become his friend? Surely, he must keep some memory of the familiarity they had; and just as we think we must do kindnesses for friends more than for strangers, so also we should accord something to past friends because of the former friendship. . . .
>
> (1165b31ff.)

This seems to be a precise description of how Martins is acting: He is still manifesting a degree of loyalty to Lime because they were once friends.[24] However, Aristotle also adds an important proviso to his discussion: "whenever excessive vice does not cause the dissolution." What this means is that a person's loyalty to a former friend should be overridden in cases where that friend has turned out to be a truly vile individual. And this certainly is the case with Lime.

So in order for Martins to act in accordance with Aristotle's account, he needs to realize the true horror of Lime's actions. Despite Calloway's attempts, Martins has not fully grasped the moral significance of Lime's evil deeds. So after his first attempt to use Martins to trap Lime is derailed by the loyal Schmidt's contempt, Calloway provides Martins with the experience he still needs before he can embrace a correct moral assessment of the limits of his loyalty to Lime. On the way to the airport, while bringing the dispirited Martins to the plane he never does manage to catch, Calloway disingenuously suggests that he has an errand to run in the biggest children's hospital in Vienna and asks Martins to accompany him because he is sure that, as a writer, he will be interested. Recall that earlier Calloway had told Martins that the unlucky children who went insane because the diluted penicillin had not cured their meningitis were hospitalized in a mental ward. Now, he wants Martins to see the actual fruits of Lime's labors – in close up and in detail. The camera, tilting once more, this time to record Martins' doubts and dismay, follows Calloway and Martins as they walk around the ward. As Martins looks at the children in their beds, the camera tracks his movement, showing him looking down into one cot in particular. A nurse shakes a thermometer. Another gives a child oxygen. Finally, one drops into the trash a teddy bear that we saw hanging on one child's hospital bed – another victim of Lime's crime has succumbed, this time before Martins' eyes. It takes only a moment longer for Martins to surrender: "I said you win," he tells Calloway, "I'll be your dumb decoy." (*The Third Man*, p. 195.)

Martins had previously refused to cooperate with Calloway because he felt that his friendship with Lime required him to be loyal to Lime. He now sees Lime's punishment as morally more significant than being loyal to him. Indeed, as Schmidt's example makes clear, unquestioned loyalty to an evil person can be a moral failing, just as Lime's example has made clear the moral failings of an absence of any loyalty to one's friends. What changes Martins' mind is a close look at the devastating effects of Lime's operations on the lives of innocent children, for this stimulates his moral judgment by showing him that Lime was truly evil.

By using the harm done to children as the proof that Martins requires, the film brings to mind Ivan's argument in the "Rebellion" chapter of Fyodor Dostoyevsky's *The Brothers Karamazov*. Ivan argues that his perspective as a human being does not let him accept a moral outlook that justifies the suffering of innocent children. His target is the argument from evil – that we should accept the existence of evil as a necessary aspect of God's creation of a world with even greater good. Ivan rejects that moral outlook as inhuman, because it relativizes the suffering of children. For him, the suffering of such innocents is an absolute evil that cannot be accounted for by a moral calculus.

Martins manifests a similar vulnerability to the suffering of innocent children, though the film does not present this as an absolute moral value. Indeed, unlike Ivan, Martins must actually see their pain up close before he is able to overcome his romanticized view of his friendship with Lime. If

Vienna is a city in which there are no absolutes, in which everyone has to compromise to stay alive – a view that Kurtz expressed earlier to explain his own presence as a nightclub musician – the film asserts that this need not be a defect. Rather, it asserts that morality requires flexibility, a refusal to treat any commitment as so absolute that it cannot be overridden in the appropriate circumstances by other commitments. Indeed, this is precisely why moral intelligence is such an important moral virtue: Without it, we would not be able to judge when circumstances warrant overriding a commitment.

Martins does not shed his loyalty to Lime easily. Nor should he. As I have said, loyalty to a friend is a virtue that we do, and should, value highly. But this does not mean that such loyalty cannot be misplaced, that there are no circumstances in which it must give way to more important moral considerations. *The Third Man* presents us with an example of one set of circumstances in which this is true. But in so doing, it does not provide a counterexample to a moral principle – as Carroll had alleged in his discussion of the film cited earlier[25] – but rather an account of when loyalty to a former friend no longer makes sense.

It is important to realize that what brings about Martins' willingness to serve Calloway is actually *seeing* the effects of Lime's crime. Once again, the film here suggests that an act of visual perception is central to achieving the appropriate moral perspective on one's situation. But what it has now added to its earlier view is that this act of perception requires that we inspect the suffering of others from a vantage point close to them, so that we can see what their lives really are like. Unlike the view from on high that Lime uses to allegorize his own moral perspective, seeing others' situations in close up mobilizes our moral sympathies in a way that, according to the film, allows us to perceive our own situation and its requirements more clearly.

Somewhat surprisingly, the film does not actually show us the children who are Lime's victims and the objects of Martins' empathy. Rather, its focus is on Martins as he looks at them, as well as on the nurses and their routines. In so doing, the film steers clear of the dangers of including exploitative images of suffering children while still providing its audience with the images it needs to understand the film's point. In particular, its use of the teddy bear to symbolize the child's death is highly effective. As a result, we do not get a direct view of the sufferings that cause Martins to change his mind; instead, we see Martins and the toy bear. Still, we are looking at things close up and with attention to details. It is this – rather than an unmediated look at reality – that affects us.

I want to suggest that the film here provides an allegory of film as capable of providing us with moral guidance because it can show things in close up – quite literally – and also in great detail. In this allegorization of film, Calloway is the stand in for the filmmakers. Despite Martins' initial hostility – he even attempts to hit Calloway while drunk – Calloway maintains a sympathetic attitude towards Martins, always seeking to keep him from harm. At the same time, he selects the visual experiences that bring about Martins' enlightenment and his reassessment of Lime, Calloway, and his own role. The film thus presents Calloway's interventions as an analogue to its own effects on its viewers.

The moral position that the film ultimately endorses requires Martins to cooperate with Calloway in Lime's capture, for the morally reprehensible actions of this man annul any loyalty that Martins may have had towards him. The penultimate sequence of the film, stunning from a visual point of view and very suspenseful, involves Lime being chased by Martins, Calloway, and the police. In the end, Martins actually kills Lime, thereby completing his rejection of his commitment to his former friend as he acts in the role he had once only imagined doing.[26]

From a philosophical point of view, the significance of the progressive growth of Martins' understanding of his situation is its illustration of a range of claims that Aristotle makes about friendship. In particular, because the film unifies these different features of Aristotle's account by placing them into a coherent narrative, it allows us to see that they also possess a systematic unity that might not initially be apparent to a philosophical reader. We see that Aristotle's assertions about a friend's imperviousness to slander, the grounds for dissolving a friendship, and the circumstances in which there is no residual loyalty owed a friend are systematically related because the film's narrative places them into relationship with one another. In doing so, the film makes a contribution to our understanding of the theory it illustrates.

Early in this chapter, I discussed the banality objection to films doing philosophy. My discussion of *The Third Man* should have put any skeptical doubts about film's philosophical capabilities to rest. There are two reasons for this. First, the film illustrates a range of Aristotle's claims about friendship in a manner that shows those claims to be more systematic than they might seem. This already qualifies the film as doing philosophy, for it contributes to our understanding of Aristotle's theory. But, even more significantly, it provides an original account of the "vicissitudes" of moral intelligence, i.e. presents two factors that inhibit its exercise, namely the baneful influence of prior commitments and pulp fiction. This latter aspect of the film is a real contribution that the film makes to the theory of moral intelligence and thus qualifies this film as doing philosophy in a particularly effective and original manner.

7 Foregrounding the background
Empire and *The Flicker*

In previous chapters, I have examined a number of different techniques that films have employed to screen philosophy. In developing my argument, I made reference mainly to fiction films and often only to popular fiction films at that. In the present chapter, I focus upon a very different type of film, the structural avant-garde film. One reason for this is that film scholars as well as filmmakers have seen these films as having unique philosophical significance. We therefore need to examine whether this film genre provides another avenue that films use in order to do philosophy.

Probably the central reason why these films have been seen as philosophical is that they are *self-reflexive*. That is, they take the medium of film as their subject matter; they are films about film. For those who see philosophy as a type of meta-discourse, a form of thinking that I discussed in **Chapter 2**, in which primary level practices are themselves taken as objects, such films ought to be paradigmatic examples of philosophy, even though it would occur on film.

But what exactly are the philosophical claims being made by these films? Because the films do not employ narratives, they allow their audiences to focus on aspects of film that they normally look past or through. That is, the films get viewers to notice features of film they normally overlook, which usually constitute the background that enables viewers to concentrate on the narratives that generally form the content of fiction films. Because these films have developed a means of getting viewers to attend to properties of film that are normally transparent, they can establish those features as essential to the medium. As a result, these structural films make a significant contribution to our understanding of the nature of film and, therefore, ought to count as doing philosophy.

The films with which I am concerned in this chapter are referred to as "structural avant-garde" films. They are made for a small, intellectual audience, not for the huge audience that Hollywood films aim to reach. As a result, they are more hermetic, harder to watch and understand, and call for a very different type of attention than do standard fiction films.

In their rejection of the formulae of popular fiction films, structural films ally themselves with progressive works in other arts. In so doing, they contest the standard assumptions about filmmaking encouraged by the dominance of popular modes of filmmaking, both narrative and documentary. In particular, they avoid both plot and character development, features typical of popular film.

The foremost theorist of avant-garde film, P. Adams Sitney, first characterized this tradition as structural in a 1969 article and this terminology has become widely accepted.[1] Sitney called these films "structural" because they caused viewers to focus upon their form or structure rather than their content. In his book, *Visionary Film*, Sitney defines the structural film as a "cinema of structure in which the shape of the whole film is predetermined and simplified, and it is that shape which is the primal impression of the film."[2] This definition shows that Sitney called the films *structural* to emphasize the dominating role played by an overarching idea that, in turn, determines the overall shape of the films: "The structural film insists on its shape, and what content it has is minimal and subsidiary to the outline." (*Visionary Film*, pp. 407–08.) Here, Sitney claims that structural films have only minimal content – narrative or characterization, say – and this content is subordinated to the films' greater concern with its overall shape and structure.

The filmmakers that Sitney identifies as structural include Michael Snow, George Landow (Owen Land), Hollis Frampton, Paul Sharits, Tony Conrad, Ernie Gehr, and Joyce Weiland. (*Visionary Film*, p. 407.) The paradigmatic structural film for Sitney is Michael Snow's *Wavelength* (1967). Sitney quotes Snow's own description of the film:

> The film is a continuous zoom that takes 45 minutes to go from its widest field to its smallest and final field. It was shot with a fixed camera from one end of an 80-foot loft, shooting the other end, a row of windows and the street. ... The room (and the zoom) are interrupted by 4 human events that include a death.
>
> (*Visionary Film*, p. 413.)

Wavelength provides a good example of the structural film because its primary emphasis is on the "zoom," the slow, continuous restriction of the visual field and consequent enlargement of the objects that is presented to viewers by means of the manipulation of the zoom lens.

The zoom lens, introduced in 1932 by Bell and Howell, had become a regular tool in the arsenal of filmmakers by the 1960s. However, most of the time, we see *through* it to the narrative content of a film. Although contemporary narrative filmmakers occasionally make rapid zooms precisely in order to get viewers to notice this technical manipulation of what they are seeing, most zooms in narrative films pass unnoticed, for viewers concentrate on what they are seeing, not how they have been enabled to see what they see. This "overlooking" of the techniques whereby objects are presented on screen is called the *transparency* of narrative filmmaking.

Wavelength attempts to undermine the transparency of the zoom, making the *zoom* of the zoom lens its primary focus. The four narrative "events" of the film are subordinate to the film's presentation of the zoom as an object for our attention. Since the film has minimal content – aside from its four minimal "events," all we see is the ever narrowing yet enlarged content of the visual field of the lens – the viewer is forced to think more about *how* the film is showing her what she sees than *what* exactly she is seeing. After all, for most of the film's 45 minutes, we see the same room in which not much is changing. This allows the zooming of the zoom lens, which ordinarily is not an object of awareness for a viewer of narrative film, to become the object of which the viewer is primarily aware. To put this aphoristically, as a structural film, *Wavelength* allows technique to become content.

Sitney also identifies the structural film through its relationship to earlier traditions of avant-garde filmmaking, such as the lyrical film or graphic cinema. However, it is also important to see it in relationship to broader artistic movements of the 1960s. For this reason, Noël Carroll suggests that such films would better be termed "minimalist," thereby making an explicit connection between them and the general artistic movement of which they are a part.[3]

Minimalism was an artistic movement that arose during the 1950s and early 1960s in which artists created works that were stripped down to what they took to be the most basic features of their artforms. In this respect, the movement was a specification of the modernist artistic program, as theorized by the influential critic, Clement Greenberg, of "eliminat[ing] from the specific effects of each art any and every effect that might conceivably be borrowed from or by the medium of any other art."[4] According to Greenberg, all twentieth century art movements were attempts to eliminate elements of the artform that had previously been seen as necessary but now, as a result of the new movement, could be seen not to be. The specific achievement of minimalism was to push this strategy as far as its practitioners thought it could go, leaving nothing remaining that could be eliminated. This strategy aimed at getting the true nature of the respective artforms to emerge. Thus, a minimalist painting might consist of a canvas completely covered with only black pigment in order to eliminate not only the depictive elements that had already been rendered contingent by various forms of abstraction, but even the presence of colors. Ad Reinhart's *Abstract Painting* (1960–66) is an example of such a monochromatic work and it can be seen as an attempt to reveal the true nature of painting. Although one might previously have thought that paintings had to represent something and use a variety of different colors, Reinhart's painting – following on the model of Kasimir Malevitch – showed that this was not so.[5]

One might find this Minimalist program odd. After all, it could be pointed out that removing all the aspects of a meal – such as the food, the settings, the table – would not be likely to reveal the essential nature of a meal. So then why should we assume that the same would not hold of Minimalism in the arts?[6]

To this, there are a number of possible responses. First, an important trajectory of 20th century art did seem to be its elimination of various "extraneous" elements from the arts, leaving a more elemental artform at each stage. Second, it might just be a peculiarity of art – though this would have to be accounted for – that the reductive strategy could reveal art's nature. But finally, and most important, the minimalist strategy, at least in the films I am talking about, allowed elements of the medium that had been transparent to emerge into the experience of audience members. It is this that I think is the crucial feature of the program from a philosophical point of view.

In any case, by the early 1960s, minimalism had become a major artistic movement with important practitioners in virtually every artform. Some examples of non-film minimalists are: Donald Judd in sculpture, Philip Glass in music, and Frederick Barthelme in literature. What all of these artists have in common is an emphasis on structure and minimal content so as to allow the basic character of their artform to emerge as the object of audience awareness.

So even though Carroll is correct to insist that we view structural films in relationship to minimalism in art more generally, I do not think that this justifies changing the terminology with which we refer to this type of film. The term *structural* has deep validity in characterizing the nature of these films. Given its nearly universal acceptance, there is not sufficient justification for jettisoning it.

Like all minimalist artists, then, the structural filmmakers attempted to make works of art that called attention to what they took to be the basic materials of their artform. The question that we need to answer is whether some of the films they made should be treated as philosophy in virtue of this fact. In answering this question, it is important to remember that minimalism – and modernism in art more generally – created a set of cultural practices and expectations in which audiences anticipated being confronted by works that attempted to reveal the essence of their medium. Although this may no longer be the dominant aim of even avant-garde art, we need to be aware of its importance at that time, so that the films I shall discuss in a moment were constructed anticipating that their viewers were immersed in and proficient at this general interpretive practice.

Trevor Ponech recognizes that certain structural films have made important contributions to the philosophical theorizing about the nature of film. Indeed, he thinks that they have done more to reveal film's actual nature than the explicit writings about film done by philosophers and film theorists:

> Frampton, Brakhage, Gehr, and others, by modeling their artform's primitive parts and processes, provide a resource for inquiry into

cinema's engineering specification, a resource unparalleled by anything arising from philosophical discourse itself.[7]

Ponech's use of the term "engineering specification" must not obscure the point he is making about structural films: their common attempt to lay bare the fundamental constituents of film as an artform. As a result, he views structural films as providing important materials for philosophers to use in reflecting about the nature of cinema, a question that has traditionally been at the center of philosophical reflection on film.

The reason for this, according to Ponech, is that structural films attempt to articulate their makers' views about the essence of the medium: "[T]hese works [of structural filmmaking] undertake artistic but nonetheless practical experiments designed to uncover cinema's rock-bottom constituent elements. ... "[8] We will soon see how a couple of specific structural films purport to exhibit film's essence. For now, we need only understand Ponech to be acknowledging the importance that these films have for a philosopher seeking to understand the nature of film as an artform.

Despite the significance that Ponech attributes to structural films for philosophy of film, he denies that these films can actually be categorized as philosophy:

> These explorations are not works of philosophy. They are hardly *rigorous truth-seeking procedures providing evidence and arguments* in support of their authors' conclusions. Rather, they are vehicles for their makers' philosophically pertinent ideas about cinema's nature.[9]

So although Ponech grants that structural films express ideas that their makers have about the nature of cinema, he nonetheless denies that this qualifies them as works of philosophy. This is because he sees philosophy as requiring certain techniques that have no cinematic equivalent. For Ponech, philosophy necessarily employs "rigorous truth seeking procedures [that] provid[e] evidence and arguments in support of their authors' conclusions." Ponech's denial that structural films themselves are philosophy on the grounds that they lack rigor and explicitness resembles objections against films counting as doing philosophy that we have canvassed previously – and, in general, rejected as invalid.

By now it should also be obvious that I do not accept Ponech's overly narrow characterization of philosophy. In previous chapters I have shown that there are aspects of philosophical practice that are not reducible to the production of evidence and the formulation of arguments, the two features Ponech insists philosophy must have. In particular, I explored thought experiments, which is a philosophical technique central to the discipline but one that cannot be reduced to Ponech's overly narrow conception of philosophy as requiring explicit argumentation and evidence production. And I have argued that films are able to screen philosophical thought experiments.

The structural films that I am interested in are not thought experiments, however. They are, of course, real films that have been made for specific purposes by their makers. And unlike scientific experiments, they are not designed to test an already articulated theory of film. While they may be seen as *explorations* of film's nature, their method of conducting their investigations is not that of a scientific experiment, as Ponech mistakenly suggests.

What is correct about Ponech's claim is that these films do not involve argumentation, though there is a sense in which they provide something like evidence. As I shall show, the structural films I am interested in are best thought of as philosophical endeavors to demonstrate that certain features of film are essential to the medium's nature.

In order to investigate the idea that certain structural films can reveal the nature of the medium of film, I turn to some claims made about Andy Warhol's films by the noted philosopher of art Arthur Danto. Warhol's films were an important stimulus to the structural film movement. In an article entitled, "The Philosopher as Andy Warhol," Danto claims that Warhol's films "have an unparalleled contribution to make in our philosophical understanding of the concept of film."[10]

The film upon which Danto concentrates his attention is Warhol's 1964 film, *Empire*. Warhol and his production team went to the 41st floor of the Time-Life Building in New York City on the evening of the 25th of June 1964 and filmed the Empire State Building with a static camera for nearly 7 consecutive hours. Although the film was shot at 24 frames per second, Warhol had it screened at 16 fps, so that the actual length of the filming is nearly an hour and a half less than the 8 hours and 5 minutes required for viewing it in its entirety. The only breaks in the filming took place when the film reels had to be changed. These are registered on the screen by various flashes of light and a slight repositioning and refocusing of the image. This was necessary because Warhol was using a single newsreel camera to make the film.

Empire thus consists primarily of a static image of the Empire State Building that remains on the screen for just over 8 hours. Nonetheless, there are a number of changes in the depicted scene that occur during the film. Aside from a light atop one of the buildings next to the Empire State Building that goes on and off in an irregular pattern, we notice the waning daylight and the illumination of the upper levels of the Empire State Building that occur as night falls.

Given the rather limited content of the objects and events depicted in this film, we might be surprised to find Danto attempting "to explain what makes *Empire* finally *so philosophical a film*."[11] Here is what he says:

> Warhol subtracted everything from the moving picture that might be mistaken for an essential property of film. So what was left was pure film. What we learn is that in a moving picture it is the film itself that moves, not necessarily the object, which may remain still. Warhol's art,

in film and elsewhere, goes immediately to the defining boundaries of
the medium and brings these boundaries to conceptual awareness.[12]

Thus, according to Danto, *Empire* is a philosophical achievement in that it
puts forward a putative essence of film. Danto's interpretation of the film
thus makes it continuous with later structural films that focus upon showing viewers the nature of film as an artistic medium.[13]

But what exactly is the essence of film, according to *Empire*? First, a bit
of context setting is required. One of the obvious features of film that distinguishes it from other art forms is its ability to present things in motion.
It is no surprise to find the noted psychologist and theorist of art Rudolf
Arnheim in 1934 treating the ability to show moving objects as one of the
essential characteristics of film: "Motion being one of its outstanding properties,
the film is required by aesthetic law to use and interpret motion."[14]

From Arnheim's attempt at a definition of film – or, at least, the positing
of one essential characteristic of it – it might seem that, in order for some
work to qualify as a film, it would have to present *moving objects*. But this
is precisely what *Empire* shows not to be the case, according to Danto.
Empire is clearly a film despite the fact that no object moves in it. Indeed, the
only objects that we see in the film are the ever-static Empire State Building

Figure 16 The Empire State Building as it appears in *Empire*.

and its neighboring buildings, though these are not illuminated and thus are not visible for most of the film, which takes place after night falls.

On Danto's account, *Empire* fits the model I presented in **Chapter** 5 of a film that is a counterexample to a philosophical thesis. Arnheim's proposed definition of film as an artform in which objects are presented in motion is shown to be inadequate because *Empire* includes no moving objects but certainly counts as a film. Still, it is important to realize that there is one relevant difference between *Empire* and the film I discussed in **Chapter** 5, *Eternal Sunshine of the Spotless Mind*. Whereas the latter functions as a counterexample by including a thought experiment as its content, *Empire* cannot have a thought experiment as its content because it does not employ a fictional narrative. Rather, film is here used in a documentary manner, allowing the nature of physical reality to be seen. Thus, the *film itself* is the counterexample to the proffered definition of film.

Still, Danto thinks *Empire* has greater philosophical significance than simply counterexampling Arnheim's view of cinema. In place of the idea that films must show moving objects, *Empire* asserts that film has the capacity to show things *either* in motion *or* at rest. While we might have thought that painting and still photography showed things in repose, Danto asserts that this is not the case. Although these static artforms could show things in motion – such as a horse in the act of running – they could not show the motion that the thing possessed. As a result, they could not show stillness either, although the objects they depicted could be in repose. Both stillness and motion were things that only could be shown on film. And it was *Empire* that established this, according to Danto.[15]

As part of his argument, Danto imagines a thought experiment that parallels *Empire*. Danto entitles the film in his thought experiment *Either/ Or* after Søren Kierkegaard's philosophical text of the same name. Danto's *Either/Or* is a film the length of *Empire* – or even longer, he allows – that consists of nothing but the title page of Kierkegaard's great work. Danto claims that his thought experiment is adequate to demonstrate that films do not have to depict motion. Warhol's film, Danto asserts, is more than a thought experiment, for *Empire* is an actual film. What is not clear in Danto's account is what difference this makes.

So we can see that there is something missing in Danto's account of *Empire*. It is a shortcoming of his account that it does not explain *how* we come to be aware of the nature of the medium of film through viewing this film. Danto simply asserts that this happens because the film presents a static image, as if no more could be said than that this thought – *film does not have to present movement* – just occurs to the viewer while watching the film. In addition, Danto claims that there are two "collateral effects" of the film that also have philosophical significance, namely its foregrounding of time and of the material properties of film. He claims these are subordinate to the film's presentation of motion/stillness as definitive of moving pictures, but we need to ask whether their presence is merely accidental. Is it possible to see these three effects of the film as having a more unified nature?

But the most pressing problem with Danto's view is that he takes Warhol to be explicating the nature of film as such in *Empire*. I think it more accurate to say that *Empire* is an examination of what is necessary in order for *objects* to be depicted on screen. This distinction is important because, as we shall see in the next section of this chapter, *Empire* takes film's photographic nature for granted or, more accurately, does not call it into question. Indeed, this is necessary for the philosophical project that I take *Empire* to embody: namely, providing the necessary conditions for objects to be displayed on screen.

So my claim is that Warhol has discovered a style of filmmaking that allowed viewers to *experience* those properties of the medium that normally are transparent, seen *through*, but are actually necessary for our being able to see objects on film. Although while viewing *Empire* we remain focused on the Empire State Building, noting its stasis and waiting to see if anything about it will alter, our attention is also drawn to other features of the film. Among these are the duration of the film and features of the screen image that are not representational.

Let's consider more carefully, then, our experience of watching *Empire*. As I've said, there is no depiction of any object in motion in the film. The only changes that occur are changes in the lighting conditions. Warhol chose to begin shooting *Empire* at 8 p.m. presumably in order to include the vanishing of the daylight and the onset of nocturnal darkness. He seems to have set the camera's aperture so that the Empire State Building would be appropriately registered on film when the sky was dark and its upper portion was illuminated. As a result, when the film begins, the screen is nearly completely white (or light grey). Only three shadowy presences indicate the Empire State Building and two much smaller buildings to its left on the screen. Over the next 36 or so minutes, the sky darkens so that, at the end of this time period, all that is left on the screen are the partially illuminated Empire State Building and a light atop the smaller building to the immediate screen left of the Empire State Building.

During this opening segment of the film, there are comparatively frequent changes in the content of what we see. As the sky darkens, more and more details of the Empire State Building and its surroundings seem to emerge from nowhere, almost as if the buildings were created by the act of filming them. These changes become the focus of our attention as we slowly wait for more of them to appear. As a result, we notice a number of features not of the depicted objects, but their manner of depiction. First, we become very aware of duration as an aspect of film. Because of the relative *lack* of any events transpiring on the screen, the fact that film involves duration becomes something that we notice, even as or precisely because we look at the buildings and their slowly changing state of illumination. As we *wait* for things to *happen* – an expectation that is gradually denied gratification – we realize that film is able to depict transitions in the state of objects even when those objects do not move. We therefore realize that film has the capacity to depict, in addition to locomotion or change of position, what we can call state changes, alterations in how a thing is or appears to be.

Because of the film's minimal narrative content, we also become aware of some additional characteristics of film as an artistic medium that are necessary for the film to be able to depict objects. We become aware, first, of the many imperfections on the surface of the celluloid because we notice that these are projected onto the screen along with the photographic images. Indeed, at times *these* become the primary object of our awareness as they appear nearly instantaneously on a surface hovering between us and the objects depicted – the screen – and then vanishing as quickly as they appeared, though not before seeming to dance before our eyes.

As the sunlight dims, the film's graininess becomes apparent, even as the buildings become more distinct and well defined. This alerts us to further features projected on the screen that are not elements of the depicted objects. Like the scratches and other imperfections, the grain of the film appears to move – both vertically and horizontally – causing the *immobility* of the Empire State Building to become something of which we are aware. That is, as we watch the film and notice a variety of phenomenal movements due to the nature of the celluloid strip by means of which the image of the Empire State Building is projected, the *static and persistent* nature of that building becomes an impressive fact. This may seem odd, for we all know that buildings, like philosophical substances, don't change – at least not very much or very often. But we may never have had the *impression* of such stasis, such persistence before. It is part of the achievement of *Empire* to allow us to *see* such *static persistence* for the first time.

Thus, two very different things happen nearly simultaneously as we watch this film. First, imperfections in the celluloid as well as the graininess of the image, elements of most films that we usually don't pay attention to, become distinct foci of our awareness. These, thus, become part of the content of the work, just as the ambient sounds become the content of avant-garde musical works like John Cage's notorious *4' 33"*, a work in which the performer in instructed to make no sound. Because the scratches on the celluloid and the grains of the film rival the representational pictorial content of the film in their interest, we become aware of the means whereby we view the film: Its projection from a strip of celluloid onto a screen. At the same time, the motion that these appear to have – the scratches seem to dance across the screen and the grains at times seem to generate moving images – allow the static nature of the image of the Empire State Building to be registered. The presence of these different pictorial elements are crucial to our ability to notice the film's presentation of features films must have in order to depict objects.

Once the building is illuminated and the sky has become completely dark, the *static persistence* of the Empire State Building emerges even more starkly, despite the repeated flashes of illumination that abruptly appear on the screen. (I imagine that these came from various activities taking place in the room where *Empire* was filmed, such as someone striking a match or opening the door to the hallway to enter or leave the darkened room.) Observing this stasis – it is composed of both a lack of motion and a constancy of properties – we realize that film has the capability to project such doubly static images.

What is truly remarkable is that viewing *Empire* gets us to notice that we've never before actually experienced static persistence in art, startling as this realization is. This is because film's ability to depict stasis (as opposed to the ability to depict static objects, which other artforms can also do) depends upon its ability to depict, and thus fuel our expectation of perceiving, alteration experientially (something unique to this artform – and cognate ones). And this, of course, depends upon its having, and therefore being able to depict and allowing audiences to experience, duration.

The point of this rather extended description of the experience of watching *Empire* is that it explains *why* this film is philosophically so significant: Warhol has here discovered a mode of filmmaking that transforms the viewer's experience from one in which she is focused upon the pictorial and narrative content of a film into one in which she also notices those aspects of the film that are normally transparent, but that are necessary for a film to present any object whatsoever to its viewers.

In the *Critique of Pure Reason*, Immanuel Kant claimed that there was an innate structure to the human mind by means of which visual input had to be structured in order for us to become aware of objects. He called these innate features of the mind *categories* and claimed that it was not possible for us to experience objects unless the categories had universal validity.[16] Kant characterized his philosophy as *transcendental* because its concern was to explain the possibility of our experience of objects.

I want to claim that *Empire* is a philosophically significant film because Warhol has discovered an analogue to Kant's transcendental philosophy. That is, Warhol's film presents an answer to the following question: What are the cinematic structures that are necessary in order for an object to appear on screen? In virtue of this, we can appropriate Kant's terminology and call *Empire* a work of *transcendental cinema*, for its concern is establishing the necessary conditions for objects appearing to us on a film screen. *Empire* presents duration, celluloid projection, and the ability to present static persistence, as well as change, as elements of the categorial structure necessary for objects to be depicted on film.

I have explained previously how I think this happens. Let me now just reemphasize how my description of the film accords with what I have just claimed about its philosophical significance. Take celluloid projection. To say that this is a feature necessary for objects to appear on screen is to say that a film is constituted by projecting onto a screen a strip of celluloid that has been appropriately exposed and developed. *Empire* makes us aware of this by calling attention to both the graininess of the photographic image (mostly visible in the empty space) and the imperfections in the celluloid – scratches, watermarks, etc. – that are projected onto the screen but that we normally look past and ignore. The film thus makes us aware of "celluloid projection" as a necessary feature for objects to be presented on screen and, for this reason, I characterize it as a work of transcendental cinema.[17]

The difference between Kant's deduction and Warhol's is that the cinematic structures Warhol uncovers can be made – as *Empire* does – part of our conscious experience of watching a film. They can be registered, as David James claims, "phenomenologically."[18] Warhol's genius was in discovering a film form that allowed this to happen. Kant, on the other hand, thinks that the categories cannot be experienced, so his attempt to deduce them and demonstrate their validity can have no experiential touchstone. His genius was to find a form of philosophical argumentation that would demonstrate their necessity.

This discussion allows us to see an additional reason for categorizing films like Warhol's as structural: their ability to expose the deep structure of filmmaking to our view. Like the structural theories of language that became popular during the 1950s and 1960s, *Empire* presents a deep structure that is necessary for a certain field to be objectively constituted and thus deserves the appellation "structural."[19]

I have argued that *Empire* presents a set of features that films must have in order to present objects to us. One question remains: Are we justified in seeing these characteristics as defining characteristics of film itself. In order to answer this question, I want to consider another film, Tony Conrad's *The Flicker* (1965).

Although I have generally followed Danto's claim that *Empire* employs the strategy of reducing its manifest content to a minimum, I explicitly noted that there was one feature of film remaining in *Empire* that Warhol had not eliminated: its use of photography. Although *Empire* has stripped away many of the usual features that characterize narrative films, it has not eliminated the use of photography, indeed the film even emphasized it, since its project was that of showing what was required for us to see objects in a film.[20] It is for this reason that I stated the film's argument as one that presented the conditions necessary for us to *see an object* on film.

Film's use of depictive photography has been treated as essential to its nature by many theorists of film including probably the most influential film theorist of the twentieth century, André Bazin. For Bazin, film's photographic basis is essential, for it allows this artform to achieve something unique in the history of art:

> For the first time, between the originating object and its reproduction there intervenes only the instrumentality of a nonliving agent. For the

first time an image of the world is formed automatically, without the creative intervention of man.[21]

Bazin takes photography to provide a unique possibility in the history of the arts, the formation of an artistic image without the active intervention of a human agent. Although a human being has to press a button in order to take a picture, once she has done so, the image forms on the film without any further human activity, the result of a physical process alone.

It is therefore essential to Bazin that film *as an artform* have a photographic basis. Only in this way can it realize the dream that he sees lying at the root of all art:

> The guiding myth, then, inspiring the invention of cinema, is the accomplishment of that which dominated in a more or less vague fashion all the techniques of the mechanical reproduction of reality in the nineteenth century, from photography to the phonograph, namely an integral realism, a recreation of the world in its own image, an image unburdened by the freedom of interpretation of the artist or the irreversibility of time.[22]

What makes film an art for Bazin is its ability to present us with a simulated world that is more realistic than the simulations attainable in any other art form.

Let us return to *Empire*. We can now see that, while challenging Arnheim's assertion that films had to present moving objects, it not only leaves in place Bazin's characterization of film as essentially photographic but emphasizes it. From the vantage point of the 21st century, with our increasing reliance on digital imaging technologies, it may seem quaint to think of film as an inherently photographic medium. What I wish to show is that a critique of the essentially photographic nature of film was made *on film* only a short time after Warhol made *Empire*.

The film in question is Tony Conrad's *The Flicker* made in 1965, a year after *Empire*. While showing that Warhol's dependence on photography in *Empire* does not yet strip film of all of its non-essential features, *The Flicker* simultaneously demonstrates the falsity of a Bazinian conception of film. As such, it deserves to be seen as another philosophical film, one that advances our understanding of the medium of film in an important way.

The Flicker is a film that is literally composed out of alternative segments of clear and opaque (black) film leader.[23] In the beginning, the segments are relatively long, so that the viewer sees only an illuminated screen that flickers, i.e. alternates between complete illumination and total darkness; there is no other content to what is seen other than the screen, devoid of objects, alternating between these two states. As the film progresses, the tempo of the flickering increases, varying between four and forty alternations or flickers per second. At a certain point, as the pace of the flickering becomes hard to discern visually, the viewer experiences a radical change in what she sees. Instead of seeing a blank screen whose only content is the flickering of projected white light, shapes moving in circular patterns appear to hover on the screen. At first, the viewer wonders whether what she is seeing is "really there" or just something she is imagining. But as the hovering images remain visible, it becomes clear that the film is actually presenting these images to her. After a while, the images even become colored and spin around rapidly.

The Flicker also has a soundtrack that consists of "a drone." Conrad describes it as follows:

> The sound for *The Flicker* was conceived as a composition of pulse trains whose frequencies would fall into the perceptual region lying between rhythm and pitch. It was performed on a custom configuration of interconnected mechanical devices, with a sine wave oscillator driver and some tape echo.[24]

The sound is very much like that made by a film projector, although it varies in pitch and intensity more than the sound made by a projector.

The Flicker continues *Empire*'s project of making a moving picture from which everything non-essential has been subtracted, so that what emerges is "pure film," to use Danto's terminology, but with important differences. If *Empire* asserted that film does not have to present its audience with moving objects, then *The Flicker* asserts that film need not photographically depict objects at all in order to depict motion. The motion that film presents is not depicted by photographing an enduring object whose motion (change of position) the film viewer perceives, but only by the flickering due to the technology of film projection. The film shows that motion can be perceived even when there is no photographed object that we see in motion.[25] The motion is the result of the impact of the rapid flickering of the screen due to the stroboscopic nature of film's technology for image projection. According to *The Flicker*, *this* is what is necessary for something being a film: its employment of the technology for stroboscopic image projection.

In thinking about *The Flicker* as philosophy, it is important to notice that it has a structure that explicitly calls attention to its claim that flickering light brings about the perception of motion in film. It begins and ends with visually perceivable flickers – slowly increasing in frequency at the outset and slowly decreasing in frequency at the end. These segments frame the main body of the film, in which the flicker has increased to a frequency where it is not visually noticeable but motion and colors appear. The film thus uses its temporal duration as a means of articulating a claim that it demonstrates concerning film's nature. And as such, I see it as qualifying as philosophizing.

It is interesting to note that *Empire* and *The Flicker* adopt very different strategies to get viewers to see what properties of film are essential in their view. While *Empire* involves a mostly static photographic image that remains on the screen for an extended period of time, *The Flicker* presents startling moving visual images. Each of these strategies results in viewers becoming aware of properties of the film that are purported to be essential to the medium.

I have called *Empire* a work of transcendental filmmaking in virtue of its concern with the possibility of objects being depicted cinematically. *The Flicker* has a different concern and a distinct method. Instead of using a static image as a means towards engendering an awareness of structural features of film, *The Flicker* shows its audience its cards: the flicker. It is as if it were saying, "See this? Well, I'm going to produce motion from the simple alternation of an illuminated and a darkened screen. There is no more to cinema than that!" And, like the proverbial magician who apparently produces a rabbit from nothing but an empty top hat, this film is able to produce color and motion from nothing more than the stroboscopic effect produced by alternating illumination and darkness on the screen.

Like *Empire*, then, *The Flicker* plays a greater role in the philosophy of film than merely providing material for philosophical reflection. The film itself makes a philosophical claim, even though it cannot do so linguistically. It presents its conception of film's nature through a temporal process that focuses its audience's attention on an aspect of film that is usually neglected, the technological process whereby motion is generated in perceivers. *The Flicker* is a cinematic and philosophical triumph of avant-garde filmmaking.

I want to end this chapter by returning to what I introduced as a terminological issue in the first chapter. There, I said that I would be arguing that films could do philosophy or philosophize, but would generally avoid asserting that they should be seen as *works* of philosophy. As I pointed out then, this latter claim was a stronger one and I generally did not think it could be sustained. What I did not do at that point, and what I would like to do now, is to enter into a discussion of what is at stake in charactering something as a work of philosophy.

A necessary condition for something being a work of philosophy is that it occupy a place within the ongoing tradition of philosophy. Although there may be other necessary conditions, something would simply not count as a work of philosophy if it were not part of the tradition that we call "philosophy." An advantage of thinking about the issue of categorizing works of philosophy in this historical manner is that, since it allows us to leave open the vexed question of whether such works must possess certain intrinsic features, we can still proceed to discuss whether non-standard works can count as philosophical works.

If we accept this strategy, we can also apply it to the concept of art, claiming that characterizing something as a work of art involves placing it within an ongoing trajectory of other works of art. Such a point of view allows us to see both *Empire* and *The Flicker* as works of cinematic art because, as my discussion has shown, they occupy an important place in the history of avant garde cinema. The question remains, though, of whether they should also count as works of philosophy.

Before answering that, let me just point out that this account of how categorization works allows us to see that the categories "work of philosophy" and "work of art" need not be mutually exclusive. If a work plays a role in the history of two different intellectual or cultural histories, it could be seen to be a work of both. Certain minimalist works, for example, could be taken to be works in two different artforms. So John Cage's *4' 33"* is arguably both a musical work and a piece of performance art or theater because it has a place in the histories of both these artforms. It is therefore possible that a film could be both a cinematic work and a philosophical one. But are *Empire* and *The Flicker* such works?

I don't think that we are now in a position to answer that question, for its answer depends on the future development of the philosophy of film. If the field develops in such a way that these two films occupy places in the ongoing philosophical discussion of the nature of film (and its cognate media), then they would count as works of philosophy. Although there is ample reason to doubt that the field will develop in this way – philosophers are, after all, jealous of their professional identities – the present chapter can be taken as a recommendation that it should, for these films present us with deep phenomenological experiences of the nature of cinema that written philosophical texts cannot rival. We may therefore hope for a more catholic philosophical tradition of thinking about cinema in which certain specific films – *Empire* and *The Flicker* are my candidates for inclusion – play a necessary role.

8 The nature of cinematic philosophy

When I introduced and explained the methodology I would employ in this book, I characterized its individual chapters as fibers that, braided together, would constitute the strong cable linking film and philosophy. I borrowed the metaphor of a cable from C. S. Peirce, the founder of pragmatism. Peirce used it to criticize the a priori method he saw dominant in the practice of Western philosophy. He criticized the idea that philosophy should involve a single chain of logically certain argumentation that linked a well accepted premise to a more dubious conclusion. In place of that, he urged philosophers to use a multiplicity of mutually supporting arguments:

> Philosophy ought to imitate the successful sciences in its methods, so far as to proceed only from tangible premises, which can be subjected to careful scrutiny, and to trust rather to the multitude and variety of its arguments than to the conclusiveness of any one. Its reasoning should not form a chain which is no stronger than its weakest link, but a cable whose fibers may be ever so slender, provided they are sufficiently numerous and intimately connected.[1]

The problem with philosophy as it had been done, as Peirce saw it, was that one weak link would compromise the strength of an entire chain of complex and intricate reasoning. If a series of linked philosophical arguments had just one illicit transition, then the whole edifice it attempted to establish would collapse in ruin.

While I disagree with Peirce's attempt to model philosophy on the natural sciences, I do think that he made an important point about the conduct of philosophical inquiry. In place of the single chain, he suggested a series of interlocking strands, none of which might be able to bear the full weight of a heavy object, for the interlocking strands would distribute the load, thereby keeping the object supported even when one of the strands was weak or, even, broken. He thought that philosophical truth would better be attained by the mutual support of interlocking strands of reasoning than from a single line of argument.

I used Peirce's metaphor because I see it as a mistake to support the possibility of film doing philosophy by positing a global, universal, or a priori connection between the two. I characterized the investigation I undertook in this book as proceeding according to Peirce's recommendation, for I would be detailing a range of specific links that bound film and philosophy, proceeding locally rather than globally. My idea was that the mutual support of these different connections would secure my sense of film and philosophy as genuinely and intimately related to one another.

In large measure, then, this book developed an account of what I take to be the central philosophical capacities of film. In order to characterize these, I explored a variety of techniques that are characteristic of philosophy – including thought experiments, counterexamples, and arguments – trying to show that films are capable of screening each of these. Turning to films as diverse as *Modern Times*, *The Matrix*, and *Empire*, I have showed how films are able to present significant philosophical insights to their viewers.

In many ways, the results of my local study of the connection between film and philosophy are surprising – at least to me. Like virtually all philosophers writing about film, I had initially rejected the idea that films could do philosophy when they illustrated a philosophical claim, theory, or position. I think this was because I wanted to claim that films could philosophize in other, what I thought of as more significant ways. But once I realized that film and philosophy could have multiple, overlapping connections, the idea that *being an illustration* was a philosophically significant way for film to do philosophy seemed much more plausible. So I began to think about what actually made a picture an illustration of a text, with the unanticipated result that I uncovered a plurality of such relations, some essentially arbitrary and others more integral. This allowed me to begin investigating how a cinematic illustration of a philosophical theory could make genuinely creative and significant points about the theory of which it was an illustration.

Like many philosophers, I had recognized that thought experiments were an important element to many significant philosophical texts, but I hadn't really thought about how to characterize their importance. Once I became interested in the issue of whether narratives could be arguments, the centrality of the thought experiment emerged. After all, thought experiments generally involve narratives, one of the features of philosophy that had been taken as a reason that film could not screen it. If one could show that a thought experiment was an essential element in certain philosophical arguments, the path would be open to showing that films could also make philosophical arguments because their narratives contained thought experiments. This proved to be an extremely fruitful avenue to go down for thinking about the ways that films could philosophize. Once films were viewed as presenting thought experiments, it seemed that a variety of different modes of philosophical investigation – including but not limited to counterexamples – were available for screening.

Although my own initial interest in film developed from an interest in fiction films – the first films I was truly engaged by and also the ones I found discussed most often by philosophers – I have become more interested in avant-garde films over the years. In part, this was simply because, as the one-time head of a film studies program, I gained increasing exposure to this inventive and challenging mode of film production. Still, as a philosopher, I remained suspicious of the claim that avant-garde films were really philosophical. My identity as a philosopher made me wary of attempts by members of different professions – actually artists in this case – to say that they were doing what was, after all, my job. But the context of this study – in which I came to see more and more connections between film and philosophy – made me want to investigate whether avant-garde films might also be a means of linking the two. I was particularly interested in the idea that self-reflexive films might be a good way to think about the nature of film. And, again somewhat to my surprise, I became convinced after viewing some of these films that they really did present original philosophical thinking about the nature of film as an artistic medium.

There is a question that I have deliberately avoided posing until this point in my argument: Is there something specific to film as an artistic medium that makes it specially qualified for presenting philosophical issues, ideas, theses, and/or arguments? The context for asking this question is the existence of influential philosophical accounts of other artforms that claim that those artforms make a unique contribution to philosophy.

Let's begin with art itself, i.e. painting and sculpture. Arthur Danto has argued that, at a certain point in its history, art became philosophy.[2] This is because art began to address the question of its own nature and, in thus becoming self-conscious, became philosophy albeit still in artistic form. The reason why, at this stage – one that Danto provocatively characterizes as the end of art – art was philosophy, is that the question of art's nature is one of those issues that belongs inherently to the philosophy of art. So in so far as art addressed this issue, it had itself become philosophy.

The paradigmatic artwork that is philosophy, according to Danto, is Andy Warhol's *Brillo Box* (1964). The work consists of a plywood cube that is painted so as to be visually indistinguishable from the grocery cartons containing boxes of Brillo pads that were to be found in the storage rooms of grocery stores at the time of the work's execution. It counts as philosophy because it raises the question of why one of two visually indistinguishable objects is an artwork while the other is not. Danto's answer – that *Brillo Box* embodies a meaning – need not concern us here, for we are only considering the question of whether there is a different type of reason why films count as philosophy on my account.

As we saw in the previous chapter, there are certain films – Warhol's *Empire* being one of them – that philosophize by putting forward a view about the nature of film as an artistic medium. Such films function analogously to *Brillo*

Box in that they pose questions – and, indeed, answers – about the nature of the type of thing of which they are an instance. But such self-reflexive films are only one species of philosophy on/in/through film. As my interpretations of films in earlier chapters has shown, films can address a wide range of philosophical issues besides that of their own nature; the films I have discussed address issues from many other fields of philosophy, from epistemology to ethics.

This suggests that film has a wider philosophical range than the two artforms – painting and sculture – that particularly concern Danto. Although he sees both painting and sculpture as raising questions about the nature of art, he does not suggest that these artforms are able to make significant interventions in other areas of philosophy. But as I have shown, the case is quite different with film, for I have provided examples of films that philosophize about such diverse matters as the alienation of the worker in a capitalist society, the possibility of skepticism, the viability of utilitarianism, and the nature of friendship – as well as the aesthetic question of film's own nature. And, of course, this list of topics could be greatly expanded by considering additional films.

Martha Nussbaum has explored the philosophical potential of another artistic medium: literature and, more specifically, the novel. She states that "there may be some views of the world and how one should live in it" that cannot be expressed adequately in standard philosophical prose but require a language and form "more complex, more allusive, more attentive to particulars," such as found in certain novels such as those of Henry James.[3] She asserts that such works should count as philosophy because they are as engaged in the search for truth as texts more widely recognizable as philosophical.

Cora Diamond has argued in a similar vein that certain texts generally accepted as philosophy – such as Plato's *Crito* – are philosophical less because of the presence of a deductive argument than because they are "an exercise of moral imagination" that enables people "to see the situation differently."[4] From her point of view, philosophy is characterized by an interest in transforming how people see the world, so that an emphasis on precision and argumentation is simply a misunderstanding of the nature of the discipline of philosophy.

From the point of view expressed by Nussbaum and Diamond, my method of procedure might seem flatfooted and even misguided. Whereas they attempt to show that there are philosophical tasks that require nonstandard means of exposition, I have emphasized film's deployment of widely recognized and quite standard philosophical techniques – most notably the thought experiment – to justify seeing the artform as capable of philosophical thinking.

I do not think there is as wide a gulf separating me from these two philosophers of literature as it might appear. First of all, my deconstruction of the "mere illustration/serious thinking" dichotomy found in the work of many philosophers of film granted that illustrating a philosophical theory could itself count as a philosophically significant achievement. But this allows the possibility that literary works count as philosophy because of their status as illustrations of philosophical theories, thereby legitimating at least some of the works Nussbaum and Diamond are interested in treating as philosophy, though perhaps from a different point of view. In addition, my emphasis on thought experiments provides another avenue for thinking of literature, with its emphasis on particulars, as counting as philosophy. Indeed, I have explicitly argued against the view that philosophy is constituted exclusively by universal principles.

In reflecting on the relationship of film to other artforms, we should note that film employs the features to be found in other artforms in a new synthesis. Thus, film is visual – as are painting and sculpture – as well as narrative – a crucial feature of literary works. This reliance on features of other artforms, even if in a novel combination, gave pause to traditional philosophers of film such as Münsterberg, Arnheim, and Bazin, who all desired to see film as unique as well as novel. Their misguided attempts to develop normative conceptions of filmmaking from an essentialist conception of the medium of film are the antithesis to my emphasis on the local, the particular, the empirical. But if we admit that films involve the unfolding of the visual in time, then we can ask whether this does not result in a unique connection to philosophy.

I do think that the fact that film is both a visual and temporally extended artform gives it an immediacy that is greater than other artforms in its presentation of philosophy. Although Descartes' written text, for example, could convince us that all of our perceptual beliefs were mistaken and even provide us with a thought experiment to render this possibility more immediate, these attempts pale in the face of a film – *The Matrix* – that succeeds in presenting us with perceptual experiences that are deceptive – even if they are about a fictional world. If there is anything unique about film as a philosophical medium – in addition to its ability to address a wider range of philosophical issues than Danto, Nussbaum, or Diamond grant to their respective media – it is the immediacy with which its temporally developing images confront us with a counterfeit of our everyday experience of the world. That this gives the medium its philosophical punch has been one of the burdens of this study to reveal.

I recognize that there are many who think that it is a mistake to view film as capable of actually doing philosophy, rather than, say, suggesting ideas to philosophically inclined viewers. In fact, I began this book by attempting to articulate a variety of reasons for holding that films could not philosophize. I explored three different objections to film being philosophy: the explicitness objection, the generality objection, and the imposition objection. Although I gave reasons for rejecting both the explicitness objection and the imposition objection in **Chapter 2**, dismissing the generality objection presupposes some of the results derived in later chapters. In general, my analyses of the films presented in the previous chapters of this study comprise the strongest argument against these objections.

Consider first the explicitness objection. This objection contrasted the precise and explicit formulation of claims in philosophy texts with the supposed imprecision and ambiguity of narrative films. Although I gave some general arguments against this view earlier, they are reinforced by the specific interpretations I have given of the films in the preceding chapters of this book. In each case, I have formulated what I take to be precise claims that the films have made, claims in virtue of which the films qualify as philosophy.

Nonetheless, the explicitness objection is well taken if it is interpreted as methodological guidance for developing philosophical interpretations of films. That is, in presenting a film as making a philosophical claim, it is important to show precisely how the film expresses the view attributed to it. Consider, for example, my claim that *Eternal Sunshine of the Spotless Mind* presents a counterexample to utilitarianism. It might be asked whether the film really targets this specific ethical view rather than a more general hedonism rooted in American society. Here, the only answer is the film itself and the way it presents its rejection of the technology of memory erasure that is its concern. What I attempted to do was to show that the film criticized an explicitly utilitarian justification for selective memory erasure.

But this leads to a further question. Let's grant that *Eternal Sunshine* presents a criticism of utilitarianism. It differs, however, in that this criticism is not an end in itself – as it generally would be in a philosophical text that employed a similar thought experiment – but a means towards the successful creation of the romantic couple that is the heart of the film. The audience of the film is not left thinking about how problematic utilitarianism is as a social theory, but how poignant it is that Clementine and Joel have gotten back together despite their knowledge of where this might lead.

An ongoing issue within film theory has been the competing roles of narrative and imagery in film. Although films generally strive for narrative closure, it has been argued that the threat to closure provided by images can be so strong that, despite the presence of an actual narrative closure, the audience can still remain caught up in the threat that the closure will not occur. I want to suggest that this is what happens with *Eternal Sunshine*. Although the film ends with something like the ending of a traditional romantic comedy in which the two romantic partners are shown frolicking, the audience remains very cognizant of the threat to their happiness that the technology of selective memory erasure has posed. As we look at the two happy people, we are aware that they have chosen to be together with real knowledge that their choice does not mean living happily ever after and that this is the correct choice because happiness is not the only, or even most significant, value in living a life.

This leads to a reconsideration of the imposition objection. Its claim was that, particularly when an interpretation was ingenious, it seemed less to be a result of something present in the film than the acumen of the philosophical critic. I can imagine someone sympathetic to this criticism pointing out that, while he found my interpretation of *Eternal Sunshine* interesting, he did not see it as really something that the film itself presented. Although as a philosopher, I could point out that the film had implications for ethical theory, these implications were not actually indicated by the film itself.

Behind this criticism is the idea that the content of a film is readily available to a viewer on a single viewing. If an interpretation points out features of the film that viewers don't immediately perceive, then the interpretation would be imposing those issues onto the film. But I don't see things that way, maybe because I have always enjoyed reading criticism of films and other works of art. This is because, unlike the hypothetical objector I have envisioned, I have felt a need to reflect on what is really at issue in these works and have welcomed interpretations that show me there is more going on in a work than I had realized. So I find myself with a different initial response to complex interpretations of films. This is not to say that it is not possible that a philosophical interpretation of a film might impose its own concerns onto a film. I cited one example of such an interpretation in **Chapter 6**, and it is a danger that we philosophical interpreters of film need to be constantly aware of. But this threat is best met by being careful to pay attention to the film itself rather than rejecting the possibility of films doing philosophy.

And my own experience in writing about films belies the thrust behind the objection. Often, as I notice a philosophical issue present in a film, I am amazed to see how the film focuses on the issue and I find it hard to believe that the filmmakers could not have intended to do so. So, for example, as *The Third Man* pursues its interrogation into the demands of friendship, the parallels to Aristotle's discussion of friendship in books VIII and IX of the *Nicomachean Ethics* were so striking – and it took a re-reading of that text for me to really notice what those parallels were – that I could not help believing that the filmmakers had intended them.

Now I have also argued that the filmmakers do not have to be acquainted with a philosophical text, but only with the issues it raises, in order for them to screen them. Because filmmakers exist in a broader cultural and intellectual context, they are aware of some of the philosophical issues prominent in their society, which animate both its philosophical texts and its more general culture. This allows filmmakers to focus upon such issues without necessarily having read specifically philosophical texts that address them. Still, it is hard for me to believe that there is not sometimes a stronger connection between the film and the philosophical issues that it screens.

Finally, let me address the generality objection. Its basis is the difference between the general truths that are the subject matter of philosophy and the specific narratives that, according to the objection, are present in films. The easiest response to this objection points out that some films do not involve narratives at all. Structural avant-garde films, as we have seen, do not employ narratives; indeed they often lack characters and anything much by way of plot or action. The generality objection simply does not apply to them. So we could dismiss the objection as failing to establish that there is no possibility of films doing philosophy.

Still, the objector is likely to persist. Sure, we can imagine her saying, there is an obscure experimental film genre that includes films that might be capable of philosophizing. But the real issue the objection addresses is whether fiction films can philosophize. Raising the issue of structural films only diverts attention from that basic question and you really do need to address it.

The objector is certainly right that I ought to answer the generality objection in regard to fiction films. But that is also not difficult, given the results of the preceding chapters. Even if we agree for the sake of argument that *all* philosophical knowledge is general, of the form "Knowledge is justified true belief," particular narratives can be relevant. In previous chapters, I have shown that philosophical thought experiments have an important role to play in the justification of the general knowledge claims that we are conceding constitutes the subject matter of philosophy. But in philosophy these thought experiments often involve particular narratives – say, of a person heading down a hill in a trolley car whose brakes have failed. If such stories play a role in the justification of, in this case, ethical claims, the door is opened for cinematic narratives to function as thought experiments that are relevant for the justification of philosophical claims.

Of course, I have not only made an abstract argument to this effect but also have actually looked at some cinematic thought experiments that make philosophically significant claims. Again, one example is *Eternal Sunshine of the Spotless Mind*, which I claimed to include a counterexample to utilitarianism. If my account of that film was convincing, then it should be clear that, *contra* what the generality objection asserts, fictional narrative films can actively philosophize.

The account of the genesis of this book with which I began this chapter might make it seem as if I have proceeded by first thinking about philosophy and then seeing whether film could mimic its methods and concerns. However, this is not actually the way that I worked. I have genuinely investigated film and philosophy in their mutual relation to one another: Sometimes, I began by thinking about a film that seemed to have a philosophical point to make and then tried to figure out what were the philosophical techniques it employed in doing so; at other times, my reflection focused initially on an important philosophical technique and then turned to the field of film to see which film might best exemplify it.

The result is, I hope, a fully integrated account of the relationship between film and philosophy, one that does not privilege either domain but which illuminates both by seeing them as interrelated in diverse ways. Although films, especially popular narrative films, are generally regarded simply as vehicles of entertainment, my exploration of film as a philosophical medium demonstrates that films can be much more than a means for people's amusement and titillation. They can also, as I have shown in some detail, be a way of reflecting upon some of the most basic questions of human existence, the home territory of philosophy.

But if even popular films acquire a new seriousness in light of being thought about in this way, philosophy does not emerge from this investigation unaffected. Many people regard philosophy as an esoteric and remote specialty practiced by a small elite that is out of touch with the contemporary world. Indeed, a number of my favorite teachers of philosophy were proud of their embrace of the esotericism of philosophy and explicitly sought to defend it from the "deadly" threat of *relevance*. But, to speak metaphorically, philosophy needs to be brought down from the mountain of its own exile from contemporary society, for philosophy can be an important voice in our contemporary world, one that can help inject some sanity into what increasingly seems like a world spinning out of our control. It can do this because it fosters a self-consciously critical attitude whereby beliefs of all sorts are subjected to rational reconsideration. In a society dominated by the sound bite, such second thoughts, in a different sense, are a welcome and beneficial addition. The promise of critical reflection is that it leads to a more fulfilling life and a more rational society. But this will only come about, not when philosophers are kings, but when ordinary people are philosophers. And this is one of the promises that might be realized were the recognition to become widespread that film is an artistic medium in which philosophically significant ideas and arguments can be found.

So film and philosophy both benefit from their juxtaposition. If film can gain some cultural weight from its association with philosophy, then philosophy can gain a wider audience and greater social impact from its connection to film.

In making my argument about film's capacity for philosophy, I have not meant to suggest that films can do everything that written philosophical texts can, so that we could dispense with those texts and simply make recourse to screened philosophy without significant loss. I certainly think that written texts are indispensable for understanding philosophy. Without sustained concentration on the difficult and often obscure texts that constitute the Western tradition of philosophy, it is difficult to fully appreciate the nature of philosophical discourse and argumentation. So I am not suggesting that film simply replace philosophy in, say, the curricula of colleges and universities. What I am saying is that awareness of philosophical issues is a prerequisite for understanding what is going on in many films – both popular and arcane.

There is thus an asymmetry in my view. I see philosophy as indispensable for film, but not vice-versa. Although philosophy has the ability to go its own way, oblivious to the ways in which its issues have enriched filmmaking, I think it would nonetheless be a mistake for philosophy to do so. This is because philosophy stands in need of a legitimation of itself as a vital intellectual practice for the twenty-first century. For, sadly, the United

States lacks an adequately philosophical culture. One means to enhance the status of philosophy is to show that it is engaged with vital realms of popular culture. While many may see this as watering down philosophy, I think that would be a mistake. In order to insure its own vitality, philosophy needs to show its relevance to contemporary people and societies. It is my bet – one on which I have staked a good portion of my life and career – that the linking of philosophy and film is one way to do so.

Of course, I am not alone in this belief. At the beginning of this book, I cast a quick glance over the rapidly expanding fields of the philosophy of film and the philosophy of popular culture. All of the philosophers who are engaged in these fields believe, I take it, that they are supporting the endeavor of philosophy by showing it to be relevant to cultural domains that seem far from its typical shores. This is not just a revolt of the culturally disenfranchised philosopher attempting to stake out a terrain for his own interests. It is also the result of a recognition of the social contribution that philosophy can make. The health of our culture, our society, our world, depends upon its acknowledging the importance of philosophy to it. And one of the first signs of such a possibility is the growing acknowledgment that films of all sorts can, and sometimes do, screen philosophy.

Notes

1 Can philosophy be screened?

1 See, for example, Bernard Williams, *Problems of the Self* (Cambridge: Cambridge University Press, 1973) and Derek Parfit, *Reasons and Persons* (Oxford: Oxford University Press, 1984).

2 Stanley Cavell, *Pursuits of Happiness: The Hollywood Comedies of Remarriage* (Cambridge MA: Harvard University Press, 1981) and *Contesting Tears: The Hollywood Melodrama of the Unknown Woman* (Chicago: University of Chicago Press, 1996).

3 Christopher Falzon, *Philosophy Goes to the Movies: An Introduction to Philosophy* (London: Routledge, 2002) and Stephen Mulhall, *On Film* (London: Routledge, 2002). The two collections are: Rupert Read and Jerry Goodenough (eds) *Film as Philosophy* (Houndmills, UK: Palgrave Macmillan, 2005) and Murray Smith and Thomas E. Wartenberg (eds) *Thinking Through Cinema: Film as Philosophy* (Oxford: Blackwell, 2006).

4 This is most notable in the book series on philosophy and popular culture that William Irvin has edited and that was first published by Open Court and is now being published by Blackwell. Over 25 titles have appeared in the two series.

5 For a discussion of Hegel's claim, see my "Hegel's Idealism: The Logic of Conceptuality," in *The Cambridge Companion to Hegel*, Frederick Beiser (ed.) (Cambridge: Cambridge University Press, 1992), pp. 102–29.

6 See the entire "Pro and Contra" section of *The Brothers Karamazov* for Ivan's arguments.

7 Martha Nussbaum, among others, has argued for this claim. See her *Love's Knowledge: Essays on Philosophy and Literature* (New York: Oxford University Press, 1990).

8 The precise claim defended is a matter of debate. I see it more about the relativity of interpretations than straightforward epistemological relativism.

9 Bert Bandman raised this objection to me in private correspondence.

10 This point is raised by Paisley Livingstone in "Theses on Cinema as Philosophy" in Smith and Wartenberg, *Thinking Through Cinema*, pp. 11–18.

11 Rudolph Arnheim, *Film as Art* (Berkeley CA: University of California Press, 1957).

12 For an interesting take on how technological changes have affected the way in which films are now viewed, see David Denby, "Big Pictures: Hollywood Looks for a Future," *The New Yorker*, 8 January 2007, pp. 54–63.

13 An example is Noël Carroll's advocacy of the term "moving image." See, for example, his *Theorizing the Moving Image* (Cambridge: Cambridge University Press, 1996).

2 Are there limits to film's philosophical capabilities?

1 Plato's dialogues generally feature his teacher, Socrates, as their main character. Although the early dialogues are taken to represent Socrates' own point of view, the later dialogues, such as *The Republic*, present Plato's views through the mouth of Socrates.

2 I will discuss the Allegory of the Cave at greater length in later chapters where I will emphasize other functions it performs philosophically.

3 The term "cinema" refers not primarily to individual films or movies, but to the entire apparatus of their production, distribution, and viewing. Whether it makes sense to still focus on the cinema as a distinct artform in a digital era is an important question for scholars of film, as I have mentioned in the previous chapter.

4 I borrow this term for film from *The Third Man*. See my discussion of the film in **Chapter 6**.

5 Murray Smith, "Film Art, Argument, and Ambiguity," in Murray Smith and Thomas E. Wartenberg (eds) *Thinking Through Cinema: Film as Philosophy* (Oxford: Blackwell, 2006), p. 39.

6 Op. cit., p. 40.

7 Herbert Granger, "Cinematic Philosophy in *Le Feu follet*: The Search for a Meaningful Life," *Film and Philosophy* 8 (2004): 76.

8 There are films that might count as cinematic painting, such as Stan Brakhage's *Mothlight* (1963), but these are very different from the one I envision in the text.

9 Granger, "Cinematic Philosophy," p. 75.

10 Op. cit., p. 85.

11 Bruce Russell, "Film's Limits: The Sequel," *Film and Philosophy* 12 (2007): 18.

12 Op. cit., p. 17.

13 Op. cit., p. 18.

14 Most notably in the infamous claim that the author is dead. See, for example, Roland Barthes, "The Death of the Author," reprinted in Thomas Wartenberg (ed.) *The Nature of Art, 2nd Edition* (Belmont CA: Wadsworth, 2007).

15 See, for example, Dieter Henrich's now-classic article, "The Proof-Structure of Kant's Transcendental Deduction," *Review of Metaphysics* 22 (1969): 640–59.

16 Noël Carroll, "Theorizing Through the Moving Image: The Case of *Serene Velocity*," in Smith and Wartenberg (eds) *Thinking Through Cinema*, pp. 173–86. I discuss avant-garde films' philosophical significance in **Chapter 7**.

17 I discuss how films can present arguments in **Chapter 6**.

18 I accept this claim now simply for the sake of argument.

19 Xenophanes, fragment 19, in Arthur Fairbanks (ed. and trans.) *The First Philosophers of Greece* (London: Kegan Paul, Trench, Trubner, 1898).

20 I leave open the question of what other types of non-fiction films there are, not intending this dichotomy to be exclusive.

21 Fiction films share with novels narrative form. In **Chapter 8**, I will consider the relationship between literature and films as non-standard ways of doing philosophy.

22 In his groundbreaking study, *The Photoplay* (New York: D. Appleton and Company, 1916), Hugo Münsterberg attempted to distinguish films from mere recordings of reality. We face here a similar problem. Münsterberg's solution of seeing films as portraying psychological reality is, however, not one we can follow.

23 Friedrich Nietzsche, *The Use and Abuse of History*, Part II. Accessed at: www.mala.bc.ca/~johnstoi/Nietzsche/history.htm

24 In some cases, the narrator and narratee may be the same person, as when we tell ourselves a story about ourselves. In what follows, I will use the term "event" in a broader sense than many philosophers do, so that an historical event such as the American Revolution will itself be comprised of many smaller "events."

25 Sydney Lens, *The Labor Wars* (New York: Doubleday, 1973), p. 338.

26 For a more complete discussion of the issues raised by the film and its significance, see my "Beyond Babies and Banners: Towards an Understanding of the Dynamics of Social Movements," *New Political Science* 14 (Winter 1985–86): 157–71.

27 My use of documentary films as a link to history might seem misguided, since I am generally worried about fictional films screening philosophy. I use them only because they help show the difficulties facing the thesis that philosophy can be screened.

28 In "Beyond Babies and Banners: Towards an Understanding of the Dynamics of Social Movements," *New Political Science* 14 (Winter 1985–86): 157–71, I argued that the film, *With Babies and Banners*, was a genuine work of history that not only documented the attempt of former members of the United Auto Workers Women's Auxiliary to have their place in the Great Flint Sit Down Strike recognized, but presented a revised narrative of the strike that showed the crucial role played by the women.

29 That documentary films can present philosophical arguments is generally agreed upon by all participants in the debate about the philosophical potential of fiction films. This is because the soundtrack of the documentary film can make the sort of universal statements taken to be characteristic of philosophy that the imagetrack can then confirm. Nothing I say here is meant to deny this possibility.

30 Christopher Grau considers the ethical issues surrounding the robots of *I, Robot* in "There is no 'I' in 'Robot': Robots and Utilitarianism" in *IEEE: Intelligent Systems* 21 (July/August 2006): 52–55. I leave open the question of whether the film itself raises the questions Grau explores in it.

31 For more on this, see my website: www.mtholyoke.edu/go/kidsphil. I should point out that many children's books do develop aporias, i.e. states of mind in which the need to go beyond standard assumptions about a concept are clear. It could be argued that this itself constitutes a philosophical achievement of the sort aimed at by Socrates.

32 I propose this dichotomy as a generalization of the distinction between an author- and a reader-oriented interpretation of literature.

33 Let me just note that, as I argued in the case of *The Man Who Shot Liberty Valance*, PCI1 does not require that the creator of a work actually be acquainted with the work of the philosopher(s) posited in the interpretation.

34 Stanley Cavell, *The World Viewed: Reflections on the Ontology of Film* (Cambridge MA: Harvard University Press, 1979), p. 25.

35 In his most recently published book on film, *Cities of Words: Letters on a Register of the Moral Life* (Cambridge MA: Harvard University Press, 2004), Cavell presents an alternative global justification of film as a mode of philosophy, its exemplifying "ethical perfectionism." I do not discuss this here, since his earlier work has had greater impact within the philosophy of film. In addition, adding a second concern to film's philosophical menu does not alter the global nature of Cavell's approach.

36 I am aware that Cavell takes himself to be only articulating the nature of traditional film prior to the 1970s. Nonetheless, his theorizing about film's relationship to philosophy obscures his own contextualizing of his claims to a particular style of filmmaking and a specific time period. For my purposes, I

thus treat his view as an essentialist one despite a tension in his thought in this regard.

37 David Bordwell and Noël Carroll (eds) *Post-Theory: Reconstructing Film Studies* (Madison WI: University of Wisconsin Press, 1996).

38 I abstract here from the contextual view of philosophy discussed in **Chapter 7** that also plays a role in our understanding of the concept.

39 C. S. Peirce, "Some Consequences of Four Incapacities," *Journal of Speculative Philosophy* 2 (1868): 140–41.

3 Illustrating a philosophical theory: *Modern Times*

1 For example, in defending the possibility of film being philosophy, Noël Carroll asks, "Can motion pictures *do* philosophy, or can they only ever illustrate philosophy?" ("Philosophizing Through the Moving Image: The Case of *Serene Velocity*," in Smith and Wartenberg, *Thinking Through Cinema*, p. 173), employing the same dichotomy as the two theorists I discuss here, Falzon and Mulhall.

2 Christopher Falzon, *Philosophy Goes to the Movies: An Introduction to Philosophy* (London: Routledge, 2002).

3 Op. cit., p. 4.

4 Op. cit., p. 6. Emphasis added.

5 This is not to deny that there may be *some* philosophy in Woody Allen's films. For example, *Crimes and Misdemeanors* might count as a counterexample to the claim that "crime does not pay," but it would be a mistake to limit the philosophic content of his films to those few instances of genuine philosophy in them. See Bruce Russell, "The Philosophical Limits of Film," *Film and Philosophy* Special Issue on Woody Allen (2000): 163–67.

6 Op. cit., p. 4. Emphasis added. Falzon here seems to conflate the *literary* images employed within a philosophical text with the *visual* images that compose a film.

7 Op. cit., p. 5.

8 I will discuss this "image" in more detail in a moment. It is worth noting that there is one dialogue where there is something like a visual image, namely the *Meno*, in which a slave boy is asked to consider a geometrical construction. Falzon does not discuss this, nor would it serve to bolster his argument.

9 Immanuel Kant, *Critique of Pure Reason*, trans. Norman Kemp Smith (New York: St Martin's Press, 1929), A235–36/B294–95. In *The Philosophical Imaginary* (Stanford CA: Stanford University Press, 1989), Michele Le Doeuff argues that images generally play a role in justifying a philosopher's position and supports her claim with this very passage. While her view would support the idea that cinematic illustrations of a philosophical position should be counted as instances of philosophy itself, I do not wish to base my argument on the acceptance of this very controversial thesis.

10 Although one might deny that this analogy really constitutes the Parable as an *illustration* of Plato's metaphysics, I simply assume here that it does.

11 *The Republic of Plato*, G. M. A. Grube, trans. (Indianapolis IN: Hackett, 1974), p. 168.

12 Ernie Alleva has pointed out that the entire Parable is a way of explaining Socrates' philosophical practice and the trouble he had with the Athenian authorities. While I do not doubt this, I am interested in thinking about the argumentative role of the Parable as a thought experiment, something that I see as not inconsistent with it also being a rationalization of Socrates' way of life.

13 There is a growing literature on thought experiments in philosophy. See, for example, Roy A. Sorenson, *Thought Experiments* (Oxford: Oxford University Press, 1998), and Tamar Szabó Gendler, *Thought Experiments: On the Powers*

and Limits of Imaginary Cases (New York: Garland Publishing, 2000). I discuss some of this literature in the next chapter.

14 Stephen Mulhall, *On Film* (London: Routledge, 2002), p. 2.

15 Ibid.

16 Ibid. Emphasis added

17 To view a photograph of the picture, go to www.artchive.com

18 Mulhall has been criticized for this by Nathan Anderson, "Is Film the Alien Other to Philosophy?," *Film and Philosophy* 9 (2005): 1–11, and by Julian Baggini, "Alien Ways of Thinking: Mulhall's *On Film*," *Film and Philosophy* 9 (2005): 12–23. Mulhall fails to elucidate the issue in his own response, "Ways of Thinking: A Response to Anderson and Baggini," *Film and Philosophy* 9 (2005): 24–29. I do think that cultural forms such as painting can philosophize, a claim that I discuss in **Chapter 7**.

19 Ibid. Emphasis added.

20 Arthur Danto makes some suggestive comments in this regard in "Illustrating a Philosophical Text: Mel Bochner's Wittgenstein Drawings," in his *Philosophizing Art: Selected Essays* (Berkeley CA: University of California Press, 1999), pp. 100–05.

21 Jasper Johns famously plays with this idea in his paintings such as *Flag* (1954–55) or *Number 9* (1969), for the paintings don't simply illustrate or represent the things they are illustrations or representations of, they are those things as well. My statement is not meant to claim that the subject of an illustration must actually exist, but only that illustrations are representational.

22 There are many illustrated versions of the book. The image used here comes from Mark Twain, *The Adventures of Tom Sawyer* (New York: Harper and Brothers Publishers, 1922).

23 Lewis Carroll, *Alice's Adventures in Wonderland* (New York: Macmillan and Co., 1877). Illustrations by John Tenniel.

24 I owe this formulation to Angela Curran.

25 In both of these cases, there is the additional issue of the relationship between the books and the films based on them, a question that I must leave to one side.

26 This is not just a philosopher's objection. In the case of another set of iconic illustrations, those of E. H. Shepherd for A. A. Milne's *Winnie-the-Pooh*, the first published Pooh story appeared with illustrations by J. H. Dowd rather than Shepherd when it appeared in the *London Evening News* of 24 December 1925.

27 Edmund Husserl, *The Phenomenology of Internal Time Consciousness* (Bloomington IN: University of Indiana Press, 1964).

28 Arthur Danto, "The Artworld," *Journal of Philosophy* 61.19 (1964): 571–84.

29 Matt Lawrence, *Like a Splinter in Your Mind: The Philosophy Behind the Matrix Trilogy* (Oxford: Blackwell, 2004), p. 5.

30 Florence Merriam Bailey, *Handbook of Birds of the Western United States* (Boston MA and New York: Houghton Mifflin Company, 1902). Virtually any birding guide can be consulted to confirm my point, so long as it contains drawings or sketches rather than photographs. More recent birding guides have more illustrations that confirm my claim.

31 I owe this point to Stephen Davies (personal communication).

32 My colleague Paul Staiti has suggested Winslow Homer's illustrations in *Harper's Weekly* and Blake's illustrations of his own poems as two other examples.

33 Heidegger is one philosopher who makes an essential link between discussions of the history of philosophy and philosophy itself. There are other philosophers, however, who reject the notion that doing the history of philosophy counts as doing philosophy in any sense. My characterization reflects what I take to be a broad, middle-of-the-road consensus on this issue.

34 Throughout, I will refer to the director of the film, and its central actor, as Chaplin and the character that he plays as Charlie, in conformity with the usual practice.
35 I take it that there is an essential continuity in Marx's writings, so that we can find this theory of alienation throughout his corpus and not only in his early writings. I have argued for this view in "Marx and the Social Constitution of Value," *The Philosophical Forum* XVI.4 (1985): 249–73. It is worth pointing out that Marx's *Economic and Philosophical Manuscripts* of 1844 were first published in 1932, so that Chaplin could have been cognizant of the issues their publication raised because of the widespread interest they aroused.
36 It could be argued, though I will not do so here, that this scene contains not only a philosophical thought, but a philosophical argument. The topic of visual arguments has had extensive discussion. See, for example, the essays in G. Thomas Goodnight (ed.) *Arguing, Communication, and Culture, Volume 1* (Annandale VA: National Communications Association, 2001).
37 Karl Marx, *Early Writings* (New York: Random House, 1975), p. 324.
38 Ibid.
39 Here, the film pantomimes Charlie's thought that Big Bill better do his job, exemplifying another possible way for films to think.
40 Marx, op. cit., p. 331.
41 Op. cit., pp. 326, 360.
42 Op. cit., p. 325.
43 On this, see my "'Species Being' and 'Human Nature' in Marx," *Human Studies* 5 (1982): 77–95.
44 It is worth emphasizing that there are various elements of Marx's theory that are not illustrated by the film. For example, nothing in the film illustrates Marx's claim that only a revolution can bring about the transcendence of alienation.
45 This objection is a version of the explicitness objection discussed in **Chapt**er 2.

4 A skeptical thought experiment: *The Matrix*

1 The anthologies are: *The Matrix and Philosophy: Welcome to the Deserts of the Mind*, William Irvin, ed. (LaSalle IL: Open Court, 2002), *More Matrix and Philosophy: Revolutions and Reloaded Decoded*, William Irvin, ed. (LaSalle IL: Open Court, 2005), and *Philosophers Explore the Matrix*, Christopher Grau, ed. (New York: Oxford University Press, 2005). The single-authored book is Matt Lawrence, *Like a Splinter in Your Mind: The Philosophy Behind the Matrix Trilogy* (Oxford: Blackwell, 2004).
2 The film also screens Plato's metaphysics, albeit in a transformed manner. Although I do not explicitly discuss this aspect of the film, it has also intrigued philosophers, especially those interested in "Cypher's argument" that the distinction between reality and appearance does not matter so long as we have the experiences themselves, regardless of their cause.
3 Julia Driver and Michael McKenna have argued that the film presents a thought experiment in their contributions to *Philosophers Explore the Matrix*.
4 Ernst Mach, *The Science of Mechanics*, trans. J. McCormack (LaSalle IL: Open Court, 1960). Cited by James Robert Brown, "Thought Experiments," in *The Stanford Online Encyclopedia of Philosophy*, retrieved 8/11/2006.
5 Roy A. Sorenson, *Thought Experiments* (New York: Oxford University Press, 1992).
6 Tamar Szabó Gendler, "Thought Experiments," in *The Encyclopedia of Cognitive Science* (London: Routledge, 2002), p. 388. Viewed online.
7 There are two recent collections of philosophical thought experiments: Peg Tittle, *What If . . . : Collected Thought Experiments in Philosophy* (New York:

Pearson Longman, 2005), and Martin Cohen, *Wittgenstein's Beetle and Other Classic Thought Experiments* (Oxford: Blackwell, 2005).

8 Judith Jarvis Thomson, "A Defense of Abortion," *Philosophy and Public Affairs* 1 (1971): 47–66.

9 Frank Jackson, "Epiphenomenal Qualia," *Philosophical Quarterly* 32 (1982): 27–36.

10 Jonathan Dancy, *Ethics without Principles* (Oxford: Clarendon Press, 2004).

11 Throughout this chapter, I translate *genie* as "demon" rather than "genius." For consistency, I have emended all quotations from Descartes' text to match this usage without specifically noting the change.

12 René Descartes, *'Discourse on Method' and 'Meditations on First Philosophy,'* Donald A. Cress, trans. (Indianapolis IN: Hackett, 1980), p. 18.

13 Op. cit., p. 22.

14 Ibid.

15 There has been a great deal of recent debate about the use of thought experiments in both philosophy and science. For a good summary of some of the issues, see James Robert Brown's article "Thought Experiments" in the *Stanford Online Encyclopedia of Philosophy*, accessible at http://plato.stanford.edu. The central issue is whether thought experiments are eliminable or whether they play a necessary role in philosophy and science.

16 Thomas E. Wartenberg and David Ross, "Quine and the Third Manual," *Metaphilosophy* 14 (1983): 267–75.

17 C. Mason Meyers, "Analytical Thought Experiments," *Metaphilosophy* 17 (1986): 111. I reject Meyers' theory of thought experiments.

18 See Derek Parfit, *Reasons and Persons* (Oxford: Oxford University Press, 1984).

19 What is missing from such observations is the production of new data, which is necessary in full-blooded experiments.

20 Galileo also proposes a thought experiment to refute the Aristotelian view. See Brown, "Thought Experiments," for an account of it.

21 Noël Carroll discusses the use of thought experiments in fiction in "The Wheel of Virtue: Art, Literature, and Moral Knowledge," *The Journal of Aesthetics and Art Criticism* 60.1 (2002): 3–26. Oddly, Carroll appears to deny that films themselves can present thought experiments while simultaneously holding that their scripts can. I discuss aspects of Carroll's view in **Chapter 6**.

22 The role of imagination in film viewing is a contested subject. See, for example, Gregory Currie, *Image and Mind: Philosophy, Film and Cognitive Science* (Cambridge: Cambridge University Press, 1995).

23 Christopher Falzon does discuss *The Matrix* as an "updating of the evil demon argument" (*Philosophy Goes to the Movies*, p. 29). But even though he recognizes that the film puts viewers in an analogous situation to the characters in the film, he does not draw any philosophical conclusions from this, merely comparing the film to others that employ similar narrative strategies. But the films he cites – such as *The Usual Suspects* (1995) – do not give us deceptive visual experiences, but only engender false interpretations of what we see, as *The Matrix* does in relation to Neo's "nightmare."

24 Strictly speaking, the film considers only perceptual beliefs and other beliefs based on them. It does not, for example, raise the question of whether we could be wrong about our mathematical beliefs. I do not think this difference affects my argument.

25 I think that the term, "The Matrix," as used by the film, refers both to the apparent world that most of the world's inhabitants believe to be real – "It is the world that is pulled over your eyes that blinds you to the truth" – and to the vast ensemble of computers, human beings, and structures that lies behind this reality. I will use it only in the former sense.

26 As has been noted frequently, this aspect of the film resembles Plato's Parable of the Cave.
27 Throughout the film, there are references to *Alice's Adventures in Wonderland*, suggesting that Neo's trip and Alice's have much in common. Here, like Alice, he is offered two pills.
28 Cypher compares Neo's journey to Dorothy's trip from Kansas to Oz. This is an inversion of what happens, for Neo, unlike Dorothy, moves from illusion to reality.
29 From the film's beginning, there have been many elements in the film's narrative that do not accord with our sense of how our world behaves. People can do physically impossible things, such as jump huge distances and even disappear. The scene I am now discussing is the one that begins to resolve the puzzles we have been experiencing all along.
30 It also seems apparent that the film is here screening Hilary Putnam's "brain-in-a-vat" thought experiment. Putnam argues that the thought experiment is incoherent, however. See *Reason, Truth, and History* (Cambridge: Cambridge University Press, 1981), chapter 1.
31 In accordance with my practice in regard to *Modern Times*, I refer to the film's director and central actor as "Keaton," and to the character he plays as "Buster."

5 Arguing against utilitarianism: *Eternal Sunshine of the Spotless Mind*

1 Structuralist films are a key group of avant-garde films that are often taken to make philosophic claims about film's nature. For example, Michael Snow's film *Wavelength* has been seen as a philosophic "discussion" of the zoom lens. I will consider the philosophical contributions of these films in **Chapter 7**.
2 Bruce Russell makes this argument in "The Philosophical Limits of Film," *Film and Philosophy* Special Issue on Woody Allen (2000): 163–67.
3 Alasdair MacIntyre, *After Virtue: A Study in Moral Theory* (South Bend IN: University of Notre Dame Press, 1981).
4 See, for example, Marya Schechtman in *The Constitution of Selves* (Ithaca NY: Cornell University Press, 1996).
5 Rawls' difference principle justifies departures from equality and is to be found in his epoch-making *A Theory of Justice* (Cambridge MA: Belknap Press, 1971). What this thought experiment envisions is people making decisions about their future well-being while in a state in which they are ignorant of their own social positions. Rawls characterizes this hypothetical scenario as one in which people are acting under a veil of ignorance.
6 Although the hypothetical *Justifying Difference* is a documentary, the case can be changed easily into a fiction film by having actors play the various roles. The same points can be made about the latter hypothetical film.
7 I discuss this issue more fully in "What Else Films Can Do," in *Film and Philosophy* 12 (2007).
8 It is interesting to note that, in his book *The Photoplay* (New York: D. Appleton and Company, 1916), Hugo Münsterberg worried that film might not be considered an independent artform precisely because it was able to record performances of other works. For this reason, he emphasized the aspects of film that distinguished it from other artforms such as theater.
9 In *Coming to Terms: The Rhetoric of Narrative in Fiction and Films* (Ithaca NY: Cornell University Press, 1990), Seymour Chatman discusses an interesting hybrid film, Alain Resnais' *Mon Oncle d'Amérique* (1980), that contains both an explicit argument and a narrative.
10 There are other forms of non-fiction film beside the documentary. I discuss some of these in **Chapter 7**.

11 Carl Plantinga, *Rhetoric and Representation in Nonfiction Film* (Cambridge: Cambridge University Press, 1997), p. 70.
12 Quotation from the book based upon the documentary, John Berger, *Ways of Seeing: Based on the BBC Television Series* (New York: Penguin, 1972), p. 28.
13 The question of whether and, if so, how documentary films can present philosophical arguments deserves further consideration than I give it here. It is also worth noting that a fiction film or television show can present an argument by having one of its characters deliver it. The famous "Argument Room" sketch of *Monty Python's Flying Circus* contains numerous arguments, despite being a work of fiction. But all these arguments are explicitly stated by the characters and thus are contained on the soundtrack.
14 Each of these films has received attention from philosophers. *Blade Runner* is the subject of an interesting discussion by Stephen Mulhall, *On Film* (London: Routledge, 2002), pp. 33–52; Joseph Kupfer discusses *Groundhog Day* in *Visions of Virtue in Popular Film* (Boulder CO: Westview, 1999), pp. 35–60; and *Memento* has been discussed by Andrew Kania, "'Write This Down!': *Memento* and Philosophy," in *The Routledge Companion to Philosophy and Film*, eds Paisley Livingston and Carl Plantinga (London: Routledge, forthcoming).
15 For purposes of this paper, I ignore non-discursive elements of the soundtrack such as music.
16 Noël Carroll, *Theorizing the Moving Image*, p. 281. Carroll has more recently changed his mind. For evidence, see his "Philosophizing Through the Moving Image: The Case of *Serene Velocity*," in Murray Smith and Thomas E. Wartenberg (eds) *Thinking Through Cinema: Film as Philosophy* (Oxford: Blackwell, 2006), pp. 173–86.
17 See Chatman, *Coming to Terms*.
18 Carroll, *Theorizing*, p. 280.
19 I have discussed the implications of this view of beauty in my "Humanizing the Beast: *King Kong* and the Representation of Black Male Sexuality," in *Classic Whiteness: Race and the Studio System*, ed. Daniel Bernardi (Minneapolis MN: University of Minnesota Press, 2001), pp. 157–77.
20 Traditionally, the Greeks treated "justice" as a disposition to treat others well. It was one of the four main virtues.
21 John Rawls, "Two Concepts of Rules," *Philosophical Review* 64:1 (1955): 3–32.
22 Op. cit., p. 11.
23 My discussion of *Eternal Sunshine* draws on the insightful analysis of the film by Christopher Grau in his essay, "*Eternal Sunshine of the Spotless Mind* and the Morality of Memory," in Murray Smith and Thomas E. Wartenberg (eds) *Thinking Through Cinema*, pp. 119–33.
24 See, for example, the *Washington Post* article by Rob Stein on 4 October, 2004 "Is Eevery Memory Worth Keeping? Pills to Reduce Mental Trauma Raise Controversy," available at: www.ajc.com/news/content/health/1004/19memory.html; Grau also discusses this issue in the appendix to his essay cited in **note** 23 above.
25 In particular, I have ignored the film's non-sequential narrative structure. I think this is an important aspect of the film, for it engenders in the audience a confusion about what is happening that is analogous to that which the characters suffer from when they have had their memories erased.

6 Moral intelligence and the limits of loyalty: *The Third Man*

1 This criticism originated with Jerome Stolnitz, "On the Cognitive Triviality of Art," *British Journal of Aesthetics* 12 (1992): 191–200. It is repeated by, among

others, Noël Carroll in "The Wheel of Virtue: Art, Literature, and Moral Knowledge," *The Journal of Aesthetics and Art Criticism* 60.1 (2002): 3–26.

2 E. M. Forster, "What I Believe," *Two Cheers for Democracy* (New York: Harcourt Brace, 1967). Cited by Noël Carroll in "The Wheel of Virtue," p. 9.

3 He is correct, however, in seeing the film as concerned with morality, something denied by Rob White in *The Third Man* (London: BFI Publishing, 2003), p. 64.

4 Carroll cites various philosophers who believe that there is a need for more fully presented scenarios of narrative fiction in philosophical contexts. See "The Wheel of Virtue," p. 25. But he does not explain why such extended narratives are needed for this particular philosophic purpose. I take this chapter to function as such an explanation.

5 Aristotle, *Nichomachean Ethics*, trans. Terence Irwin (Indianapolis IN: Hackett Publishing Company, 1985), 1141a25–28.

6 Op. cit., 1141b15–23.

7 Iris Murdoch, *The Sovereignty of Good* (London: Routledge and Kegan Paul, 1970); Martha Nussbaum, *Love's Knowledge: Essays on Philosophy and Literature* (New York: Oxford University Press, 1990); and Lawrence A. Blum, *Friendship, Altruism, and Morality* (London: Routledge and Kegan Paul, 1980).

8 All quotations are taken from the film script to *The Third Man* by Graham Greene (Shepperton, UK: London Film Studios, n.d.). Page references will be given parenthetically as *The Third Man*.

9 The original American version of the film had a different voiceover narrator than the British version. The version currently available has the voiceover restored.

10 In *The World Viewed: Reflections on the Ontology of Film* (Cambridge MA: Harvard University Press, 1971), Stanley Cavell argues that films embody philosophical skepticism. Rather than make such a general claim, I pinpoint specific techniques that *The Third Man* uses to present skepticism. This is a specific instance of my local approach and its advantages.

11 I am using the term "alignment" here in the sense specified by Murray Smith in *Engaging Characters: Fiction, Emotion, and the Cinema* (Oxford: Clarendon Press, 1995). We do not yet give Martins our "allegiance."

12 In his translation of this passage, Irwin mistakenly inserts "to a friend" after "injustice." This distorts Aristotle's claim by limiting it to actions taken in regard to one's friends.

13 This is the main theme of "The Wheel of Virtue."

14 It is also plausible to see the film as presenting Martins, Calloway, and, later, Schmidt as representing the different moralities of their nations. Martins' vulnerability to the moral categories of the western would be characteristically American; Schmidt's loyalty to an evil person, perhaps, typically Austrian; and Calloway's perceptive handling of the complex situation a mark of British cultural superiority.

15 Although the secondary literature on the film stresses the interest that both its producer Michael Korda and director Carol Reed had in post-war Vienna, I can't help but see the film as here also reflecting on a broader issue posed by the war itself: How can an evil person convince basically decent people to support his endeavors? Why don't these people see evil for what it really is and oppose it? Although there have been many answers proposed to this question, I think *The Third Man* contributes an intriguing one to the discussion. Despite not being a complete account of the rise of fascism, its depiction of how deficient moral intelligence fueled by pulp fiction can aid the triumph of evil strikes me as contributing to our understanding of evil's ability to command people's loyalty.

16 The qualification is that, if we misjudged the friend, then it is not the friend's fault and it may not be all right to simply dissolve the friendship.

17 Because Martins has lost Lime – whom he has admired and viewed as his best friend – he puts himself in Lime's place by falling in love with the object of Lime's desire, Schmidt. This odd substitution is later employed by Neil Jordan in *The Crying Game*. I discuss its significance in my *Unlikely Couples: Movie Romance as Social Criticism* (Boulder CO: Westview, 1999).

18 Although Aristotle thought that there could not be cross-gender friendships, I take it that the film simply departs from this problematic assumption.

19 Lawrence A. Blum, *Friendship, Altruism, and Morality* (London: Routledge and Kegan Paul, 1980). Blum's discussion of friendship as requiring a friend to pay attention to his friend's welfare does involve questions of loyalty to a friend, though Blum does not discuss the issue in those terms.

20 Schmidt clearly has some knowledge of Lime's dealings on the black market, since he secures false papers for her. Depending on how much she actually knew, this might account for her not changing her attitude towards Lime as a result of Calloway's information.

21 It may seem odd that I treat (sexual) love as a form of friendship, but I am simply following Aristotle's usage.

22 So *The Third Man* is another example of a twist film. It differs from *The Matrix* in not deceiving us about our perceptual beliefs but only our interpretations of what we see.

23 Lime's association of people with dots recalls Walt Whitman's characterization of the poet in "As I Sat Alone by Blue Ontario's Shore": The poet, he says, "bestows on every object or quality its fit proportion, neither more or less/. ... He sees eternity in men and women – he does not see men and women as dreams or *dots*." (Lines 144 and 147, emphasis added.)

24 It could be argued that Lime was never a true friend to Martins. But because Martins took him to be one, Aristotle's discussion of dissolving a friendship still applies.

25 See, Carroll, "The Wheel of Virtue," pp. 9ff.

26 In another sense, Martins' killing the injured Lime is an act of mercy, sparing him from a trial and imprisonment.

7 Foregrounding the background: *Empire* and *The Flicker*

1 P. Adams Sitney, "Structural Film," *Film Culture* 47 (1969).

2 P. Adams Sitney, *Visionary Film* (New York: Oxford University Press, 1974), p. 407. Future references to this text will be cited parenthetically as *Visionary Film*.

3 Noël Carroll, "Philosophizing Through the Moving Image: The Case of *Serene Velocity*," in Murray Smith and Thomas E. Wartenberg (eds) *Thinking Through Cinema: Film as Philosophy* (Oxford: Blackwell, 2006), p. 176. Carroll claims that *Serene Velocity* is a philosophical thought experiment. As I will show, it is a mistake to think of structural films as thought experiments because they are real films, not hypothetical ones, like the one envisioned by Danto that I discuss later in this chapter. That imaginary film – *Either/Or* – is part of a thought experiment. The two films I discuss also predate *Serene Velocity*, so Carroll's claim about that film's originality is mistaken.

4 Clement Greenberg, "Modernist Painting," in *Clement Greenberg: The Collected Essays and Criticism, Volume 4*, ed. John O'Brian (Chicago: University of Chicago Press, 1993), p. 85.

5 As we shall see, the reason why this minimalist strategy was able to succeed is that it enabled aspects of artforms that were transparent to their audiences to become objects of awareness. I will explain how this works in the case of structural films in a moment.

6 This is a version of an objection put forward by Derek Matravers.

7 Trevor Ponech, "The Substance of Cinema," in Murray Smith and Thomas E. Wartenberg, *Thinking Through Cinema*, p. 197. Future references to this work will be given parenthetically as *Substance*.
8 Op. cit., p. 187.
9 Ibid., emphasis added.
10 Arthur Danto, "The Philosopher as Andy Warhol," *Philosophizing Art: Selected Essays* (Berkeley CA: University of California Press, 1999), p. 63.
11 Op. cit., p. 65, emphasis added.
12 Op. cit., p. 67.
13 Sitney sees the relationship between Warhol's films and structural films differently: "[T]he structural film is not simply an outgrowth of the lyric [an earlier type of avant garde film that Sitney characterizes as an 'investigation of the consciousness confronting (and constructing) external nature.' (*Visionary Film*, p. 202.) It is an attempt to answer Warhol's attack by converting his tactics into the tropes of the response." (*Visionary Film*, p. 412.)
14 Rudolf Arnheim, "Motion," in *Film as Art* (London: Faber and Faber, 1958), p. 150. Cited in Noël Carroll, "Philosophizing Through the Moving Image: The Case of *Serene Velocity*," p. 184, fn. 12.
15 It is worth noting that Alexander Calder's mobiles are a parallel example of an artform capable of showing things in motion.
16 For simplicity, I leave off Kant's limitation of the categories to objects of experience alone. This does not affect my argument here.
17 It is true, of course, that we would now deny that films require celluloid projection, since we conceive of television, video, DVDs, etc., to be part of a more generic medium of which the celluloid film is a specific instance. However, *at the time*, film was thought of as a distinct artistic medium and I take *Empire* to be concerned with the nature of *that* specific artform.
18 David James, *Allegories of Cinema: American Film in the Sixties* (Princeton NJ: Princeton University Press, 1989), p. 65.
19 It could be objected that this sense of "structural" differs from that claimed for the films by Sitney. Nonetheless, I believe it gives added support for retaining that terminology.
20 This formulation does not acknowledge the possibility of objects appearing via animation. This is an important qualification, but one that is not relevant to my argument here.
21 Andre Bazin, *What is Cinema?*, *Volume 1*, trans. Hugh Gray (Berkeley CA: University of California Press, 1967), p. 13.
22 Op. cit., p. 21.
23 In this respect, *The Flicker* uses the same elements as Peter Kubelka employed in his graphic film *Arnulf Rainer* (1960). Conrad uses them to a markedly different effect, however. For the purposes of this chapter, I will ignore the title sequence for the film that contains facetious warnings about the possible health effects of the film. My description refers only to the main body of the film.
24 Tony Conrad in a web posting found at www.music.columbia.edu/pipermail/0xff/2004-April/000555.html
25 In this respect, *The Flicker* differs from *Serene Velocity*, even if we accept Carroll's claim that that film also presents motion as essential to film.

8 The nature of cinematic philosophy

1 C. S. Peirce, "Some Consequences of Four Incapacities," *Journal of Speculative Philosophy* 2 (1868): 140.
2 He has made this argument throughout his extensive writings on art. For a way of making the case that intersects my concerns in a particularly interesting way,

see his "The Philosopher as Andy Warhol," in *Philosophizing Art: Selected Essays* (Berkeley CA: University of California Press, 1999), pp. 61–83.

3 Martha Nussbaum, *Love's Knowledge: Essays in Philosophy and Literature* (New York: Oxford University Press, 1990), p. 3.

4 Cora Diamond, *The Realistic Spirit: Wittgenstein, Philosophy, and the Mind* (Cambridge MA: MIT Press, 1991), p. 310.

Bibliography

Philosophy and film websites

The range of information on the web about philosophy in/on/through films is increasing rapidly. Here are three very different sites that are useful for further information.

Film-Philosophy: www.film-philosophy.com An "International salon-journal" that has all sorts of information about philosophy and film.
The Film and Philosophy Database: http://arts.anu.edu/Philosophyandfilm/videodata Lots of information about the philosophical content of films.
Ethics in Film: http://ethicsinfilm/ An online journal that has discussions of ethical issues presented on film.

Books and articles

Anderson, Nathan. "Is Film the Alien Other to Philosophy?" *Film and Philosophy* 9 (2005): 1–11.
Aristotle. *Nicomachean Ethics*. Trans. Terence Irwin. Indianapolis IN: Hackett Publishing Company, 1985.
Arnheim, Rudolph. *Film as Art*. London: Faber and Faber, 1958.
Baggini, Julian. "Alien Ways of Thinking: Mulhall's *On Film*." *Film and Philosophy* 9 (2005): 12–23.
Bailey, Florence Merriam. *Handbook of Birds of the Western United States*. Boston MA and New York: Houghton Mifflin Company, 1902.
Barthes, Roland. "The Death of the Author." *The Nature of Art, 2nd Edition*. Ed. Thomas Wartenberg. Belmont CA: Wadsworth, 2007.
Bazin, André. *What is Cinema? Volume 1*. Trans. Hugh Gray. Berkeley CA: University of California Press, 1967.
Berger, John. *Ways of Seeing: Based on the BBC Television Series*. New York: Penguin, 1972.
Blum, Lawrence A. *Friendship, Altruism, and Morality*. London: Routledge and Kegan Paul, 1980.
Bordwell, David, and Noël Carroll (eds) *Post-Theory: Reconstructing Film Studies*. Madison WI: University of Wisconsin Press, 1996.
Brown, James Robert. "Thought Experiments." http://plato.stanford.edu
Carroll, Lewis. *Alice's Adventures in Wonderland*. New York: Macmillan, 1877.

Carroll, Noël. *Theorizing the Moving Image*. Cambridge: Cambridge University Press, 1996.
—— "The Wheel of Virtue: Art, Literature, and Moral Knowledge." *The Journal of Aesthetics and Art Criticism* 60.1 (2002): 3–26.
Cavell, Stanley. *The World Viewed: Reflections on the Ontology of Film*. Cambridge MA: Harvard University Press, 1971.
—— *Pursuits of Happiness: The Hollywood Comedies of Remarriage*. Cambridge MA: Harvard University Press, 1981.
—— *Contesting Tears: The Hollywood Melodrama of the Unknown Woman*. Chicago: University of Chicago Press, 1996.
—— *Cities of Words: Letters on a Register of the Moral Life*. Cambridge MA: Harvard University Press, 2004.
Chatman, Seymour. *Coming to Terms: The Rhetoric of Narrative in Fiction and Films*. Ithaca NY: Cornell University Press, 1990.
Cohen, Martin. *Wittgenstein's Beetle and Other Classic Thought Experiments*. Oxford: Blackwell, 2005.
Conrad, Tony. Web posting at: www.music.columbia.edu/pipermail/0xff/2004-April/000555.html
Currie, Gregory. *Image and Mind: Film, Philosophy, and Cognitive Science*. Cambridge: Cambridge University Press, 1995.
Dancy, Jonathan. *Ethics without Principles*. Oxford: Clarendon Press, 2004.
Danto, Arthur. "The Artworld." *Journal of Philosophy* 61.19 (1964): 571–84.
—— "Illustrating a Philosophical Text: Mel Bochner's Wittgenstein Drawings." *Philosophizing Art: Selected Essays*. Berkeley CA: University of California Press, 1999. 84–105.
—— "The Philosopher as Andy Warhol." *Philosophizing Art: Selected Essays*. Berkeley CA: University of California Press, 1999. 61–83.
Descartes, René. *'Discourse on Method' and 'Meditations on First Philosophy'*. Trans. Donald A. Cress. Indianapolis IN: Hackett, 1980.
Diamond, Cora. *The Realistic Spirit: Wittgenstein, Philosophy, and the Mind*. Cambridge MA: MIT Press, 1991.
Doeuff, Michele Le. *The Philosophical Imaginary*. Stanford CA: Stanford University Press, 1989.
Dostoyevsky, Fyodor. *Notes from Underground and the Grand Inquisitor*. Trans. Ralph E. Matlaw. New York: E. P. Dutton, 1960.
Fairbanks, Arthur (ed. and trans.) *The First Philosophers of Greece*. London: Kegan Paul, Trench, Trubner, 1898.
Falzon, Christopher. *Philosophy Goes to the Movies: An Introduction to Philosophy*. London: Routledge, 2002.
Forster, E. M. "What I Believe." *Two Cheers for Democracy*. New York: Harcourt Brace, 1967.
Freeland, Cynthia. *The Naked and the Undead: Evil and the Appeal of Horror*. Boulder CO: Westview, 2000.
Gendler, Tamar Szabó. *Thought Experiments: On the Powers and Limits of Imaginary Cases*. New York: Garland Publishing, 2000.
—— "Thought Experiments," in *The Encyclopedia of Cognitive Science*. London: Wiley, 2002. 388.
Gilmore, Richard A. *Doing Philosophy at the Movies*. Albany NY: SUNY Press, 2005.

Goodnight, G. Thomas (ed.) *Arguing, Communication, and Culture, Volume 1*. Annandale VA: National Communications Association, 2001.

Granger, Herbert. "Cinematic Philosophy in *Le Feu follet*: The Search for a Meaningful Life." *Film and Philosophy* 8 (2004): 74–90.

Grau, Christopher (ed.) *Philosophers Explore the Matrix*. New York: Oxford University Press, 2005.

—— "*Eternal Sunshine of the Spotless Mind* and the Morality of Memory." *Thinking Through Cinema: Film as Philosophy*. Eds Murray Smith and Thomas E. Wartenberg. Oxford: Blackwell, 2006. 119–33.

—— "There is no 'I' in 'Robot': Robots and Utilitarianism." *IEEE: Intelligent Systems* 21 (2006): 52–55.

Greenberg, Clement. "Modernist Painting." *Clement Greenberg: The Collected Essays and Criticism, Volume 4*. Ed. John O'Brian. Chicago: University of Chicago Press, 1993. 85–93.

Greene, Graham. *The Third Man*. Shepperton, UK: London Film Studios, n.d.

Henrich, Dieter. "The Proof-Structure of Kant's Transcendental Deduction." *Review of Metaphysics* 22 (1969): 640–59.

Horowitz, Tamara, and Gerald J. Massey (eds) *Thought Experiments in Science and Philosophy*. Savage MD: Rowman and Littlefield, 1991.

Husserl, Edmund. *The Phenomenology of Internal Time Consciousness*. Bloomington IN: University of Indiana Press, 1964.

Irvin, William (ed.) *The Matrix and Philosophy: Welcome to the Deserts of the Mind*. LaSalle IL: Open Court, 2002.

—— *More Matrix and Philosophy: Revolutions and Reloaded Decoded*. LaSalle IL: Open Court, 2005.

Jackson, Frank. "Epiphenomenal Qualia." *Philosophical Quarterly* 32 (1982): 27–36.

James, David. *Allegories of Cinema: American Film in the Sixties*. Princeton NJ: Princeton University Press, 1989.

Kania, Andrew. "'Write This Down!': *Memento* and Philosophy." *The Routledge Companion to Philosophy and Film*. Eds Paisley Livingston and Carl Plantinga. London: Routledge, forthcoming.

Kant, Immanuel. *Critique of Pure Reason*. Trans. Norman Kemp Smith. New York: St Martin's Press, 1929.

Kupfer, Joseph. *Visions of Virtue in Popular Film*. Boulder CO: Westview, 1999.

Lawrence, Matt. *Like a Splinter in Your Mind: The Philosophy Behind the Matrix Trilogy*. Oxford: Blackwell, 2004.

Light, Andrew. *Reel Arguments: Film, Philosophy, and Social Criticism*. Boulder CO: Westview, 2003.

Litch, Mary M. *Philosophy through Film*. New York: Routledge, 2002.

Livingstone, Paisley. "Theses on Cinema as Philosophy." *Thinking through Cinema: Film as Philosophy*. Eds Murray Smith and Thomas E. Wartenberg. Oxford: Blackwell, 2006. 11–18.

Mach, Ernst. *The Science of Mechanics*. Trans. J. McCormack. LaSalle IL: Open Court, 1960.

MacIntyre, Alisdair. *After Virtue: A Study in Moral Theory*. South Bend IN: University of Notre Dame Press, 1981.

Marx, Karl. *Early Writings*. New York: Random House, 1975.

Meyers, C. Mason. "Analytical Thought Experiments." *Metaphilosophy* 17 (1986): 109–18.

Mulhall, Stephen. *On Film*. London: Routledge, 2002.
—— "Ways of Thinking: A Response to Anderson and Baggini." *Film and Philosophy* 9 (2005): 24–29.
Münsterberg, Hugo. *The Photoplay*. New York: D. Appleton and Company, 1916.
Murdoch, Iris. *The Sovereignty of Good*. London: Routledge and Kegan Paul, 1970.
Nietzsche, Friedrich. *The Use and Abuse of History*, Part II. Accessed at: www.mala.bc.ca/~johnstoi/Nietzsche/history.htm
Nussbaum, Martha. *Love's Knowledge: Essays on Philosophy and Literature*. New York: Oxford University Press, 1990.
Parfit, Derek. *Reasons and Persons*. Oxford: Oxford University Press, 1984.
Peirce, C. S. "Some Consequences of Four Incapacities." *Journal of Speculative Philosophy* 2 (1868): 140–57.
Plantinga, Carl. *Rhetoric and Representation in Nonfiction Film*. Cambridge: Cambridge University Press, 1997.
Plato. *The Republic of Plato*. Trans. G. M. A. Grube. Indianapolis IN: Hackett, 1974.
Ponech, Trevor. "The Substance of Cinema." *Thinking Through Cinema: Film as Philosophy*. Eds Murray Smith and Thomas E. Wartenberg. Oxford: Blackwell, 2006. 187–98.
Porter, Burton. *Philosophy through Fiction and Film*. Upper Saddle River NJ: Prentice-Hall, 2004.
Putnam, Hilary. *Reason, Truth, and History*. Cambridge: Cambridge University Press, 1981.
Rawls, John. "Two Concepts of Rules." *Philosophical Review* 64.1 (1955): 3–32.
—— *A Theory of Justice*. Cambridge MA: Belknap Press, 1971.
Read, Rupert, and Jerry Goodenough (eds) *Film as Philosophy*. Houndmills, UK: Palgrave Macmillan, 2005.
Rowlands, Mark. *The Philosopher at the End of the Universe: Philosophy Explained through Science Fiction Films*. London: Ebury Press, 2003.
Russell, Bruce. "The Philosophical Limits of Film." *Film and Philosophy* Special Issue on Woody Allen (2000): 163–67.
—— "Film's Limits: The Sequel." *Film and Philosophy* 12 (2007).
Schechtman, Marya. *The Constitution of Selves*. Ithaca NY: Cornell University Press, 1996.
Singer, Irving. *Reality Transformed: Film as Meaning and Technique*. Cambridge MA: MIT Press, 1998.
Sitney, P. Adams. "Structural Film." *Film Culture* 47 (1969): 1–10.
—— *Visionary Film*. New York: Oxford University Press, 1974.
Smith, Murray. *Engaging Characters: Fiction, Emotion, and the Cinema*. Oxford: Clarendon Press, 1995.
—— "Film Art, Argument, and Ambiguity." *Thinking through Cinema: Film as Philosophy*. Eds Murray Smith and Thomas E. Wartenberg. Oxford: Blackwell, 2006. 33–42.
Smith, Murray and Wartenberg, Thomas E. (eds) *Thinking through Cinema: Film as Philosophy*. Oxford: Blackwell, 2006.
Smith, William G. *Plato and Popcorn: A Philosopher's Guide to 75 Thought-Provoking Movies*. Jefferson NC: McFarland, 2004.
Sorenson, Roy A. *Thought Experiments*. Oxford: Oxford University Press, 1992.

Stein, Rob. "Is Every Memory Worth Keeping? Pills to Reduce Mental Trauma Raise Controversy." *Washington Post* (2004) www.ajc.com/news/content/health/1004/19memory.html

Stoehr, Kevin L. (ed.) *Film and Knowledge: Essays on the Integration of Images and Ideas.* Jefferson NC: McFarland, 2002.

Stolnitz, Jerome. "On the Cognitive Triviality of Art." *British Journal of Aesthetics* 12 (1992): 191–200.

Thomson, Judith Jarvis. "A Defense of Abortion." *Philosophy and Public Affairs* 1 (1971): 47–66.

Tittle, Peg. *What if . . . : Collected Thought Experiments in Philosophy.* New York: Pearson Longman, 2005.

Twain, Mark. *The Adventures of Tom Sawyer.* New York: Harper and Brothers, 1922.

Wartenberg, Thomas E. "'Species Being' and 'Human Nature' in Marx." *Human Studies* 5 (1982): 77–95.

—— "Marx and the Social Constitution of Value." *The Philosophical Forum* XVI.4 (1985): 249–73.

—— "Beyond Babies and Banners: Towards an understanding of the Dynamics of Social MOvements," *New Political Science*, 14(Winter 1985–6): 157–71.

—— "Hegel's Idealism: The Logic of Conceptuality." *The Cambridge Companion to Hegel.* Ed. Frederick Beiser. Cambridge: Cambridge University Press, 1992. 102–29.

—— *Unlikely Couples: Movie Romance as Social Criticism.* Boulder CO: Westview, 1999.

—— "Humanizing the Beast: *King Kong* and the Representation of Black Male Sexuality." *Classic Whiteness: Race and the Studio System.* Ed. Daniel Bernardi. Minneapolis MN: University of Minnesota Press, 2001. 157–77.

—— "What Else Films Can Do." *Film and Philosophy* 12 (2007).

Wartenberg, Thomas E. and David Ross. "Quine and the Third Manual." *Metaphilosophy* 14 (1983): 267–75.

White, Rob. *The Third Man.* London: BFI Publishing, 2003.

Williams, Bernard. *Problems of the Self.* Cambridge: Cambridge University Press, 1973.

Wilson, George. *Narration in Light.* Baltimore MD: Johns Hopkins University Press, 1986.

Yanal, Robert J. *Hitchcock as Philosopher.* Jefferson NC: McFarland, 2005.

Index